SEX LIVES

OF THE
ROMAN EMPERORS

SEX
LIVES
OF THE
ROMAN EMPERORS

Nigel M. Cawthorne

First published in 2005 by
Prion
an imprint of the
Carlton Publishing Group
20 Mortimer Street
London W1T 3JW

A catalogue record for this book is available from the British Library

ISBN 1-85375-556-7

Typeset by e-type, Liverpool
Printed in Great Britain by Mackays

The publishers would like to thank The Bridgeman Art Library for their kind
permission to reproduce the pictures in this book: p.1 Erotic Scene, House of the
Centurion (fresco), Roman, (1st century BC) Pompeii, Italy, Alinari; p.2: Head of
Caesar Augustus / Private Collection; p.3: The Romans of the Decadence, detail of
the central group, 1847 (oil on canvas) (detail of 36568), Couture, Thomas (1815-79) /
Musee d'Orsay, Paris, France, Giraudon; p.4: Agrippina wife of Tiberius (engraving),
Sadeler, Aegidius (1570–1629) / Private Collection, The Stapleton Collection; p.5:
Tiberius Caesar (10 BC–54 AD) Emperor of Rome 14-37 AD engraved by Aegidius
Sadeler (1570–1629) (engraving), Titian (Tiziano Vecelli) (c.1488–1576) (after)/Private
Collection, The Stapleton Collection; p.6: A Banquet in Nero's palace, illustration
from Quo Vadis by Henryk Sienkiewicz (1846–1916), c.1910 (colour litho), Checa y
Sanz, Ulpiano (1860–1916) / Bibliotheque des Arts Decoratifs, Paris, France, Archives
Charmet; p.7: Caligula Caesar (12–41 AD), 1596 (engraving), Italian School, (16th
century) Private Collection, The Stapleton Collection; p.8: Rape of Lucretia (oil on
canvas), Procaccini, Giulio Cesare (1574–1625) / © Collection of the Earl of Leicester,
Holkham Hall, Norfolk. Every effort has been made to acknowledge correctly and
contact the source and/or copyright holder of each picture and Carlton Books
Limited apologises for any unintentional errors or omissions that will be corrected in
future editions of this book.

CONTENTS

INTRODUCTION

Civilisation in Rome was spawned by its northern neighbours, the Etruscans, who were a thoroughly sexy lot. Although the Romans later conquered them and destroyed their written language – making it hard to know what they got up to – accounts of their goings-on were left by the Greeks. According to the Greek historian Timaeus, writing in the fourth century BC, the Etruscans lived a lifestyle so extravagantly luxurious that it was customary for slave girls to wait on men naked.

While the men were suitably distracted, Theopompus of Chios, another Greek writing in the fourth century BC, said that Etruscan women "gave themselves to men that were not their husbands".

He described a drunken feast that quickly degenerated into a public orgy. After eating, he said, all the men and women swapped partners and watched each other having sex. For *ferae festivae*, it was just like California in the 1970s. Theopompus was particularly impressed by the way the Etruscan women "shaved their bodies and engaged in gymnastic sexual positions with the men".

Some historians and archaeologists doubt the legitimacy of Theopompus's account and think that he was describing one religious festival, a particularly sexy cult, rather than the general practice of all the Etruscan people; Etruscan pottery and other surviving artwork usually shows men and women paired off into couples and not having sex in groups.

Etruscan men depicted on this pottery are always nude, while the women are often fully clothed, with long robes and sometimes with a veil covering their face. Goddesses or other deities are the only women who are depicted naked. Even when couples are shown together, the women always have their clothes on; in contrast, their male counterparts are stark naked. The only occasions in which Etruscan men are shown clothed are in war scenes – they wore skirts – but even then soldiers were shown naked most of the time. But then, as Ovid said: *"Militiae species amor est."*

While the Greeks' top god was Zeus and the Romans' Jupiter, the Etruscans worshipped the female deity Uni as their chief god. She was depicted naked on carved mirrors and was later called "Uni-Astarte" – Astarte is the Phoenician name for the Ishtar, the Sumerian goddess of war and sexual love. This suggests that the Etruscans, like the Phoenicians who settled in Carthage, near Tunis, North Africa, migrated from the Middle East. Indeed, it also seems possible that they intermarried with the Carthaginians. So it is argued that the orgy Theopompus was describing may have been a festival of the Uni-Astarte cult and that the women involved were the temple prostitutes who were employed by the cult.

However, Theopompus made it clear that he was writing about everyday life in old Etruria – the Etruscans' home in northwest Italy.

"Sharing wives is an established Etruscan custom," he wrote.

He also admired the females of the tribe.

"Etruscan women take particular care of their bodies and exercise often, sometimes along with the men, and sometimes by themselves," he said. And, belying the pottery: "It is not a disgrace for them to be seen naked."

According to Theopompus, regular dinner parties were a time for fun.

"The women do not share their couches with their husbands but with the other men who happen to be present," he said, "and they propose toasts to anyone they choose. They love to drink and are very beautiful."

Such promiscuity meant that it was impossible to tell who had fathered which child. So Etruscan families were organised around the matriarch and lineage had to follow the maternal line.

"The Etruscans raise all the children that are born without knowing who their fathers are," said Theopompus. "The children live the way their parents live, often attending drinking parties and having sexual relations with all the women..." So they had early training in *artis amatoriae* in a rather more graphic fashion than in our own, less enlightened times. "... Also, Etruscan men do not consider it shameful to have sex openly with other males, either in the active or the passive role, for that is the custom in their country. So far from thinking such sexual variation disgraceful, when someone asks to see the master of the house, the servant answering the door says that he is doing this or that, crudely specifying the name."

Theopompus described a normal evening at home with the Etruscans: "When they are having sexual relations, either with courtesans or within their family, they do as follows: after they have stopped drinking and are about to go to bed, while the lamps are still lit, servants bring in courtesans, or boys, or sometimes even their wives. Once the husbands have enjoyed themselves with any of these, the servants fetch lusty young men, who also fool around with these courtesans, boys or wives. They adore sex and sometimes make love while people are watching them, but most of the time they put screens woven of sticks around the beds, and throw cloths on top of them."

It was their own version of *spectacula tv veri similia*.

However, because Theopompus was godly and pompous he was quick to condemn Etruscan men as both *pathice* and *cinaede*.

"They are keen on making love to women," he said, "but they particularly enjoy boys and youths. The youths in Etruria are very good-looking and take great care of their bodies, because they live in luxury and keep their bodies smooth. In fact, all the barbarians in the West use pitch to pull out and shave off the hair on their bodies."

It seems that Etruscan men liked their boys smooth, the same way that they liked their women. Indeed, there were many shops on the street where men and women went for depilation. Etruscans would get their *volva et natis pilosas* waxed publicly, "without any reserve or without having any shame of being seen, even by passers-by".

"*Admonui, ne trux caper iret in alas, Neve forent duris aspera crura pilis,*" as Ovid said in *The Art of Love*. ("Let no rude goat find his way beneath your arms, or let that your legs be rough with bristling hairs.")

Although the Romans obliterated the Etruscan language, other artefacts survived. In the Tomb of the Bulls in the Etruscan town of

Tarquinia, 45 miles northwest of Rome, there are murals that depict both heterosexual and homosexual couplings. And, as you would perhaps expect in the Tomb of the Bulls, bulls are also involved. Alongside the gay couple, a bull is shown in an aggressive pose; alongside the straight couple, the bull is passive. This has been interpreted by some authors as a suggestion that the Etruscans disapproved of homosexuality, but the watching bulls have human faces, which possibly indicates some mythological context – or that voyeurism was alive and flourishing in Ancient Etruria.

Scopophilia, it seems, had a great many outlets in Etruscan society. In the Tomb of the Bigas, in Tarquinia, a homosexual couple are depicted making love in full view of a crowd at a chariot race. As nobody is throwing anything – not even up – I guess homosexuality was widely accepted in Etruscan society. The city of Pompeii – situated to the southeast of modern Naples – was also founded by the Etruscans. From a wall painting left after the city was covered in volcanic ash following the eruption of Vesuvius in AD 79, it seems that all varieties of sexuality were openly, and blatantly, pursued. Homosexuality, group sex and even paedophilia were accepted as normal behaviour.

Meanwhile, back in Tarquinia, there are more erotic scenes to be found on the walls in the Tomb of the Floggings. One shows a woman – naked except for a *tutulus*, a fancy hairdo – bending and holding the hips of a bearded man who is facing her. He has a big smile on his face – for obvious reasons. Although the mural is damaged, it is plain that she is in the act of providing him with oral pleasure. Behind her, there is a youth who has one hand on her buttocks. In the other, he holds a raised whip and is plainly about to beat her for *postrema lascivia*.

Another mural shows a woman embracing a youth, while being penetrated from behind by a bearded man. The other walls are covered with scenes of musicians, drinking and dancers, all of which suggest the influence of the cult of Dionysus, the Greek god of wine, inspiration, madness and generally getting carried away.

Pottery found in Tarquinian tombs, particularly those of the sixth and fifth centuries BC, show similar erotic scenes and tend to back up Theopompus's view of Etruscan society. They show men in an aroused state and depict numerous acts of copulation and fellatio. Indeed, the imagery used in the tombs is so blatant that it tends to reinforce the idea that Etruscan society was much more permissive than other societies around at that time.

The Greek philosopher Plato, not known for this love of the fairer sex, condemned the Etruscans as immoral and, in Roman times, the word Etruscan became synonymous with a prostitute. In the first century AD, the Roman historian Livy contrasts virtuous Roman wives with their liberated Etruscan counterparts in his tale of the rape of Lucretia, which we will come to.

However, according to legend, Rome itself was founded as a result of a bit of *lascivia*. The story goes that Amulius deposed his older brother Numitor as king of Alba Longa, a city in the Alban Hills to the south of Rome said to have been founded by the son of Aeneas, a survivor of the Trojan war, who himself was the son of the goddess of erotic love Venus and a high-born Trojan. To secure his position, Amulius forced Numitor's daughter, Rhea Silvia, to become a Vestal Virgin. This would prevent her from giving birth to any rival claimants to the throne.

Even though she had taken the Vestal's vow of chastity, Rhea Silvia managed to get herself *cum chavvi*. She claimed that she had been raped by Mars, the god of war – although I suspect that a passing soldier must have acted as his earthly stand-in. She gave birth to the twins Romulus and Remus. Amulius ordered them to be drowned in the River Tiber, which separates Etruria from Latium to the south. However, they were washed ashore at the site of the future city of Rome, where they were suckled by a she-wolf before they were found by a herdsman called Faustulus, who, along with his wife, brought them up.

That Romulus and Remus were suckled by a she-wolf is an interesting aspect of the story, one that is central to the legend of the founding of Rome. The Latin word for she-wolf is *lupa*. However, *lupa* also means a prostitute and a *lupanar* is a brothel: it seems, therefore, that the founders of Rome may well have been saved by a hooker. But as Ausonius said: "*Quae casta est?*"

When they grew up, Romulus and Remus, along with a band of other exiles, killed Amulius and put Numitor back on the throne. Then they founded the city of Rome on the site where they had been saved. Romulus built the city wall, but when Remus jumped over it, Romulus killed him. So the city was named Rome after Romulus, not Reims, which is in France.

That, at least, is the Roman version of events surrounding the founding of Rome. The Greeks say that Rome was founded by Romus, the son of Odysseus by Circe, the enchantress who lived on the nearby island of Aeaea and who was one of the many extra-marital conquests he made during his odyssey. The more banal explanation is that Rome was founded by traders at a convenient crossing point of the Tiber on the route from the Apennine mountains to the sea. Rome also happens to be situated at the meeting point of the regions of three distinct peoples who, together, became Romans – the Etruscans to the north, the Sabines to the east and the Latins to the south.

The history of Rome begins with another famous rape – the rape of the Sabine women. It was all very well for Romulus and his warlike bunch to found a city, but they needed women to give them children – otherwise Rome would only have lasted for a single generation. So, after a discussion in the Senate, Romulus sent out emissaries to neighbouring peoples offering an alliance in return for some *mulierculae*.

According to Livy, these emissaries were not given a fair hearing because Rome's neighbours feared that a great power was growing in their midst. Many considered the Romans to be little better than criminals and asked why, if Romans wanted women, they did not offer asylum to women law-breakers who, after all, were of their own rank.

This was an insult. Some of the hot-headed Roman youths took it badly and wanted to take up arms, but Romulus was an awful lot smarter than that. He proposed staging a games in honour of the local Italian god Consus. And, as a gesture of reconciliation, they would invite the neighbours. A lot of people came simply to see the new city. The entire Sabine population turned out for the event, including the women and children. It was a nice day out.

The Romans laid on the hospitality and gave them a guided tour of the city. Then everyone settled down to watch the games. At a prearranged signal, the Romans began to grab the Sabine women. This pre-planned abduction demonstrated the Roman mastery of organisation, an asset that would soon become legendary. According to Livy: "Many just snatched the nearest woman to hand, but the most beautiful had already been reserved for the senators and these were escorted to the senators' houses by plebeians who had been given this assignment."

The story goes that one woman, the most beautiful one by far, was carried off by the gang of a man named Thalassius. Everyone wanted this *über*-babe and wanted to know where they were taking her, but Thalassius's men told them to keep their hands off her because they "were taking her to Thalassius". According to Livy, this was the origin of the Roman "wedding cry".

The Romans drove off the Sabine men and got down to the raping. It has to be said that this was considered a normal way to attain a bride in ancient times. When the *fututum* was over, the grieving parents of the Sabine women accused the Romans of having violated the laws of hospitality. They invoked Consus, who the Romans were supposed to have been honouring at that day's festival, but the Sabine women, who had been well and truly raped by this point, did not hold out much hope that Consus, who was essentially the god of storage bins and a distinctly second-class deity, was going to do much to help them. However, Romulus took it upon himself to placate the women. According to Livy: "Romulus then went among them in person to assure them that none of this would have happened if their fathers hadn't been so inflexible in not letting them marry their neighbours, but now they would have the status of wives with all the material rewards and the civil rights of citizenship and they would have children."

He asked them to cool their anger and give their hearts to the men who had already taken their bodies.

"A good relationship often begins with an offence," he said.

He promised that their husbands would now treat them with extra kindness in an effort to make up for the loss of their parents and their country. The other men added their blandishments to those of Romulus, saying that they had been motivated by love and passion. According to Livy, these entreaties were "very effective with women".

And he seems to have been right. When the Sabine men returned, heavily armed, under their king Titus Tatius, the Sabine women – now Roman wives – persuaded their fathers not to fight their new husbands. The Romans then accepted Titus Tatius as joint ruler with Romulus.

Later, the Roman poet Ovid, who wrote around the time of Christ, celebrated the rape in verse:

The ravished girls were led away to marriage;
Their very shame made them more beautiful.
And when one struggled hard against her captor,
He carried her away in eager arms,
And said: "Why spoil your pretty eyes by weeping?
Your father took your mother, now I take you!"

Rape was very much the order of the day in ancient times and the Romans continued to make similar abduction-led alliances with their neighbours while simultaneously building the institutions of the Roman state under a series of kings. The first king was crowned in 616 BC. He was an Etruscan called Tarquin and it is said that he brought all the habits of his people to Rome with him.

Rome's seventh and last king, who reigned from 534 to 509 BC, lost the throne as a result of another rape. He was another Etruscan, called Tarquinius Superbus or "Tarquin the Proud", who had also come to power as a result of a little jiggery-pokery, with a bit of incest thrown in for good measure. Tarquin's father, Tarquinius Priscus, the fifth king, had been murdered in 579 BC. His wife, the prophet Tanaquil, then managed to put her son-in-law Servius Tullius on the throne, thus making him the sixth king. Tarquin, however, would not be denied the crown. He murdered Tullius and his wife – Tarquin's sister – in 534 BC. Tarquin then murdered his brother, married his brother's wife and made himself king of Rome. He was an absolute despot and put many senators to death in the reign of terror that followed his accession.

In 509 BC, the Romans attacked Ardea, the capital of the wealthy Rutuli people, 23 miles south of Rome. Unable to take the city, they began a prolonged siege. To while away the time, the Etruscan princes passed their idle hours indulging in long dinners and drinking bouts. One day they were drinking in the quarters of Tarquin's son, Sextus Tarquinius, when the topic of who had the most virtuous wife came up. Nearly every man praised the virtue of his own wife with enthusiasm and the argument grew heated.

Another guest, Tarquinius Collatinus, said that there was no need to waste any more words on the subject. In a couple of hours, they could ride to Rome and check on the disposition of their wives. If they did that they would soon see how far their wives were outshone by the virtue of

Collatinus's own wife Lucretia. As by this time they had all had a little too much wine, they agreed and set off on horseback for Rome.

Arriving there at early dusk, they found most of their wives at a luxurious banquet, whiling away their time with their young friends and other Etruscan distractions. They then moved on to Collatinus's home in nearby Collatia. Although it was now late at night, according to Livy, they found the beautiful Lucretia "busily engaged upon her wool, while her maidens toiled about her in the lamplight as she sat in the hall of her house". They were courteously received. It was plain that Collatinus had won and he graciously invited the other Tarquinii to stay for dinner.

However, Sextus Tarquinius fancied Lucretia. He was turned on not just by her beauty, but also by her virtue. He had to have her, by force if necessary. A few days later, Sextus Tarquinius slipped out of the camp again without letting on to Collatinus. He went back to Collatia, where he was welcomed as an honoured guest as no one suspected what he was up to. After dinner, as it was too late to return to camp, he was shown to a spare bedroom.

By now Sextus Tarquinius was burning with passion, but he waited until everyone in the house was fast asleep. Then, he drew his sword and crept into the bedroom where Lucretia was sleeping. Seizing her breast with his left hand to hold her down, he said: "Be still, Lucretia! I am Sextus Tarquinius. My naked sword is in my hand. Utter a sound and you die!"

The startled Lucretia awoke to find herself facing imminent death with no help in sight. Then Tarquinius began to declare his love to her. According to Livy, he pleaded with her, "mingling threats with prayers, to bring every resource to bear upon her woman's heart". None of it did any good.

As Lucretia did not even seem to be moved by fear of death, he went further and threatened her with disgrace. He said that after he had killed her, he would kill a slave and lay him naked by her side, so that it "might be said that she had been put to death in foul adultery with a man of base condition".

"At this dreadful prospect, her inflexible modesty was overcome by his lust," said Livy, "and when he had raped her, Tarquinius departed, exulting in his conquest of a woman's honour."

Lucretia sent a message to both her husband and her father, Spurius Lucretius, begging them to come. When they arrived, they found Lucretia sitting alone in her chamber. Tears welled up in her eyes as they entered.

"Are you all right?" asked Collatinus.

"Far from it," she replied, "for what can be well with a woman when she has lost her honour? The print of a strange man is in your bed, Collatinus, but only my body has been violated. My heart is guiltless, as death shall be my witness. Now pledge with your right hands and your words that the adulterer shall not go unpunished. It was Sextus Tarquinius who, last night, returned hostility for hospitality. He brought ruin on me, and no less on himself – if you are men – when he had his pleasure with me."

Both her husband and her father swore that they would avenge her. Then they tried to console her, saying: "It is the mind that sins not the body, and where there has been no intent there is no guilt."

Lucretia, however, would not be comforted and thought only of punishing Sextus Tarquinius.

"It is for you to determine what is due to him," she said. "For my own part, though I acquit myself of the sin, I do not absolve myself from punishment; nor in time to come shall ever an unchaste woman live through the example of Lucretia."

Then she pulled out a knife that she had concealed beneath her robe and plunged it into her heart. Falling forward on it, she died as her husband and her father cried out in grief. Lucius Junius Brutus, who was with them, pulled the knife from Lucretia's wound, and, holding it up, dripping with gore, said: "By this blood, which was so chaste until a prince befouled it, I swear before you and the gods that I will pursue Lucius Tarquinius Superbus and his wicked wife and all his children, with sword, with fire and with all the violence I can command, and that I will suffer neither them nor any other to be king in Rome!"

The others took the knife one by one and swore a similar oath. Then they carried Lucretia's corpse from the house and took it to the marketplace in Collatia. A crowd soon gathered. Each man there had a similar tale to tell about Sextus Tarquinius and the behaviour of the royal retinue. Brutus urged them all to take up arms.

When word reached Rome, an outraged mob gathered in the

Forum. Tarquin and his entire family were driven from the city. The king died in exile. Rome became a republic and for the next 478 years it was governed by two consuls, both of whom were nominated by the Senate, elected by the people and held office only for one year.

CHAPTER 1

The era of the Roman republic, which lasted from the expulsion of Tarquin the Proud in 509 BC to Caesar Augustus taking sole control of the state in 27 BC, saw the power of Rome spread across most of the known world. This expansion was led by the Roman army, which conquered the Italian peninsula, Carthage and North Africa, Spain, Syria, Macedonia, Greece, Egypt and Gaul.

At the head of the Roman army as it marched into battle rode on horseback a half-naked girl with her breasts exposed. She was the Venus Victrix or the Venus of Victory. This practice dates back to Ancient Mesopotamia and Ishtar, the goddess of war and sexual love. Ishtar and her Roman equivalent Venus were seen as the restorers of life and were said to be able to bring back the dead – an important consideration if you are about to risk your life in battle.

Being led into battle by a topless babe must have done wonders for morale. In simple terms, nubile young women are indeed the restorers of life, by dint of the fact that they have babies. Unfortunately, homosexuality was rife in the army.

The sex lives of Roman soldiers – and their opponents – often had huge historical consequences. It had an effect on the outcome of the Punic Wars between Rome and Carthage. After crossing the Alps and taking most of Italy in 216 BC, Hannibal then prepared to take Rome, but while wintering in Capua, his troops, it is said, "lost their hardiness in the luxuries and debaucheries of that wicked city". Hannibal was forced to withdraw.

Then, when the Roman army was besieging Carthage in 149 BC, the soldiers were happy to spend their time being entertained by a large number of slaves and prostitutes, both male and female. They were also supplied with new-fangled luxuries, such as hot baths with attendant bath-boys, which were all the rage at the time, and no progress was made.

When Scipio Aemilianus was given command of the army in 147 BC, he got rid of both the boys and the baths. In 146 BC, his newly disciplined army took Carthage, enslaved its people and destroyed the city for ever. The lesson had been learnt. In 123 BC, a new Army Law was introduced which banned anyone under the age of 17 from joining the army as, traditionally, younger boys had been encouraged to enlist so that the older soldiers could indulge themselves in the joys of pederasty.

Instead, soldiers had to indulge their desires while they were on home leave. According to the first-century historian Tacitus, Rome was often overflowing with soldiers who spent their time "weakening alike their bodies and their minds by indulging in all the pleasures and unmentionable vices of the city".

Be that as it may, even when they were a long way from home, Roman soldiers still had plenty of opportunities to enjoy all the luxuries and vices of the older civilisations they conquered. On a tough campaign, they could also take some of the comforts of home along with them. When Marcus Crassus – the third member of the First Triumvirate with Julius Caesar and Pompey the Great – was governor of Syria in 54 BC, he mounted an ill-advised invasion of Parthia to the east and was beaten by the Seleucids, who triumphantly paraded the pornography they had looted from the luggage of Crassus's officers through the streets. Crassus's own head was delivered to the Parthian king Orodes in the middle of a play.

Victorious Roman soldiers often indulged themselves in a way that is now unknown. Their actions were described by the Latin transitive verb *irrumare*. This means literally "to fuck someone in the mouth". It is quite different from being fellated or having your penis sucked. It is more akin to oral rape. For the Roman male, honour lay in being the penetrator – it did not matter whether what he penetrated was male or female. So *irrumatio* was the ultimate humiliation a Roman could inflict on an enemy. It is plain that the services of a good *dentifrangibus* — tooth-smasher – were called for first. On occasions when *irrumatio* wasn't the order of the day, victorious troops would rape both the enemy's womenfolk and any good-looking boys they found. They would then carry the best looking of them away with them. Boys would be castrated to keep them youthful and their bodies would be stripped of all hair.

Women would never be subjected to *irrumatio*. They were generally treated lovingly and tenderly. Even those who had been raped – like the Sabine women – would be treated kindly and compassionately afterwards. Marriage by conquest was the most popular way of courting – for men at least – in the ancient world. Wives and other women of rank would not be expected to provide oral sex, though prostitutes often boasted of their great expertise at fellatio, and surviving art work shows that regular lovers enjoyed *ligurio*.

To maintain the class system, men would marry close relatives, often their cousins. They would also marry for political advantage, but beauty in a bride was also highly prized. Generally, with so many slave-girls and prostitutes around, a wife was not expected to be skilled in bed. She was largely there to provide children. In the first century BC, the writer Lucretius clearly spelt out the distinction between the duties of a wife and those of a prostitute.

"The sexual position is also important," he wrote. "For wives who imitate the manner of a wild beast and quadrupeds – that is, breasts down, haunches up – are generally thought to conceive better, since the semen can more easily reach the proper place."

"*Oppida tota canem venerantur, nemo Dianam*," as Juvenal said in his *Satires*.

"And it is absolutely *not* necessary for wives to move at all," said Lucretus. "For a woman prevents and battles pregnancy if, in her joy, she answers the man's lovemaking with her buttocks, and her soft breasts billow forward and back; for she diverts the ploughshare out of the furrow and makes the seed miss its mark. Whores practise such movements for their own reasons, to avoid conception and pregnancy, and also to make the lovemaking more enjoyable for men, which obviously isn't necessary for wives."

Per amor patriae, as they say.

It was also common for men to marry much younger women. Tacitus was in his late 20s when he married a 13-year-old – girls could marry at the age of 12 and boys at 14 under Roman law, as was the case in Britain until the late 19th century. But then, as Tacitus said, "The true Roman married without love and loved without refinement or reverence."

For the Roman male, the ideal woman would be a buxom 16-year-old with "skin as white as wax, sparkling eyes, sweet breath, lustrous dark or auburn hair" – no blondes or redheads – "a scented, sensuous, lissom body and a shaved clitoris, glowing like a pearl". *Noli appropinquare me cum illo novacula.*

In the second century BC, the statesmen Cato the Elder had a successful marriage to a young girl, and didn't stop there. According to the first-century historian Plutarch: "Cato had such a sound and strong constitution that he was able to have intercourse with women even when he was old and to marry a wife much younger than himself. This was the cause of his marriage. After the death of this wife, he married his son to the daughter of Paulus Aemilius, Scipio's sister; he himself used to make love to a young girl who came to his house in secret."

Cato's house was small and his daughter-in-law soon realised what was going on. The girl seemed to walk around the house a little too boldly and Cato's son grew jealous. So Cato decided to resolve the situation. A man called Salonius had just joined his retinue and Cato asked him whether he had married his daughter off yet. Salonius said that he had not and would not do so without consulting Cato.

"Well," said Cato, "I have found a suitable husband for her, unless she objects to his age. He has no other faults, but he is very old."

Salonius then gave Cato permission to marry off his daughter to anyone he thought suitable. Cato then told him that he was asking for the girl in marriage himself. According to Plutarch, Salonius was astonished, "thinking that Cato was beyond marrying age and that he himself was too far beneath a man who had been consul and had celebrated a triumph" – that is, being given a triumphal parade back into Rome after winning a great victory on the battlefield – "but when he saw Cato was in earnest he accepted the offer with pleasure".

And the union was a successful one.

"From this marriage Cato had another son, who took the by-name Salonius from his mother," said Plutarch.

Cato may have lived to regret taking another wife, for he once remarked: "All other nations rule their wives; we rule all nations, but our wives rule us." Certainly, the Roman wife ruled the household and was called *domina* – "mistress" – by everyone, including her husband.

In early times, the bride would have to have sex with her husband's friends before the marriage. Many must have echoed Plautus when he said: *"Edepol ne hic dies pervorsus atque advorsus."* Later, in more enlightened times, the first intercourse merely had to be performed in the presence of witnesses while the husband's friends threw nuts into the bridal chamber. Often, though, having done his duty on his wedding night, the groom would absent himself with another woman. *Mulier dicit quo vadis?* perhaps.

The wedding itself was accompanied by rude songs praising Priapus, the god of the erect penis. The ceremony took place in a temple of the god of fertility, Mutunus Tutunus. He was represented by statues of erect penises, sometimes crowned with flowers. On the wedding day, the groom would undo the bride's girdle and she would sit naked on one of these phalluses. This would have been painful if she was a virgin, as St Augustine* remarked that both clowns and priests liked to exaggerate the size of the male organ. (See p. 233 for an explanation of the Daisy Chain.) Even if she was not, it would certainly have been cold. Older women returned to the phallic god and did the same thing to encourage fecundity, or perhaps they did it just for the fun of it.

A man would almost certainly not have been a virgin when he married. Prostitutes of both sexes were freely available. They worked out of open cells, where they displayed themselves completely naked to encourage potential clients. A board hung above the doorway with the name of the prostitute – usually an assumed one – and the price. Sometimes there was a bed, but the cells normally contained just a few cushions or a mat and a bronze lamp to illuminate obscene frescoes on the walls, allowing practitioners to say, *"Veni et vide picturas meas."* Female prostitutes were compelled by law to wear blonde wigs – *quo magis mutat, eo magis perstat* – and prostitutes were taxed; they provided the state with a healthy income.

A man was expected to put aside his catamites and concubines when he married, but few did. If he could afford it, he would keep his boy on as a cupbearer and find his mistresses other jobs around the house.

There were no laws against adultery for husbands until the prudish Augustus came to power. For women, though, during the early part of the Republic, the punishment for adultery or drinking was death. Indeed, a husband could take the law into his own hands and kill his wife if he caught her with another man. He could kill the man too, but he would often inflict a far worse punishment on his wife's lover. He would dishonour him by handing him over to his servants and retainers to sexually abuse him in any way they thought fit. Again, for the Roman male, to be penetrated was to be dishonoured.

As the Republic rolled on, divorce was legalised. By 306 BC, a man could rid himself of a troublesome wife simply by repudiating her. Up until then, a man could only divorce his wife if she was shown to be barren. Later, a divorce could be obtained by mutual consent. With men often away for long periods, fighting on the far-flung borders of the empire, women began to divorce their husbands while they were away if they found another man that they wanted to marry. Soon it was not uncommon for both men and women to marry four or five times.

It has been noted that there is no Latin word for dildo, though such devices – made out of leather – were common in Ancient Greece. Because of the huge number of slaves in Rome, masturbation was unnecessary. While husbands might fill their houses with young boys and girls for sexual use, older women would also take their pleasure with male slaves, particularly slaves who had only been partially castrated, so that their testicles had been removed but their penises were still intact and in working order. This meant that Roman matrons could have all the fun of sex without any danger of having a slave's baby.

Young men and women would be displayed naked in the slave markets so that their sexual delights could easily be assessed. The prettiest and most well endowed fetched stiff prices. Slaves did not only come from nations overrun by the Roman army: unwanted babies, abandoned by their parents in the hope that they would die a natural death, were collected by pimps, brothel-keepers and slave traders. They were then reared and, when they were old enough, were sold into the sex trade. This ensured a plentiful supply of girls, who were abandoned more often than boys.

Pirates provided another source of slaves. They would sell off anyone they found on a ship they captured. The first-century writer Lucius Annaeus Seneca described the sale of a young woman taken by pirates: "Naked she stood on the shore, at the pleasure of the purchaser.

Every part of her body was examined and felt. Would you hear the result of the sale? The pirate sold; the pander bought. For this the pirates spared their captives, that she might be sold to a pander. For this the pander bought her, that he might employ her as a prostitute."

It was not just pimps and private individuals who bought. Restaurant-owners, innkeepers and bathhouse proprietors also bought pretty young slaves and hired them out to their customers. Barbershops were particularly notorious for their prostitutes, who would hang around while clients, completely naked, submitted themselves to depilation.

In general, male prostitutes charged more than female ones. Although most brothels were mixed, there were also some men-only houses. The highest prices were charged by men who performed oral sex, as this was considered the most depraved and degrading act. Many male prostitutes wore earrings, grew their hair long and crimped it in feminine ways. The most effeminate, it was said, were the Syrians.

Specialist services were also available. You could organise three in a bed, so you could be both the active and passive partner at the same time, or you could join the *spintriae* – "the links of a bracelet" – who formed a daisy chain.* There were also *tribades*, now known as lesbians, who catered for other tastes. Women charged top whack for triple penetration.

There was also a great deal of casual trade. Publicans would hire out rooms for amorous couples, and cook-shops, eating-houses of all kinds, bakers' shops, perfumeries, money-changers, theatres, circuses and slave-markets were all well-known centres for prostitution involving both sexes. Even the arrival of Christianity did not curb business. St Augustine* said: "Banish prostitutes from society and you reduce society to chaos through unsatisfied lust."

There was no escaping sex in the theatre, either. The Romans had little time for the classic drama of Ancient Greece. They put on mimes, which usually included erotic scenes – often rapes and seductions from Greek myths – that were originally acted out by men; women appeared in them after the second century BC. Performers were often naked and no licentious detail of the action was missed out. And, for a price, the actors and dancers were available after the performance.

At private parties, troupes of dancing girls performed in the nude. Spanish girls were particularly prized for the lasciviousness of their dancing. Then, in the latter period of the Republic, came the introduction of the orgy, a custom that originated in the east and which was generally favoured among the wealthy. These orgies took place in chambers whose walls were covered with erotic murals; provocative images greeted the eye wherever you looked. Guests were waited on by nude boys and by handmaidens – the latter were even employed to direct the penis of a urinating guest – while naked performers performed indecent tricks. Nude acrobats would have sex on a tightrope, which must have been dangerous. The rich vied with each other to see who could lay on the most outrageously lascivious event.

Religious festivals also provided an excuse for more sexual excess. At the Saturnalia, which ran from 17 to 24 December, all moral and social restraints were thrown out of the window. During the Lupercalia, the forerunner of St Valentine's Day, which followed in the middle of February, naked youths ran through the streets whipping all those they met with strips of hide cut from sacrificial victims. This was thought to increase the fertility of the women who were whipped. Even the handsome Mark Antony took part.

At the end of April came the Floralia, the festival of the prostitutes. According to St Augustine:* "The more foully they were presented, the more devotion was shown." Extreme indecency was the order of the day and nude dancers gave obscene performances.

The Bacchanalia, or Dionysia, in the middle of March, was originally celebrated by women only. When men were admitted to the celebrations, things got out of hand. Young men under the age of 20 were "forcibly debauched". When the authorities found out, seven thousand people were arrested, many from prominent families. In 186 BC, the Senate banned the public worship of Bacchus and restricted celebrations to groups consisting of no more than three women and two men – and even then only with official permission.

Then there were the ceremonies of the Bona Dea, women-only affairs in which they gave themselves up to "the most unbridled licentiousness and tribadism, in all its forms, reigned supreme". Juvenal left a description of the all-girl rites of Bona Dea:

> Shrieking flutes excite the women's loins, wine and the trumpet madden
> them. Whirling and shrieking, they are rapt by Priapus. Then, when

their hearts are ablaze with lust, the voices stutter with it, the wine gushes in torrents down their soaking thighs ... This is no pantomime. It is the real thing. Even [the old king of Troy] Priam's aged loins and [Trojan heroes' ageing mentor] Nestor cold with age would burn to see it. Their itching cannot bear delay. Women are shrieking and crying everywhere in the house: "It is time, let the men in!" If the lover sleeps, let him grab his coat and rush here. If not, they will grab the slaves. Not even slaves. They will take the scavengers of the street.

It was a bit like a modern American *feriae vernales*.

In Rome, there was a Temple of Isis where men and women prostituted themselves as an act of propitiation. Temple prostitution had long been a part of the worship of Aphrodite in Greece and of Ishtar, and other female deities, in the Middle East. The Greek historian Herodotus recorded what went on in Ancient Babylon in the fifth century BC:

The most shameful law among the Babylonians is this: every woman, once in her lifetime, is required to sit down in the courtyard of the Temple of Aphrodite and have sexual intercourse with a stranger. Many wealthy women disdain to mingle with the riffraff and travel to the temple gates in closed carriages, with many handmaidens following them. But most just walk in and seat themselves in the sacred plot of Aphrodite wearing a garland of rope around their heads. There is always a great hubbub, with some women arriving, some leaving.

Pathways are marked out in all directions among the women so that strangers can conveniently pass among them and make their choices. Once a woman has become seated, she may not return home until one of the strangers has tossed a coin in her lap and has had sexual intercourse with her outside the temple. When he casts the coin, he must say: "I invited you in the name of the goddess Mylitta [Mylitta is what the Assyrians call Aphrodite]." It doesn't matter how little money he gives because he won't be rejected, for that would be a sin, since the money belongs to the temple. She follows the first man who tosses a coin and she never rejects anyone. Once she has finished having sex, she has fulfilled her vow to the goddess and can go home. Afterwards no gift, no matter how generous, will buy her.

Beautiful and shapely women are, of course, claimed quickly and can go home, but ugly ones must often wait a long time because they cannot fulfil the law – some of them stay three or four years.

There were other sexual scams going on in the temples. The historian Tacitus said that in AD 19, two priests of Isis were crucified, along with a woman accomplice, for helping a Roman knight impersonate the god Anubis so that he could seduce a very pious married woman called Pauline. The Christian Eusebius also reported that a priest of Saturn called Tyrannus would tell the husband of any beautiful woman he fancied that Saturn himself had requested that his wife spend a night alone in the temple. The woman concerned would think this to be a great honour. She would get dressed up and take a gift along with her.

In front of everyone, the woman would go into the temple. Tyrannus would then shut the doors, lock them, hand over the key and leave. Once everything was quiet, he would creep through a hidden underground passageway and emerge in the temple inside the statue of Saturn itself. By this time, the woman would be on her knees, deep in prayer in the candle-lit temple. Suddenly, Tyrannus would speak from inside the hollow bronze statue. The woman would think that Saturn himself was talking to her and would tremble with mixed feelings of fear and joy that she was being so blessed.

"After this, the base divinity said what he pleased, either to cause great consternation or to incite lustfulness," said Eusebius. "The curtains were somehow drawn and all the candles were suddenly extinguished. Then he came down and by his godless deceits brought the stain of adultery upon the confused and dismayed women."

One cannot be too sure how confused and dismayed they were. They could, of course, have been complicit in the whole charade. On the other hand, they could also have been true believers. Greek and Roman mythology is full of examples of gods who assume some mortal form to come down to earth and *futuo*.

Anyway, Tyrannus got away with the scam for a long time. Numerous victims had passed through the temple without anyone saying a dicky bird about it. Then everything went belly up. He picked out a woman of a particularly chaste disposition. She was shocked by the things Saturn said to her, then recognised that the voice instructing her to take her clothes off and assume the position was that of Tyrannus himself – though she seems to have gone through with it. When she got home, she told her husband about the outrage. He was furious at the wrong that had been done to his wife – or rather to himself, as a Roman would see it. He accused Tyrannus, who was taken off to be tortured. Tyrannus confessed and was convicted.

"When the dark deceit stood exposed, all shame and dishonour pervaded the homes of the pagan, since mothers had been found to be adulterous, fathers defiled and children illegitimated," said the Christian Eugebus, gloatingly.

Fellatio appears to have been one of the rites practised by the priests of Dea Syria, while the followers of Cybele castrated themselves and gave themselves anally in her temple. There was even a religious sect whose rites included whipping naked boys.

The most widely worshipped god, however, was Priapus. The son of the Greek gods Dionysus and Aphrodite – Bacchus, the god of wine, and Venus, the goddess of love, in the Roman pantheon – he was born at Lampsacus on the Hellespont, which then separated Greece from Anatolia and still marks the division of Europe from Asia today. But Juno, the queen of the gods, was angry with Venus. She touched her and with her magic power caused Venus to give birth to a male child of extreme ugliness, but with monstrous genitals. He became a favourite with the people of Lampsacus, but they eventually expelled him because of his extreme lasciviousness. They then came down with a terrible disease of the genitals, so they begged Priapus to come back and erected a temple in his honour.

The worship of Priapus, in the form of an erect penis, thus spread across the ancient world. After all, who wants the *morbus gallicus*? It was said that an erection turned a man into a god – *tuis opugis pignore*. Little boys wore phallic pendants around their necks. Posts, with an erect penis carved on them, were erected on every street corner and everyone who passed one would touch it for luck.

Priapus's constant *rigidus* made him so popular that he was the only one of the ancient pagan gods Romans refused to give up when Constantine turned the empire Christian, and his image was seen everywhere. Carved phalluses appeared on walls, outside doors and on the sides of houses, sometimes with bells and wings on them, and everywhere they were found they were thought to bring good luck.

In Rome, Priapus was seen as a fertility god, and statues of him, replete with his huge erect penis, were put up in gardens as a scarecrow and perch rolled into one. They were also supposed to scare off thieves and often had a crude piece of verse inscribed on the bottom. One said:

> A sculptor saw me where once I stood
> As useless as a piece of wood,
> Now scared birds dart from leaves
> While my biggest stump scares the thieves.

Or:

> Hey, thief, you think it's funny standing there
> Laughing at me, insulting me, giving me two fingers.
> I know that, although my dick looks terrifyingly huge
> It is only made of wood. But hold on, let me call my horny master.
> As a favour to me, he'll give you something to gag on.

Or:

> Steal once and I'll give you it in the rear.
> Steal twice and I'll overflow your mouth.
> And if you steal a third time, I'll do both:
> Both mouth and rear packed beyond capacity.

Or again:

> When you get an urge to steal a fig,
> Stare long and hard at me
> Then try and imagine what shitting
> A 20-pound, two-foot-long turd would feel like.

Iurisperiti hac lingua utuntur ut alvum evacues ex metu.

In the countryside, there would be festivals to Priapus where huge stone penises would be paraded around and where normally respectable women would strip naked and masturbate or perform other carnal acts publicly to encourage the fertility of the fields.

Another phallic god called Liber also had a widespread following. During his visit to Italy, St Augustine* witnessed the sect's rites: "That shameful part of the body was, during the festival of Liber, placed with great pomp on wagons and carried about the roads in the country and at last to the city. In the town of Lanvium [Lanvio, 19 miles southeast of Rome] a whole month was dedicated to Liber. During it, the citizens shouted obscenities until the phallus had been carried to the market place and erected there. The highest rank of lady of the town then had to put a wreath on it. The god Liber had to be propitiated to ensure the future of the crops, and the evil eye had to be driven from the fields by compelling a married woman to do in public what not even a harlot would do under the eyes of married women in the theatre."

The bathhouse also presented ample opportunities for sex. Early Romans washed their arms and legs daily and their whole body only once a week. The rich had a small bathroom next to the kitchen so that they could get warm water easily. Around the middle of the third century BC, wealthy Romans began to build large bathing halls in their town houses and country villas. Although these were for private use, there was a strict code on how they should be used. Leaders of the Republic, such as Cato the Censor, would not take a bath in the presence of his son.

Later, public baths were built for use by the lower orders who had no access to a private bath. When Rome began to become wealthy, after the Second Punic War around 200 BC, luxurious public baths, or *thermae*, began to spring up. These became meeting places with gardens, libraries and gymnasiums where most Romans could wile away the hottest hours of the day. As well as bathing and exercising, they would meet, gossip, have their bodily hair plucked and listen to poets recite their latest works. And Roman poetry often had a high erotic content.

Bathers would be completely nude. In early times, the Romans had frowned on the Greek practice of performing gymnastics and exercising nude, but that too came into fashion in the gymnasiums and the games areas attached to the baths. At first the sexes were separated, or men and women used the baths at different times, but they quickly became unisex and outside they displayed the image of the half-man, half-woman Greek deity Hermaphroditus – the union of the beautiful son of Hermes and Aphrodite and the nymph of the fountain of Salmacis in Caria, in southwest Anatolia. A good deal of sexual activity occurred in these baths and a large number of prostitutes plied their trade there. Some of the single-sex baths operated in much the same fashion as San Francisco bathhouses in the 1970s – with the added advantage of male prostitutes and lascivious slave-boys supplied by the management for the use of their patrons. It is also hard to imagine that, in the girls-only baths, casual lesbianism did not take place.

To try to prevent freeborn boys of Rome being corrupted, they were encouraged to bathe in the Tiber. In the first century BC, the poet Catullus wrote about his mistress Clodia, who bought a garden on the banks of the river overlooking a spot where she could see the boys bathing naked. Later, the baths began allowing boys under a certain age to use the baths for no charge.

Segregated or not, the baths were a hotbed of sexual activity – primarily because everybody could see what a lover had to offer. As the first-century Roman poet and epigrammatist Martial said: "When you hear clapping in the baths, you know some moron with a giant dick has just arrived."

Size, however, was not everything. Juvenal, another first-century Roman writer, said: "If you've run out of luck, it doesn't matter how long your penis is."

And things are not always what they seem to be. Writing in the first century AD, in a serious book about earthquakes and tides, Seneca explained the use of the latest Roman sex toy – the magnifying mirror:

> Let me tell you a story so that you may learn why a lusty man never rejects an instrument for arousing pleasure and how ingenious he can be with it. Take Hostius Quadra. His sex life was so notorious that they made a stage play out of it. He was a wealthy miser and, when he was murdered by his own slaves, the Emperor Augustus let them off, thinking him unworthy of vengeance.
>
> Hostius swung both ways and lusted after both men and women. He ordered magnifying mirrors to be made that made a finger look as long and thick as an arm. These mirrors were placed so that, when he was

surrendering himself to a man, he could watch the thrusts of the young
stallion behind him. Reflected, the mirror made his partner's penis look
really huge.

He would go to the public baths and slyly measure men up as
potential partners. But no matter how big they were, his insatiable lust
delighted in further optical enhancement. Now tell me that the mirror
was invented just to check your hair and make-up.

According to Seneca, Hostius went even further in "those secret acts –
the ones that, if accused, every man denies". We are talking *verpam
comedo* here. With the aid of his magnifying mirrors, Hostius, Seneca
said, could "experience them not just with his mouth but with his eyes".

Not satisfied with just simply watching, he surrounded himself with
mirrors strategically placed so that he could divide up his deeds and view
them independently. For example, as he could not scrutinise the goings-
on closely enough when being ridden from behind, he would suck
another man's dick at the same time and watch himself doing it in the
mirror. That way he could admire the obscene artistry of his own
mouth and could watch men taking him in both orifices.

Sometimes he would be sandwiched between a man and a woman,
using his whole body to service both of them. And with his mirrors he
could witness his most deviant behaviour.

He did not like doing it in the dark. Far from being ashamed, he
wanted to see his most monstrous copulations and was proud to have
them well lit. He even wanted to have himself painted in these positions.

Seneca commented: "Even prostitutes hide their subservience in the
brothel ... but he wanted to turn his obscenities into a spectacle."

Hostius was unrepentant.

"Yes," he said. "I play the passive partner to a man and a woman at
the same time" – enjoying sodomy and cunnilingus simultaneously –
"but still a part of my body is left free. So I violate another man. Thus
all my organs are occupied in lechery. Let my eyes too share in the nasty
fun and be witnesses and judges of it. By means of mirrors, let even
those acts be seen which the contortions of our bodies hide from sight,
so that no one claimed I don't know exactly what I am doing ... And let

me, in my lust, see organs larger than they are in real life and marvel at what I'm able to handle."

Like Seneca, Martial gave everyone the rough edge of his tongue in the baths.

"Chrestus, you appear with your parts all shaven," he jibed. "So your penis looks like a vulture's neck."

Labienus came in for some stick, too.

"You pluck the hair from you chest, legs and arms," said Martial. "You keep your penis cropped and ringed with short hair; all this we know you do for your mistress's sake. But Labienus, for whom do you depilate your arse?"

For first-century AD polymath Pliny the Elder, female nudity was the cure for all evils. According to his great encyclopaedia *Natural History*, a compilation of knowledge from all over the Roman world, naked, menstruating women could drive away hailstorms and tornadoes. They could also drive caterpillars, worms, beetles and other pest from the fields. Menstrual blood and breast milk would combat almost any disease known to man. As a cure for a headache, he recommended wrapping around the head the primitive brassiere Roman women used to support their breasts. And much of Books XX through XXXII of *Natural History*, which cover medicine and drugs, focuses on the preparation of aphrodisiacs and ointments that, when applied to the penis, will make the woman penetrated less promiscuous.

Male nudity was on display at the games and gladiators either fought in a minuscule loincloth or, sometimes, completely naked in the arena. Young girls swooned; Roman matrons often had affairs with the champions. In the ruins of Pompeii, in the gladiators' crude sleeping chambers, a dead gladiator was found holding in his arms a rich woman still wearing her jewellery – perhaps shielding her from hot ash while giving her *amor fervidus*.

When not practising, gladiators would usually be surrounded by an entourage of prostitutes and fans, who were known as the "screaming whores". Many groupies hung around the entrance to the gladiators' barracks at night in the hope that they would be invited in to pleasure one of the heroes, or several of them. Gladiators would also be propositioned by wealthy men to take part in more extreme sexual acts. The night before the men fought, they would often spend their time in amorous combat, buggering each other in a competition of virility to see who could get the upper hand.

As the gladiators marched into the arena, the audience would stamp their feet in anticipation. During the bouts, excitement would mount to fever pitch and the screams of pain and the rattle of death heard from the arena were often matched by orgasmic cries from the tiers above. Men from the wealthy classes would bring pretty young companions of either sex to fellate them discreetly during the carnage. These would be schooled by retired prostitutes, known as "fuck-masters", and would be trained on slaves who were tied down and compelled to suffer sucking sessions that lasted up to 14 hours.

On the higher tiers, women would offer their lovers sex from the rear, so that both partners could watch the games. If the woman was particularly turned on by a particular gladiator or the action, she would open the front of her robe so that her breasts and pudenda would be exposed, while her lover could be seen entering her vagina or anus. And, of course, between bouts, there would be ample opportunity to pick out someone fresh for sex.

The poet Ovid pointed out that men and women were frequently struck by Cupid's arrow at the arena:

> Love oft in the arena fights a bout,
> Then 'tis the on-looker who's counted out.
> While chatting, buying a programme, shaking hands,
> Or wagering on the match, intent he stands,
> He feels the dart, and groaning 'neath the blow
> Himself becomes an item in the show.

In the highest tiers, men would be offering other men sex from the rear. Sometimes the *spintriae* would sit on each other's laps, creating towers that could easily collapse on the audience below, often with fatal results. For health and safety reasons, the back rows were often cordoned off.

The most accomplished lovers – particularly skilled prostitutes – would know how to bring their partners off at the very moment of the kill. When the emperors came to power in Rome and had the power of life and death by raising or lowering a thumb, all action had to cease while he contemplated the fate of the defeated gladiator. This could cause a problem if a dog had been brought along to provide pleasure. The emperors would often teasingly delay the decision, and the execution that followed would often be greeted by waves of orgasm.

The life-or-death decision often depended on whether the emperor fancied the man or not; whether or not the gladiator had a lascivious look or if he had a large penis. If the action was unsatisfactory, the crowd would turn against the *editor* who organised the games and he would be crucified and then disembowelled in the middle of the arena. *Denique caelum.* However, some of the more bloodthirsty emperors, including Caligula and Nero, liked to act as the *editor* themselves.

The action reached a climax when hordes of naked criminals armed with rusty swords were herded into the arena to fight to the death. Attendants lashed them into action with whips, and any who refused to fight risked having a red-hot brand thrust at their sexual organs. The crowd grew frenzied as the men fought until only one of them was standing. There was no reprieve even for him, though. He would raise his arms like a victorious gladiator, then a black-helmeted, eight-foot giant carrying a two-handed axe would enter the arena and slice him in half.

Out-and-out sex shows were also staged in the arena. Romans particularly enjoyed the re-enactment of mythical couplings between humans and animals. A re-staging of "Pasiphaë and the Bull" – as a result of which the legendary queen of Crete conceived the Minotaur – must, surely, have been fatal. The bull was lowered in a cage and harnessed to the female victim; it seems certain that this hideous act was performed as an execution.

All this would take place amidst the most awful stench. Members of the audience would not risk losing their place to urinate or defecate. They would do what they had to do where they sat, pissing on people in the tier below out of fun or malice. Games could last weeks, or even months.

Some men took particular pleasure from ejaculating on those below. The bald pates of senators were favoured targets and prostitutes polished their manual dexterity so that a client's semen could hit any enemy several rows in front. The more philosophical merely wanted to see how far their sperm could fly, and the high walls that surrounded the arena itself – erected ostensibly to keep wild animals in – also stopped semen from splashing onto the contestants, either as a mark of respect or contempt. Even men without a partner or a prostitute were expected to contribute, even if they only passed water at the moment of mass ejaculation.

At night, while slaves removed severed body parts from the arena and covered pools of blood with fresh sand, others did their best to keep their footing as they climbed the stands to clean off faeces, urine, semen and other bodily fluids. The dead bodies of those overcome with excitement also had to be cleared away, but there was little that could be done about the smell, as the cocktail of excreta flushed from the stands flowed into ducts which directed it out of the building and deposited it on the heads of the great unwashed who would sleep in the open air surrounding the arena. Prostitutes working out of the arches around the bottom of the Colosseum would only add to the funk.

The air would also be filled with the sounds of religious or political dissidents who, on their last night on earth, were being tortured or sexually abused by their jailers. There would also be the roars of wild animals, the most feared of which was the Libyan lion, with his razor-sharp claws and testicles the size of a man's head. They were so ferocious, it was said, that there was only one way to catch them. An attractive slave had to get on all fours and offer the animal his anus. When the lion had mounted and was fully engaged, a gang made up of other slaves would wrestle it to the ground and sedate it with copious quantities of Armenian brandy. The process was almost inevitably fatal for the bait and probably lethal for a number of his companions. Still sedated, the lion would then be shipped across the Mediterranean to Ostia, and then up the river to Rome. There it would be caged and starved. Then, when it was ravenous and fully sober, it would be released into the arena to face a gladiator or, perhaps, a crowd of defenceless dissidents or cultists.

Some magicians claimed to possess the power to halt a lion in its tracks with a series of hand gestures. The *editor's* response to this was to release more lions. One lion could be mesmerised; ten could not.

Chariot racing also offered a bloodthirsty spectacle. Competitors deliberately ran each other down, forced opponents into the walls or cut down anyone hurled from his chariot onto the track with the sabres attached to their wheels. Chariot races usually took place on the last day of the games, as the arena had to be modified to accommodate the track. Eventually, a purpose-built stadium was erected which could house three hundred thousand spectators. Chariot racing at the new stadium attracted a younger crowd, all of whom dressed in their finery. The women wore brightly coloured dresses that offered the occasional glimpse of an erect nipple or a depilated vulva. Again the action made spectators highly aroused and men's togas were folded back to reveal bulging erections. If you could get no satisfaction in the stadium, a shanty town of prostitutes' huts grew up around it where every kind of sexual taste was catered for.

There was also action to be had at the circus. Ovid recommended picking up women there:

> Many opportunities await you at the circus. No one will prevent you from sitting next to a girl. Get as close to her as you can. That's easy enough, for the seating is cramped anyway. Find an excuse to talk to her ... Ask her what horses are entering the ring and which ones she fancies. Approve her choices ... If, as is likely, a speck of dust falls on her lap, brush it gently away; and, even if no dust falls, pretend it has done and brush her lap just the same. She will certainly let you have a glimpse of her legs ... The deft arrangement of a cushion has often helped a lover ... Such are the advantages that a circus offers a man who is looking for an affair.

However, the Roman masses did not find the circus or chariot racing as much of a turn-on as the bloody slaughter of the gladiatorial arena. This was a world where public executions, burnings, floggings and torture were considered to be entertainment. The Romans, as we have seen, enjoyed all kinds of sex, but they loved sadism most of all. It will come as no surprise then that the men who later became emperors were, for the most part, totally depraved.

CHAPTER 2

Julius Caesar was not a Roman emperor, but it was feared that he intended to become one. That is why he was assassinated on the steps of the Senate on 15 March – the Ides of March – 44 BC.

Gaius Julius Caesar was a member of one of the original aristocratic families of Rome who could trace their lineage back to Venus, the goddess of love. A tall Lothario with piercing brown eyes, he was famed for his over-active libido. As a youth he was described as "exquisite" and was looked upon as effeminate, and throughout his life he was renowned for being fastidious about his appearance.

"He was somewhat over-nice in the care of his person," said the second-century Roman biographer Suetonius,* "and not only kept the hair of his head carefully trimmed and his face smoothly shaved, but has also been accused of having certain other hairy parts of his body depilated with tweezers."

This meant that he had smooth *nates*, for purposes that have already been discussed.

His father died when he was 16 and, the following year, he broke off his engagement to the wealthy heiress Cossutia, to whom he had been engaged as a child. Instead he married Cornelia, the daughter of Lucius Cornelius Cinna, who had been consul four times. Soon after, she gave birth to their daughter Julia.

Rome was then taken over by the dictator Lucius Cornelius Sulla. He was not happy that Caesar had allied himself with Sulla's enemy Cinna and tried to force him to divorce Cornelia. When Caesar resisted, he was sacked from his position as priest of Jupiter, stripped of his privileges and divested of his wife's dowry. He was then accused of siding with another of Sulla's political enemies, Marius, the leader of the people, and was forced to flee. He hid out in the Sabine territory, but eventually won a pardon through the intercession of the Vestal Virgins.

However, it was still politic to stay out of Sulla's way, so Caesar went out east to do military service. He spent so long in Bithynia, northwest Anatolia, that there were rumours that he was having a homosexual affair with its king, Nicomedes. In fact, no sooner had Caesar left Bithynia than he found some excuse to go back. The taint of what went on in Bithynia stuck with him for the rest of his life. Indeed, his affair with Nicomedes was celebrated in a notorious poem by Calvus Licinius, which began:

> Whate'er Bithynia and her lord possess'd,
> Her lord who Caesar in his lust caress'd

The politician Marcus Tullius Cicero wrote that Caesar had been conducted by royal attendants from his own bedroom to that of the king. There he had been laid "upon a bed of gold with a covering of purple, where the flower of youth and innocence of him who was descended from Venus became defiled in Bithynia".

Later, when Caesar pleaded the cause of Nysa, the daughter of Nicomedes, before the Senate, he recounted the king's many kindnesses to him. In reply, Cicero said: "Pray tell us no more of that. We all know what he gave you and what you gave him in return."

The governor of nearby Cilicia, Gnaeus Cornelius Dolabella, called Caesar "the queen's rival and the inner partner of the royal bed", while the tribune Gaius Scribonius Curio the Elder, then Sulla's legate in Asia, called Caesar "the brothel of Nicomedes and the Bithynian stew".

Even Caesar's friend Catullus said that he was a passive pederast and compared him to the notorious pathic – the "girl" in a gay relationship – Mamurra. In the poem "On Mamurra and Julius Caesar", Catullus wrote:

> A comely couple of shameless catamites,
> Mamurra and Caesar, pathics both,
> No wonder, they share the same stain ...
> Both morbidly affected through pathic vice, the twin-like twain

Lie in a single bed,
One not more than the other greedy for lechery.
Allied rivals of the girls.
A comely couple of shameless catamites.

And Catullus was supposed to be Caesar's friend.

Eventually Caesar won his laurels for taking Mytilene, the capital of Lesbos. The island had been renowned since the time of Ancient Greece for immorality of all varieties, not just for what is now known as lesbianism. In fact, in the Classical Greek spoken by educated Romans, the verb "to lesbianise" means to perform fellatio. (See *Sex Lives of the Famous Lesbians*.) Caesar later made Mytilene a free city to please his boyfriend Theophanes, who was a Mitylenian.

The winning of his laurels was important for Caesar. He was going bald and liked to disguise his condition by wearing a crown of laurel leaves on his head. He also combed his hair forward in a manner later emulated by Napoleon,* even though the French emperor was not going bald.

When Sulla retired to spend more time in the brothel and at all-boy orgies, Caesar returned to Rome and quickly climbed the greasy pole. However, to fulfil his over-reaching ambition, he needed to study oratory. The place to do that was at Rhodes, but on the way there he was taken prisoner by pirates who found themselves captivated by his good looks and charm. After arranging his own ransom, Caesar raised a naval force, captured his captors and had them crucified.

After his wife Cornelia died, Caesar made a smart political move and married Sulla's granddaughter Pompeia. The marriage did not last due to some untoward hanky-panky. Caesar had an effeminate called Clodius Pulcher – also known as *Pulchellus Puer*, "the pretty boy" – who was notorious for seducing all three of his sisters. He too had been taken by pirates off Cyprus and saved his life by satisfying their lusts. In 62 BC, a group of women gathered at Caesar's house to celebrate the all-girl festival of Bona Dea. Pulcher dressed up in women's clothing and got past security, only to be unmasked by Caesar's mother, the sharp-eyed Aurelia. However, the rumour circulated that Pulcher had taken the opportunity to penetrate not only the rites of Bona Dea, but also Caesar's wife, Pompeia. Caesar, it appears, grew jealous that his Pompeia had been turned on by a man *in stola*.

"Tum Caesar... respondit: quia suam uxorem etiam suspicione vacare vellet," wrote Plutarch.

As Caesar's wife was now not above suspicion, he divorced her. Pulcher was later knifed to death on the Appian Way.

Caesar's taste for sumptuous living left him deeply in debt, and it is said that he invaded Britain in the hope of grabbing the precious gems reputed to be found there. His greatest extravagance, however, was buying fine young slaves. He paid so much for them that he was too embarrassed to enter the figures in his household accounts.

When Caesar became consul, he married Calpurnia, daughter of Lucius Piso who succeeded him to the consulship. He broke his daughter Julia's engagement to Servilius Caepio and gave her to Gnaeus Pompey, simultaneously organising Caepio's engagement to Pompey's daughter. This tied Caesar to Pompey, who – with Marcus Crassus – formed the First Triumvirate that took power in Rome in 59 BC. The important thing was to keep it in the *gens* – the Roman word for clan.

Despite his reputation as a *cinaede*, Caesar had numerous affairs with women. According to Suetonius, he "spent much energy and money on his lusts, and seduced many women of high rank". Among his posh lovers were Postumia, wife of Servius Sulpicius; Lollia, wife of Aulus Gabinius; Tertulla, wife of Crassus; and Mucia, Pompey's first wife. So Caesar had slept with the wives of the other two triumvirs, which must have made cabinet meetings a little strained.

Pompey had divorced Mucia over her affair with Caesar, which left him free to marry Julia, but Curio the Elder, now a supporter of Caesar, criticised Pompey for divorcing Mucia, the mother of his three children, and marrying Caesar's daughter. At the same time, privately, Curio called Caesar "Aegisthus", after the cousin of Agamemnon who seduced Agamemnon's wife Clytaemestra while he was away fighting the Trojan War.

Despite Curio's earlier slur that Caesar was a "Bithynian stew", he now spoke with some admiration of Caesar's reputation for swinging both ways, calling him in a speech "Every woman's husband and every man's wife." This was echoed by Suetonius, who said that Caesar was "a man to every woman and a woman to every man".

As a triumvir, Caesar took control of Gaul – that's France, Belgium and western Germany – where he built his reputation as a military leader.

It was noted that Caesar was a fierce fighter and a skilled politician who bent everyone to his will – "not an easy thing for a woman to do," said one senator, alluding to Caesar's time with King Nicomedes.

But Caesar was unashamed.

"Even in Assyria there reigned for some time Queen Semiramis," Caesar retorted – she was said to have planted the Hanging Gardens of Babylon – "and that the Amazons in times past held a great part of Asia in subjugation."

In other words: *"Lege labris volumen inguinale mihi."*

Even Sulla joined the sexual criticism. Noting that Caesar wore his purple-edged senatorial robe, trimmed with fringes around the wrists, girded about him rather loosely, Sulla would admonish him to "beware of the ill-girt boy" – though the boy in question might have been the young Demetrius, Caesar's catamite, who was generally shunned because "he submitted without complaint to his caprices".

Despite Caesar's growing power, political rivals still called him the "Queen of Bithynia". One of them, Marcus Calpurnius Bibulus, fearful of Caesar's ambition, said: "He had formerly been in love with a king, but now coveted a kingdom."

Caesar's assassin, Marcus Brutus, told the story that a man called Octavius, a well-known practical joker, saluted Pompey as king and Caesar as queen and, while entertaining him at dinner, arranged for Caesar to sit with the catamites. Pompey himself was said to be a great lover of boys, but in Roman eyes it was much better to give than to receive.

Pompey was also very much in love with his wife Julia, who was Caesar's daughter, but she died in childbirth in 54 BC, thus breaking the political alliance between the two men. So it was all change again. Caesar promised Pompey his sister's granddaughter Octavia – who had been married to Gaius Marcellus – and asked to marry Pompey's daughter, who had recently been promised to Faustus Sulla. Unfortunately, the two men were about to fall out in the worst kind of way.

Caesar's victories in Gaul made him both popular and powerful, but his troops still teased him, singing as they marched:

> The Gauls to Caesar yield, Caesar to Nicomede,
> Lo! Caesar triumphs for his glorious deed,
> But Caesar's conqueror gains no victor's mead.

Nevertheless the Senate grew afraid and ordered Caesar to disband his army. He refused and marched on Rome. Reaching the River Rubicon, he camped. That night he had a dream where he had sex with his mother. The following morning, he addressed his troops. If they crossed the river, it would be an act of war. Then he tore off his clothes and begged his men to pledge their fidelity. Together, they swept across the Rubicon and pushed Pompey, Crassus and the Senate out of Italy.

As Caesar's army marched on Rome in triumph, they sang another ribald song, this time about his reputation as a womaniser. It went:

> Lock your wives away, you Romans,
> A bald whoremonger home we bring.
> In Gaul his tarts cost you all your gold,
> So now he'll be just borrowing.

When he was in power, Caesar became positively prudish. Despite his own louche behaviour, he had a freed slave, who had been a particular favourite, put to death because he had dishonoured the wife of a Roman knight, even though the knight concerned had made no complaint. He also dissolved the marriage of a man who had wed a woman two days after her divorce, even though there was no hint of impropriety.

As well as the wives and daughters of aristocrats, Caesar also loved dark-skinned beauties and fell for Eunoë, a Moor and the wife of a man called Bogudes. He lavished expensive gifts on both the willing wife and the compliant husband. Then there was Cleopatra, who famously had herself delivered to him in a rolled-up carpet.

Caesar had arrived in Egypt in 48 BC in pursuit of Pompey, after defeating him at the Battle of Pharsalus in Greece. Pompey was murdered as soon as he stepped ashore in Egypt by Cleopatra's brother and husband, King Ptolemy XIII, in an effort to ingratiate himself with Caesar. It didn't work.

Cleopatra's full name was Cleopatra VII *Thea Philopator* – Greek for "Goddess Loving Her Father". The pharaohs were notoriously incestuous. After the Macedonian general Ptolemy I took control of Egypt, following the death of Alexander the Great in 323 BC, the Ptolemaic dynasty had intermarried to maintain their pure Macedonian blood, but the Egyptian pharaohs of Ancient Egypt had kept it in the family long before that. As property passed down the maternal line, when a pharaoh's wife died, he would marry his daughter, then his granddaughter and so on, to keep his hands on the loot. It was traditional.

Cleopatra herself was married to two of her brothers. She was ruling jointly with her brother-husband Ptolemy XIII when Caesar turned up. With the aid of her womanly wiles, she enlisted Caesar's help to rid herself of her troublesome brother and place herself on the throne, alone.

Modern forensic reconstructions have shown that inbred Cleopatra was no great beauty, as Shakespeare assumed, but she was *postrema lascivia*. She was thought to have taken her first lover at the age of 12 – nine years before she met Caesar. According to one account, she fellated a hundred Roman noblemen in a single night. The Greeks called her *Meriochane*, which means "she who gapes wide for a thousand men". Even the famous baby-killer King Herod claimed that she had tried to seduce him, even though she was nowhere near Palestine at the time. Known for her lewd jokes and sexually provocative conversation, the 21-year-old Cleopatra's quick tongue soon captivated the 52-year-old Caesar.

Although Caesar was already married, he went through an Egyptian wedding ceremony with her and took Cleopatra and their son Caesarion to Rome, putting them up in one of his homes. He publicly declared his love for her by installing her statue in the Temple of Venus. The idea of deifying a foreigner angered the people of Rome, who felt that Cleopatra exerted undue influence over Caesar, and who had no wish to be ruled by a foreign queen.

In an effort to salvage Caesar's reputation, his friend Gaius Oppius published a book saying that Cleopatra's child was not Caesar's at all. However, Mark Antony later testified to the Senate that Caesar had acknowledged paternity and Greek historians said that the boy resembled Caesar both in features and in gait.

Although it was said that by the time he died Caesar's strength had been undermined by his incessant debauchery, leaving him increasingly vulnerable to the epilepsy that afflicted him throughout his life, it was all too easy to believe that the child was Caesar's. He was renowned for his sexual vigour and he was a sparing drinker of wine. His political opponent Marcus Cato said: "Caesar was the only sober man who ever tried to overthrow the state" – though Cato still referred to Caesar as "that woman".

It was clear, however, that Caesar did intend to take supreme power in Rome with Cleopatra by his side. While he was away in Egypt, he had written to the tribune Helvius Cinna, asking him to draw up a bill to legitimise any marriage Caesar made to whatever woman or women he pleased "for the procreation of children".

Before he could legitimise his marriage to Cleopatra and make her his empress, though, Caesar was stabbed to death at the age of 65 in 44 BC by, it is said, 23 conspirators. His last words were not *"Et tu Brute?"* It was Shakespeare who put those Latin words, meaning "You too, Brutus?", in his mouth. Roman historians said that his last words were in Greek not Latin, and that he said to Brutus: *"Kai su, technon?"* – which means "You too, my child?"

It is likely that Brutus was indeed his son. Brutus's mother, Servilia, was one of Caesar's many mistresses. So even his death was contingent on his sex life.

As dying Caesar fell, he pulled the skirts of his toga around his legs so that he would die decently covered. He knew it was an historic moment and he did not want to be remembered two thousand years later as an *expositicor obscenus*.

The same cannot be said of the mourners at his funeral, many of whom stripped off their clothing and threw it onto his funeral pyre. With death, came silence. But as Horace remarked in his *Epistles*: *"Migravit ab aure voluptas Omnis ad incertos oculos, et gaudia vana."*

CHAPTER 3

B oth Julius Caesar and Caesar Augustus lend their names to summer months, but Augustus shined on a good many more summers of love than Julius. He died in his bed in his 76th year, was the first proper Roman emperor, and lent his name to those who followed him to the throne.

Born Gaius Octavius on 23 September 63 BC, he was Julius Caesar's grandnephew. It was said that he was conceived when his mother, Atia, and a number of her married women friends attended a solemn ceremony at the Temple of Apollo. She fell asleep on a couch and a snake glided up, entered her and then slithered away again. When she awoke, she washed and purified herself as she would after having sex with her husband. Later, a mark in the shape of a serpent appeared on her body, and from then on she avoided going to the baths.

Nine months after the snake incident, Atia gave birth to the future Augustus – known in his youth as Octavian – leading to the idea that he was descended from Apollo. A similar tale was told about the birth of the conqueror of the ancient world Alexander the Great, whose mother was also supposed to have been impregnated by a sacred asp.

At the time of Octavian's birth there was a portent that, after four centuries as a Republic, Nature herself was preparing to give Rome a new king. This caused such consternation that the Senate drew up a decree banning the raising of any male child for a year. However, a number of senators' wives who were pregnant at the time prevented the decree from being enacted.

While she was pregnant, Octavian's mother had a dream in which her womb was carried up to the stars and stretched out to encompass the whole of heaven and earth – which must have been painful. His father, Octavius, also dreamt that he had seen a sunbeam shine from his wife's womb and the sun itself rise between her thighs. Octavian's birth made him late for a Senate debate and, when he arrived, the astrologer Publius Nigidius Figulus said portentously: "The ruler of the world is now born."

"Everyone believes this story," said Augustus's credulous biographer Suetonius. *Fac ut vivas*.

Octavian came to be great-uncle Julius's favourite after he made an oration at the funeral of his grandmother Julia, who was Caesar's sister. When he was 17 years old, he accompanied Caesar on the triumphal procession after his victory in Africa, and the following year fought alongside him in Spain. When Caesar was assassinated, Octavian discovered that Caesar had adopted him as his heir.

He immediately found himself in conflict with Mark Antony, who had been Caesar's favourite and who had assumed that he would be his successor. Mark Antony said that Octavian had robbed him of his inheritance by having sex with Caesar as the price of his adoption. This was rich coming from Antony, whose interests also lay in that direction. As a youth he had been exhibited for sale in a woman's toga and the garb of a prostitute. He was also said to have been attached to an effeminate youth called Curio. After gossip that they were "husband" and "wife" became widespread, Curio's father forced his son to break off the friendship.

While he was in Rome, Antony kept a harem of both sexes and bought two pretty boys for a hundred thousand sesterces – around $4,000. Cicero said that Antony conducted all-male orgies in the villa he rented from Marcus Varro. There, it was said, he had sex with both nobly born boys, something that was against the law, and *pueri meritorii*, or boys who were especially trained and hired out for such debauchery.

Suetonius's description of the young Octavian does make him sound rather *pulchrae*: "He was unusually handsome and exceedingly graceful at all periods of his life, though he cared nothing for personal adornment. His expression, whether in conversation or when he was silent, was calm and mild ... He had clear, bright eyes, in which he liked to have it thought that there was a kind of divine power, and it greatly pleased him, whenever he looked keenly at anyone, if he let his face fall as if before the radiance of the sun."

On the other hand: "His teeth were wide apart, small and ill-kept; his hair was slightly curly and inclining to golden; his eyebrows met ... His complexion was between dark and fair. He was short of stature, but this was concealed by the fine proportion and symmetry of his figure, and was noticeable only by comparison with some taller person standing beside him."

This did not matter because he, famously, wore lifts.

Thanks to Antony's scuttlebutt, it was widely rumoured that Octavian "earned his adoption by his uncle Caesar through unchastity". And Antony's brother, Lucius, said that Octavian had also given himself to the military governor Aulus Hirtius when he was fighting in Spain for three hundred thousand sesterces – $12,000 – adding that he had singed the hairs on his legs with red-hot walnut shells to make them softer for the occasion. Another enemy, Sextus Pompeius, the son of Pompey the Great, also accused him of effeminacy. The rest of Rome thought so, too. In the theatre one afternoon, one actor playing the eunuch priest of Cybele, the mother of the gods, was playing a drum when another actor said: "Videsne ut cinaedus orbem digito temperet!" – which means: "See how the fingers of the sodomite sway the world!" The audience took this to be a reference to Octavian and broke into wild applause.

Octavian was not going to take such slights lying down, though. First, he took on Mark Antony, driving him into Gaul. Then he patched things up with Antony by dropping his fiancée, the daughter of Servilius Isauris, and getting engaged to Antony's stepdaughter Claudia, even though she was almost too young for marriage. He forced the Senate to give him the vacant consulship, then formed the Second Triumvirate with Mark Antony and Marcus Aemilius Lepidus – the new pontifex maximus, or high priest, and one of Caesar's prominent supporters.

However, then he had a row with Claudia's mother, Antony's wife Fulvia, and divorced Claudia before the marriage was consummated. He then made another politically motivated marriage to Scribonia, whose brother was a supporter of Sextus Pompeius, who was a potential rival for Octavian's place on the triumvirate. Octavian was 23 and Scribonia was in her 30s. She had already been married twice to men of consular rank and was already the mother of at least one daughter, Cornelia, who died in childhood. Nevertheless, when the marriage received her brother's blessing, Octavian effectively cancelled out any threat to his position that may have come from Sextus.

The triumvirate had dictatorial powers for five years and their enemies – including three hundred senators – were ruthlessly purged. Although Antony was seen as the leading triumvir, Octavian's prestige received a boost when, in 42 BC, Julius Caesar was elevated to the status of a god. Octavian was now officially the son of a god.

While Lepidus took control in North Africa, Octavian and Antony took their armies across the Adriatic and dispatched Caesar's principal assassins, Brutus and Cassius, who were holed up there. Antony then went on to secure the East, while Octavian returned to Italy.

Antony's wife Fulvia, his brother Lucius and his chief lieutenant Manius did not like this arrangement. They decided that holding Italy gave Octavian too much power and took him on in the Perusine War. This situation seems to have been exacerbated by another bit of *concubitum*. Having pacified the East, Antony was having his jollies with the noted beauty Glaphrya in Anatolia. Martial quoted Augustus's explanation of the situation:

Because Anthony fucked Glaphrya,
Fulvia decided I had to fuck her – in revenge.
Me, fuck Fulvia? Supposing Manius begged me to bugger him.
Would I do it? Not if I had any sense! "Either fuck me or we fight,"
    she said.
But my cock is dearer to me than my life. So sound the trumpets of war!

This epigram is quoted by the 16th-century essayist Michel de Montaigne as a classic example of how wars start.

Sextus Pompeius then sided with what he thought was the Antonyian faction, but when Fulvia and her accomplices were besieged and then defeated at Perusia, modern Perugia, Antony went behind everyone's back and made a fresh agreement with Octavian, carving up the Roman Empire between them. Pompeius fought on alone, but was defeated by Octavian's friend and ally Agrippa.

To seal the deal between Antony and Octavian, Antony agreed to marry Octavian's sister Octavia, but Antony had been a busy boy out East. As well as *futuendi* the beautiful Glaphrya, he had already spent the winter with the Queen of Egypt, Cleopatra. He had been in Tarsus, in modern Turkey, when he had sent for her. Cleopatra realised that fate was offering her a second bite of the cherry; Antony offered her another chance to achieve what she had so nearly achieved with Julius Caesar.

Determined to seduce him, she sailed up the river into Tarsus on a barge with a deck of gold, silver oars and purple sails. Suetonius said that her arrival was announced by the music of flutes and lutes. She was dressed – or, perhaps, undressed – as Venus, attended by Cupids and the three Graces.

Plutarch described the scene:

Getting ready to leave, Cleopatra prepared elaborate gifts, lots of gold and ornaments befitting the ruler of a prosperous land. But when she departed, she placed her greatest trust in herself and her ability to bewitch.

Despite many urgent letters from Mark Antony himself and his colleagues demanding her presence, she chose to toy with him from the very beginning. She sailed slowly up the river Cydnus [Tarsus] in a boat with a gilded prow and sails of deep purple. Her rowers dipped silver oars to the cadence of flutes and lyres.

Cleopatra herself lay beneath a canopy splashed with gold, posed like Venus in a painting, while boys as handsome as Eros gently fanned her. Her most beautiful handmaidens, resembling river goddesses and the Graces, were placed artfully around the ship. Beguiling perfumes billowing from incense burners engulfed the riverbanks. Local people came from far and wide to gawp. In Tarsus itself, everyone flocked from the marketplace to the riverfront, leaving Mark Antony all by himself, seated on a dais, waiting.

Then word spread that Aphrodite had arrived to sport with Dionysus for the good of Asia.

The goddess of love had come to seduce the god of fruitfulness in a game of power politics. Plutarch continued:

Antony sent a messenger to invite Cleopatra to dinner, but she insisted that he come to her. Antony, wanting to show good will and a devil-may-care attitude, agreed and went.

When he arrived, he was dazzled by a magnificent display of lights. They arched into the night sky, creating mesmerising patterns. It was one of the most astonishing sights he had ever seen.

The next day, Antony tried to outdo Cleopatra with an even more luxurious banquet, but failed and was the first to complain when the food did not come up to standard.

Cleopatra noted that Antony had the crude humour of a soldier or a workman. So, like a chameleon, she quickly dropped her airs and played along in the same unrestrained and brazen fashion.

We have been told that her beauty was by no means flawless, or even remarkable at first glance, but anyone listening to her for even a moment was captivated by her irresistible charm. She had a natural presence. Her voice was rich, sweet and beguiling and she used her tongue like a many-stringed instrument [it was ripe for plucking, as we have already established]. And when she talked to foreigners, she rarely needed an interpreter, answering Ethiopians, Troglodytes, Hebrews, Arabs, Syrians, Medes and Parthians in their own language.

Being of Macedonian descent, she would have spoken in Greek to Mark Antony who, as an educated Roman, would also have been fluent in Greek. Plutarch remarked on her unusual linguistic ability. Many of the other Macedonian pharaohs had never even bothered to learn Egyptian. Some had not even dropped their crude Macedonian dialect.

Knowing Antony's tastes, Cleopatra laid on special entertainment at her extravagant banquets, provided by *cineadii* – effeminate men – who performed lewd dances for him. Even though Fulvia was taking up arms for him in Italy and the Parthians were threatening to invade Syria, Cleopatra had little difficulty in persuading Antony to return to Egypt with her and they spent the winter of 41–40 BC in a pleasure resort outside Alexandria. While he was there, he lived surrounded by concubines and eunuchs, and Cleopatra, sensing where his tastes lay, made him a leader of the "Inimitables", the gilded youths who, it was said, possessed sole knowledge of the supreme refinements of oriental sensuality. They put on erotic theatrical shows. At one, another Roman guest played the Greek sea god Glaucus, writhing naked on the floor, painted blue.

According to Plutarch:

> Cleopatra flattered Antony, always dreaming up some fresh delight, careful never to let him stray from her either day or night. She rolled dice with him, drank with him, hunted with him and faithfully watched him exercise and play war games. And even when he scrambled about the city hiding in doorways and windows, taunting and teasing complete strangers, she went along with it. For Antony liked to disguise himself as a servant and, on occasion, wounded up being cursed and sometimes beaten, even though most people recognised him. Nonetheless, the Alexandrians enjoyed his crude jokes and joined in his pranks in their own elegant and cultured way.

Cleopatra also liked a joke. When Mark Antony was out fishing one day, he did not catch a thing and was annoyed that Cleopatra was there to witness his failure. So he secretly arranged for a servant to swim underwater and attach fish to his hook. Then he pulled up three or four big fish and Cleopatra praised him for his skill at fishing.

Even when she had figured out what was going on, she continued to fawn over his angling ability and hatched a plan of her own. Still pretending to be impressed, she told all her friends that they must come and watch the mighty Mark Antony fishing the next day. A huge party turned up to watch Antony cast. This time, Cleopatra got one of her own servants to swim down. Antony felt a tug on his line and reeled it in; he found a dried, salted herring on the hook. Everyone laughed, but Cleopatra had a serious point to make.

"Oh Imperator," she said. "Give your rod to the men of Pharos and Conobius. Your sport is to hunt cities, kingdoms and continents."

Antony's relationship with Cleopatra caused political problems, so he returned to Italy to patch things up with Octavian – leaving Cleopatra pregnant with twins. He married Octavia, an action that helped prolong the triumvirate for another five years, but Octavia was widely known to be "virtuous" – not a quality that keeps a man interested in the bedroom. Antony divorced her after five years and returned to Egypt to marry Cleopatra; his actions made the political split with Octavian inevitable. Even so, Antony wrote to Octavian in an attempt to heal the rift.

"What has come over you?" he wrote. "Why do you object to my sleeping with Cleopatra? We are married; and it is not as if it were anything new – the affair started nine years ago. And what about you? Are you faithful to Livia Drusilla? My congratulations if, when you receive this letter, you are not in bed with Tertullia, Terentilla, Rufilla, or Salvia Titisena – or all four of them. What does it matter where, or with whom, you have sex?"

By this time, Octavian had divorced his first wife, the "serious and respectable" Scribonia, on the day that she bore him his daughter Julia, and had married Livia. Octavian said that he had got rid of the ageing Scribonia because he was "sick of her crabbed character". The divorce petition accused her of "moral perversity". In reality, she had fallen out with one of his mistresses.

Meanwhile, Octavian had fallen in love with Livia, the 17-year-old wife of Tiberius Claudius Nero who, though he bore the names of three emperors, was merely the father of one, Tiberius, whom Augustus adopted. Livia was six months pregnant at the time and Octavian had to ask the chief priests whether marrying a pregnant woman was allowed. They gave the go-ahead, but not everyone thought that Octavian's divorce of Scribonia, and his subsequent remarriage to Livia, was legal and it caused a schism in the royal line between the Julians – who were the descendants of Scribonia's daughter Julia – and the Claudians – who were Livia's kin.

Livia's long-suffering husband even had to stump up a dowry as if he was her father. At the wedding banquet, one of the beautiful naked pages who attended the ladies saw Livia reclining beside Octavian, some distance from Tiberius Claudius Nero. So he ran up to her and said: "What are you doing here, my lady? The master is over there!" pointing at Nero.

The marriage between Augustus and Livia seems to have been a happy one. Tacitus is flattering about her, but the only good thing the second-century Roman historian Cassius Dio said about Livia was that she had a good and calming influence on Augustus's sometimes irritable nature, claiming that Augustus was "also in love with the beautiful wife of his friend Maecenas", the man who had arranged his

53

marriage to Scribonia in the first place. Nevertheless, the marriage continued as Augustus found his wife useful, not least as a procurer for his seemingly insatiable sexual appetite.

Maecenas, who was criticised by Seneca for the luxury of his lifestyle, was not bothered either that Augustus was venerating his wife. He divorced and remarried 20 times, but then there was a lot of temptation on offer. Seneca described the women's fashions of the time: "I see silk clothes, if these qualify as 'clothes', which do nothing to hide the body, not even the genitals. Women wearing them can barely swear in good conscience that they are not naked. These clothes are imported from distant lands and cost a fortune – and the end result? Our women have nothing left to show their lovers in the bedroom that they haven't already revealed in the streets."

It was said that Augustus was always susceptible to a pretty face – though with the proliferation of see-through women's fashion on the streets it is hard to imagine that he was looking at their faces. He was renowned as a great womaniser, even into his 70s.

"Not even his friends deny that he often committed adultery," said Suetonius, "but they claimed that he did it for reasons of state, not just out of lust, as he could more easily discover what his enemies were up to by sleeping with their wives and daughters."

He was even accused of having an incestuous affair with his own daughter Julia. No woman was safe from him and, according to Suetonius: "His friends acted as panders and stripped matrons and ripe virgins naked and made an intimate inspection of them for him, as if they were Toranius the slave-dealer putting them up for sale."

Mark Antony said that Octavian once openly took the wife of an ex-consul from her husband's dining room into a bedroom and brought her back again with her hair tousled and her ears all red. He also maintained that Octavian had married Livia in haste after "putting Scribonia away because she complained too much about the influence of his concubine".

Even though Antony's accusations were plainly true, Octavian reacted badly to them. According to Suetonius, he seized the opportunity to tell the Senate that Antony had declared Cleopatra to be "king of kings" – which was a slightly confusing comment. Antony, he said, had put aside the "virtuous" Octavia and was now a slave to a queen who worshipped dung beetles – an accurate, if not entirely respectful, way to refer to the Egyptians' sacred Scarab. Octavian claimed that Antony intended to divide the empire up between the children that he had had with Cleopatra and Caesarion, the son that she had borne for Julius Caesar. He then read out the will that Antony had lodged with the Vestal Virgins, where many people kept their wills for safekeeping. In it, Antony said that he wanted to be buried beside Cleopatra. According to Octavian, this implied that Antony intended to move the capital of the empire from Rome to Alexandria. Outraged Italians swore an oath of allegiance to Octavian, who cleverly declared war not on Antony, but on Egypt, and moved his troops into Greece.

Antony and Cleopatra mustered their combined forces at Ephesus in modern Turkey. Seizing their opportunity, every prostitute and dancing girl in the East descended on the city, which rapidly turned into a scene of revelry and debauchery and weakened the soldiers' will to fight. Fortunately, when the battle finally took place, it took place at sea. It is now thought that the combined naval forces of Antony and Cleopatra could have won the Battle of Actium, off the west coast of Greece, but Cleopatra turned tail and fled and Antony followed her, thus snatching defeat from the jaws of victory.

Octavian then pursued the couple back to Egypt, where Cleopatra retreated to her mausoleum and barricaded herself in. Thinking that she was dead, Antony fell on his sword. Mortally wounded, he was informed that she was still alive. He was then carried to her mausoleum, where he died in her arms.

Cleopatra was now at the mercy of Octavian. When she threatened to kill herself and destroy her treasures, he sent a silver-tongued freedman, an ex-slave, to tell her that Octavian was already half in love with her from a distance – and that soon that distance would shrink. It led her to believe that she now had a third bite of the cherry: Octavian was going to become the ruler of the Roman Empire and if she could get him into bed, she could rule alongside him.

When Octavian arrived in Alexandria and entered her luxurious apartments, he found her draped carelessly across an ornate chaise-longue, her skin recently softened after having had a bath of freshly drawn asses' milk. Surrounded by busts of Julius Caesar, she pulled out some of his love letters she had stuffed in her bosom and read them out in a plaintive voice. For once, however, her seductive powers failed. She was now 39 years old and no longer the 21-year-old who had beguiled Caesar. When Octavian remained unmoved, she threw herself to her knees before him and begged to be allowed to die.

Octavian wanted her alive, though, so that he could parade her down the Via Sacra in Rome as his captive. Cleopatra had no intention of being displayed in chains in front of the Roman mob and decided to commit suicide. Aware of her intentions, Octavian had her food closely examined so that she could not poison herself. Eventually, she had two asps – small, poisonous snakes that were endemic to Libya and Egypt – smuggled to her in a basket of figs. In Graeco-Roman times, it was considered honourable to die from their bite.

When Octavian heard that she had killed herself he was distraught and tried to revive her. But with Cleopatra dead, Octavian could now do what he liked with Egypt. He used her treasury to pay off his soldiers and had Cleopatra's son by Julius Caesar – who was now Ptolemy XV Caesar – killed. Octavian spared Antony and Cleopatra's children Helios and Selene – "Sun" and "Moon" – and they were brought up by the still-virtuous Octavia. Then he annexed Egypt. Now master of the Graeco-Roman world, he named himself Caesar Augustus and went to visit the tomb of Alexander the Great in Alexandria, though he seems to have knocked the nose off the corpse by mistake.

Despite his proclivities, Augustus passed tough new laws on adultery, unchastity and pederasty, and he prevented youngsters from seeing "secular" plays. The statute he drew up encouraging marriage was so rigorously framed that there was an open revolt against it. He was forced to drop the fines for failing to marry and allowed a widow or widower three years' grace after the death of their spouse before having to marry again. Rewards were increased for those who had a large family, something that was not generally the fashion in Rome. There was no primogeniture under Roman law, so having many children meant that the family's wealth got distributed. Despite the amendments to the statute, there were demonstrations demanding the law's repeal.

Augustus himself had not done too well in the siring stakes. Livia had only provided one still-born baby and his childless marriage was a great disappointment to him. He married off his one daughter by Scribonia,

Julia, to Marcellus, the son of his sister Octavia, who was then little more than a child. When Marcellus died, he married her off to his closest friend and ally, Marcus Agrippa, even though he was twice her age and was then married to one of Octavia's daughters and had had a baby by her. Julia had three sons by Agrippa – Gaius, Lucius and Agrippa Postumus – whom Augustus adopted as his own, and two daughters – Julia the Younger and Agrippina the Elder.

When the populace protested against his marriage laws, Augustus sent for the children Agrippina had had with Germanicus, the grandson of his sister, and appeared in public with them sitting on his lap, indicating that the rest of the population should follow his example and have lots of children.

He introduced tough new laws when he discovered that men were getting engaged to under-aged girls, so that they could put off having children. The statutory period allowed between betrothal and marriage was shortened and a restriction on the number of divorces you could have was introduced. Meanwhile, to up the birth rate, he rode around Italy offering cash incentives to have babies. They had to be legitimate, though. Cities where they became *fervidus* about employing *adulterium* to increasing the birth-rate were told to: *"Futue ti ipsum."*

Although Augustus's Julia had had five children by the aged Agrippa, she was notoriously promiscuous and took a series of lovers. These included some of the great names of Rome – Antonius, Gracchus, Pulcher and Scipio. Asked why all her children looked like Agrippa when she had had sex with so many men, she said that she did not give herself to another man until she was already pregnant. The actual words she used were: *"Numquam enim nisi navi plena tollo vectorem."* This means: "I do not drop the pilot [Agrippa was an admiral] until the boat is full."

When Agrippa died, Julia was engaged to Mark Antony's son Julius Antonius and then to Cotiso, the king of the Getae who lived along the banks of the lower Danube. Augustus offered to marry Cotiso's daughter in exchange. When that deal fell through, Julia was married off to Augustus's step-, now adopted, son, Tiberius, though she refused to give up her current lover, Sempronius Gracchus.

In the past, Julia had made several attempts to seduce Tiberius, but he had resisted and had married Vipsania Agrippina instead. They had

had one child and were expecting another. Nevertheless, Tiberius was forced to give up a happy marriage to marry a sexually rapacious princess, a woman he had already rejected.

At first Julia and Tiberius seemed happy enough. They even had a son, who died quite young. After that, Julia went out on the pull again. To escape his wife's constant adulteries, Tiberius volunteered to put down a rebellion in Armenia, then put himself into voluntary exile on Rhodes. Julia, now 38, gave herself up entirely to pleasure. A gentleman visiting her house remarked on her luxurious lifestyle, compared to that of Augustus, who lived a relatively frugal existence, eating and drinking little. Julia replied: "My father may forget he is an emperor, but I am mindful that I am an emperor's daughter."

The fourth-century historian Macrobius remarked that her "gentle and humane character, and her broad moral outlook, won her affection wherever her lusts were not known". Another commentator said: "Such was Roman society of the Augustan age, and such it appears to us was its finest flower, Princess Julia – a conjunction of contradictory elements: the finest culture and the coarsest materialism, the most enchanting physical beauty and the crudest sensuality, brilliant aesthetic refinement and cynical immorality."

The soldier and amateur historian Velleius Paterculus, who lived under Augustus, said: "His daughter Julia, entirely forgetting what she owed to her father and her husband, exceeded in lust and debauchery the utmost limits of shamelessness. She considered her sins should be equivalent to her high position, and considered anything that gave her pleasure was permissible."

Seneca was even harder on her.

"She counted her lovers in scores," he said. "At night, she roamed the city in nocturnal revels, and chose for the scene of her embraces the very Forum and platform from which her father had promulgated his law against adultery. She made daily rendezvous at the statue of [the Greek god] Marsyas [which stood in the Forum], for she had now turned from adulteress into whore and permitted herself any licence with unknown lovers."

This might sound a little harsh, but Pliny agreed, even claiming that Julia was unique in the rampant promiscuity that prompted her to prostitute herself publicly for pleasure.

"The only Roman example of this licentious practice was provided by the daughter of Augustus," he wrote, "who in her nightly revels used to crown the statue of Marsyas – this being mentioned in her divine father's letter of complaint."

Until Julia began putting it about so publicly, Augustus had tried to overlook his daughter's behaviour – even though under his own laws on adultery she should have been put to death. However, when Augustus learnt of her latest excesses, he could not keep it to himself and wrote to the Senate about it.

Suetonius said: "He bore death in his family more easily than disgrace. He was not overwhelmed by the deaths of Gaius and Lucius, and he informed the Senate about Julia's misdeeds by a letter read in his absence by the quaestor [treasurer]. For a long time he avoided appearing in public because he was ashamed to be seen, and even thought of having her killed. Indeed, when a freedwoman called Phoebe, one of Julia's accomplices, hanged herself, he said he would rather have been Phoebe's father."

The final straw came when Julia organised a Bacchic orgy in the middle of the night in the middle of the Forum where, in the midst of the action, Julia plotted to kill her father. When Augustus heard of the conspiracy, everyone who had attended the orgy was arrested. Julius Antonius was executed. The other men were banished. Julia herself was exiled to the tiny rocky island of Pandateria, one of the Ponziane Islands situated off the coast of Campania, southern Italy. She was guarded like a dangerous criminal and forbidden wine; even worse, male visitors were prohibited. Her mother Scribonia was sent along with her for good measure.

Augustus was softer on the other women who had been at the orgy.

"Although in consequence of this case many other women were liable to similar charges," wrote Cassius Dio, "Augustus did not allow them all to be prosecuted."

Tiberius interceded on his wife's behalf, but Augustus was adamant.

"Fire and water will mix before she comes back to Rome," he said. She was, he said, a "disease in my flesh".

After five years, she was allowed to move into a more comfortable exile in the small fort at Rhegium – now Reggio – on the mainland at the Strait of Messina opposite Sicily. Although Tiberius had stuck up for her and had even allowed her to keep the presents he had given her, he was even harsher on her than her father had been when he came to power. He stopped her allowance and she starved to death in AD 14 at the age of 51.

Her daughter Julia the Younger was almost as bad as her mother Julia the Elder had been; she was said to be another example of "the tempest that raged in the emperor's own house". She was found guilty of adultery and banished to the lonely island of Trimerus off the coast of Apulia – the modern-day region of Puglia – in southeast Italy. She lived there for 20 years and was supplied with food and drink by Augustus's wife Livia. When either of the two Julias were mentioned in his hearing, Augustus would say: "Would that I was wifeless and had died childless." He referred to the two Julias and his wayward grandson Agrippa as "my three boils" or "my three running sores".

The poet Ovid was also banished at that time to the freezing port of Tomis on the Black Sea – now Constanta in Romania. His friend Silanus had been a lover of the younger Julia and Ovid may have been, too. He admitted that his exile did have something to do with Julia, though his erotic poetry was the principal cause of his lack of popularity with Augustus. Some years earlier he had incurred Augustus's displeasure with his book the *Art of Love*; the book was totally at odds with the new morality that the emperor was championing.

It began: "If anybody here does not know the art of loving, let him read this. After reading my poem, he will be an expert lover." And to those who find love a disappointment, he promised: "I will reveal the cause of your downfall: you did not know how to love. You lacked art: it is only by art that love survives."

Ovid went on to tell young men: "The first thing to get into your head is that every single girl can be caught and that you'll catch her if you work at it right. Birds will sooner fall dumb in spring-time, cicadas stop in summer or a hunting dog turn its back on a hare, than a lover's bland inducements can fail with a woman ... She will perhaps resist at first and say, 'You naughty man,' but even while she is resisting she will show you that she desires to be overcome."

Ovid then presented an example of his own forthright seduction technique:

Finally, I ripped off her tunic, which was so thin it hardly covered anything, but she still tried to cover herself with it. She struggled as if she did not wish for victory, betrayed herself and was overcome. When she stood naked in front of me, I could see that her body had not a single flaw. What shoulders and what arms I saw and felt. How well formed her breasts were and how fit to be caressed. How firm her body was below her swelling breasts. Unspoilt by wrinkles, how beautifully formed it was. How wanton her buttocks. How slender and youthful her thighs. Why go on? Everything I saw was perfect. I pulled her naked body on to mine … May I often enjoy such happy hours of love.

That may sound awfully sexist, but Ovid was a bit of a New Man and, in verse, told a man how to be a considerate lover:

> Love's climax never be rushed, I say,
> But worked up softly, lingering all the way.
> The parts a woman loves to have caressed
> Once found, caress, though modesty protests.

He also said: "A woman does not have to be teased to be worked up into a frenzy … I do not want a woman who sees it as a duty. She should say, 'Don't come too soon,' or, 'Wait a while.' I want a woman whose eyes admit her excitement. And after she comes, let her want no more for a while. Young people know nothing of delight. These things should not be rushed. After thirty, lovers start learning how."

He also had useful advice for women:

> If your face is pretty, lie on your back.
> If your buttocks are cute, let him have you from behind.
> Atalanta used to put her legs on Milanion's shoulders.
> Do this if you have beautiful legs.
> Small women should get on top, as if they are riding a horse.
> Hector's Andromache did not do this because she was too tall.
> Press against the bed with your knees and bend backward slightly.
> If your naked body is something a lover should crave to look at,
> If your breasts and things look lovely,
> Let the man stand while the woman lies at an angle on the bed.

Whether Augustus followed Ovid's advice, we do not know. However, we do know that, while his second marriage was childless and he banned adultery for others, he regularly enjoyed the company of courtesans. One day, he sent a litter to collect one of his favourites. When it returned, it was carrying his old tutor Athenodorus, who, when he had seen the litter pick up the prostitute, had kicked her out and taken her place. When he arrived at Augustus's home – the modest Domus Livia – he upbraided Augustus for his immorality and left the ruler of the known world looking decidedly sheepish.

This had no effect. Augustus held a famous banquet known as "The Feast of the 12 Gods" to which the guests came dressed as various gods and goddesses. Augustus himself came as Apollo. According to a lampoon that did the rounds at the time:

> Caesar assumed what was Apollo's due,
> And wine and lust inflamed the motley crew.
> At such debauchery the gods avert their eyes,
> And from his golden throne great Jove indignant flies.

This behaviour was all the more scandalous because Rome was suffering from a famine at the time.

Augustus also had a passion for gambling. He could not resist a good massage and loved to be rubbed down with oil. His womanising continued into old age. Suetonius said, not without a note of admiration: "He could not free himself from lust – they say that in his later years he had a special liking for deflowering virgins, who were even procured for him by his wife."

Tacitus, who is less approving, said of Livia: "Her friendly and complaisant disposition went beyond the limit that would have been approved of by the ladies of the old school."

He cracked down on the licentious behaviour of actors and, when he discovered that the leading man Stephanio had a married woman with her hair cropped short wait on him at table like a page boy, had him whipped through the streets and then banished. A comedian called Hylas who made an obscene gesture with his middle finger at a member of the audience who hissed was publicly flogged and banished, not just from Rome, but from the whole of Italy. However, Augustus did not mind indulging in a bit of pantomime himself. Although he controlled all the levers of state, he pretended that the institutions of the Republic were still active and when people begged him to take the dictatorship – absolute authority invested in one man for a limited period during an emergency – he would bare his breast and beg them not to beg him further.

He could also be kind. When he was dining with the poet and orator Gaius Asinius Pollio, who was particularly proud of his collection of crystal, one of Pollio's slaves dropped a bowl and begged to be thrown to his master's lampreys to be eaten alive as a punishment. Augustus ordered the man to be freed and for the rest of the crystal to be smashed.

To the end of his days, when he thought that no one was watching, he would bang his head against the wall, ruing the loss of three legions under Publius Quintilius Varus, ambushed by German tribes in the Teutoburg Forest in AD 9. Varus had alienated the Germans by sexually abusing their sons and daughters. The Romans were cut down and their entrails were used to decorate the trees. Those who survived were tortured and sexually abused for years, before finally being dispatched by bloody emasculation.

Toward the very end of his life, Augustus developed a taste for pretty boys who were sent to him from all over the empire. Despite his new laws against pederasty, new spectacles involving young boys were introduced at the games and the women, with the exception of the Vestal Virgins, were restricted to the back rows during gladiatorial displays. Because of the male nudity involved, no women at all were allowed at athletic contests.

During Augustus's last visit to Capri, shortly before his death, Suetonius said: "He continually watched the exercises of the *ephebi* – young men – of whom there was still a goodly number at Capri according to the ancient usage."

Greek training survived in Capri, so the young men he would have been watching would have been performing their exercises completely nude.

"He also gave these youths a banquet at which he himself was present, and not only allowed but even required the perfect freedom in jesting and scrambling for tickets for fruit, dainties and all kinds of things which he threw to them."

Augustus died on 19 August AD 14 . His deathbed scene was interrupted by news that his daughter Julia was ill. He kissed his wife and said: "Goodbye, Livia, never forget our marriage."

Then suddenly he cried out: "Forty tall and lusty young men are carrying me off."

This was more of a premonition than a hope, as 40 of his Praetorian Guard carried him on their shoulders to his lying in state.

His last words were: "Well, I performed quite well, didn't I?"

It is not known what he was referring to – or whether Livia replied. Less than a month later, on 17 September, he was made a god.

CHAPTER 4

"Mention Tiberius and the name evokes a sceptred butcher ill with satyriasis" – excessive craving for sex in the male – "a taciturn tyrant, hideous and debauched; an unclean old man, devising in the crypts of a palace infamies so monstrous that, to describe them, new words were coined." So said one of the foremost modern classics scholars. That's quite a reputation.

In fact, this assessment is based purely on the works of Tacitus and Suetonius, both of whom seem to have had it in for Tiberius. However, after being forced to give up his beloved Vipsania and delivered into the clutches of the veteran adulteress Julia, it is not surprising that his sex life went a little awry. On top of everything else, Vipsania was the daughter of Marcus Agrippa. Julia was her stepmother. So Tiberius had been forced to marry his mother-in-law.

After putting down the rebellion in Armenia, he was back in Rome briefly on leave when he chanced to see Vipsania. By this time, she had been forced to marry a senator. They met in the home of a friend. According to Suetonius, Tiberius was so overcome with grief that, afterwards, he followed her through the streets with "tears in his eyes and intense unhappiness written on his face". When Augustus heard of this, he gave orders that Tiberius was never to see Vipsania again.

Tiberius then went into exile in Rhodes, but Augustus did not mind, as he did not like his stepson Tiberius very much; he then adopted three grandsons by Agrippa and Julia and groomed them to succeed him. However, Gaius and Lucius then died and Agrippa Postumus went off the rails and, like his mother and sister before him, had to be banished. So when Tiberius asked Augustus if could return to Rome, Augustus consented and named him as his successor. However, in a typical jibe, Suetonius said that Augustus only chose Tiberius because he was so ugly and unpleasant that Augustus's own reign would be remembered with even greater affection. Augustus was also kind enough to grant Tiberius a divorce from Julia, even though Tiberius did his best to reconcile father and daughter.

Tiberius was of Sabine origin and was descended from the rapist Claudius Regilianus, a famous Roman lawgiver who had to flee after he tried to "enslave and seduce a free-born girl".

When Tiberius came to power, he reversed Augustus's laws on adultery and revived the old custom that stated that married women caught at it should be punished, not by the courts, but within the family. He released a Roman knight from his oath that he would never divorce his wife when she was caught in bed with his son. However, women, like his ex-wife Julia, who renounced the privileges of their class and became prostitutes for the hell of it, were still to be exiled.

Tacitus said that in the reign of Tiberius "the Senate ruled that no woman whose father, grandfather or husband had been a Roman knight could sell her body. Vistilia, the daughter of a Praetorian family, as registered on the aedile's [interior minister's] list as a prostitute out of sheer lust – the standard procedure had been set up by our ancestors who thought that the shame of such an action would be punishment and prevention enough. Her husband, Titidius Labeo, also had to explain why, despite his wife's obvious guilt, he had not imposed the penalty demanded by the law. Although he pleaded that his 60-day deliberation period had not yet expired, it was deemed the right time to pass judgement on Vistilia. She was deported to the barren island of Seriphos."

A man was stripped of his government position after divorcing a wife that he had won in a lottery the day before. Then again, Tiberius reinstated a man called Sestius Gallus – whom Augustus had dismissed – on the condition that he invited him to dinner and that they would be served, in Gallus's usual fashion, by naked waitresses. All that naked female flesh seems to have turned his head.

In AD 27 at the age of 67, Tiberius left Rome and moved to the island of Capri, where he spent the remaining 11 years of his life. He built a palace on the island that contained a special chamber called a *cellaria*. It was fitted with numerous couches where troupes of naked boys and girls from all over the empire performed for him. They would have sex in front of him in groups of three to "excite his waning passion". He would then indulge in orgies of sodomy, fellatio and coprophilia. He even set up an office "for the originating of unfamiliar carnal pleasures", run by a former censor. This was a government department.

A number of small rooms were furnished with the most indecent pictures and statues he could lay his hands on and the walls of the rooms were decorated with pornographic friezes. The rooms also contained sex manuals from Elephantis in Egypt, so that the men and women he brought there knew exactly what was expected of them. The wall of his own bedroom was adorned with a painting of the goddess Atalanta performing fellatio on the warrior Meleager. The painting was bequeathed to him on the condition that, if he did not like it, he could have ten thousand gold pieces. Tiberius was a miser, but he kept the painting anyway.

He was also a keen gardener. In the woods and glades that surrounded the palace, he had boys and girls dressed as Pans and nymphs prostituting themselves in nooks and caves.

It was also said that he accrued a team of young boys from noble families and called them his "minnows". According to Suetonius, they were trained to dive between his legs when he was swimming to nibble and suck on his private parts. He was also said to cover his genitals with crumbs to entice mullets to nibble on them as he reclined in a warm rock pool. Suetonius's accusations went even further, though. He claimed that Tiberius covered his private parts with milk and honey and forced unweaned babies to suck on his penis as if it were its mother's teat. But this may testify to the depravity of Suetonius's imagination rather than to the behaviour of Tiberius.

Suetonius also said that Tiberius took such a fancy to the beautiful boy holding the censer during a sacrifice that, before the religious rites were over, he took him aside and sexually abused him, along with his brother who was playing the flute. Then, when they both protested about his disgusting behaviour, he had their legs broken.

Tiberius, it was said, was just as bad with women, even those of high birth and reputation. A Roman matron called Mallonia was forced into his bed. He was known to be an extremely ugly man in old age and, after she showed a certain repugnance at what was required of her, he had paid informers lay false accusations against her. He even showed up at her trial and kept shouting out: "Are you sorry now?" When she left court, she went home and, after a tirade against "that filthy-mouthed, hairy, stinking man", stabbed herself to death.

It is plain that what she objected to was the fact that wrinkly old Tiberius performed cunnilingus on her as a joke at his expense after lines about what an "old goat" does with his tongue had been inserted into a play. Goat is *caper* in Latin and is a pun on the name Capri. Indeed, Tiberius's sexual theme park on Capri was known as Caprineum, which means "Goatland".

Recently discovered inscriptions in his ruined palace have revealed that Tiberius was into triple anal penetration and that every member of his household had to bow down before his wizened, diseased penis every morning. He was also devoted to sexual research, measuring the maximum capacity of the anal cavity and setting up a mile-long daisy chain with male slaves, each of whom was to be strangled at the moment of orgasm. His aim was for everyone in the empire to participate, so that the entire known world would explode in one giant simultaneous eruption of semen.

While Tiberius was busy in Capri, the empire was run by Lucius Aelius Sejanus. As a youth, Sejanus seems to have made money as a gigolo, or perhaps even as a rent boy, before joining the staff of Gaius when it was thought that he was Augustus's heir. With the help of Tiberius he rose to become the prefect of the Praetorian Guard, but his ambition did not stop there. He seduced Livilla, the wife of Tiberius's son Drusus, promising her a share in the empire that he aimed, some day, to rule. First they had to get rid of Drusus. This would have been no great loss to Livilla as Drusus was a bad-tempered, wife-beating bully. When Drusus died in mysterious circumstances in AD 23, everyone except Tiberius suspected that he had been poisoned by Sejanus and Livilla. However, when Sejanus divorced his wife, Tiberius would not, at first, allow him to marry Livilla as, officially, she was still in mourning.

Sejanus then started spreading rumours that Tiberius's stepdaughter,

Agrippina the Elder, the mother of Tiberius's possible heirs, was plotting against him. When Tiberius left for his fun in the sun on Capri, Sejanus banished Agrippina, imprisoned or exiled her sons and then married Livilla. In AD 31, Sejanus became consul alongside Tiberius; with Tiberius away on Capri, Sejanus must have seemed like the emperor to the inhabitants of Rome.

Tiberius was warned of Sejanus's ambitions in a letter from his brother's widow Antonia, Livilla's mother. Tiberius sent for his great nephew, the exiled Gaius Caesar Germanicus – the future Emperor Caligula – who was the son of Agrippina the Elder and the popular general Germanicus Caesar. Having secured his heir, Tiberius sent a series of messages to Sejanus promising future advancement, while systematically opposing everything that he was doing. It soon became apparent to the Romans that Sejanus no longer wielded any real power and the crowd of people around his door asking for favours quickly thinned.

Then Tiberius sent the new prefect of the Praetorian Guard, Naevius Setorius Macro, to Rome to tell Sejanus that he was going to be given the powers of a tribune. Sejanus then made off to the Senate where the announcement was going to be made. Meanwhile Macro told the Praetorian Guard, who might still have been loyal to their former prefect Sejanus, to return to their barracks. He then had the Senate building surrounded by the city's Night Watch. While this was going on, what the first-century Roman poet Juvenal called a "long and wordy letter from Capri" was being read out in the Senate. It began by praising Sejanus, who still thought that he was going to be made tribune, but, little by little, the letter began to undermine him. The other senators began to back away from Sejanus, who sat slumped in his seat unable to believe what he was hearing. When the reading of the letter was finished, the consul Regulus asked whether there was any reason why Sejanus should not be imprisoned. When the answer no was given, Sejanus was led away by the Night Watch to be executed. There was rejoicing when his body was dragged through the streets before being thrown into the Tiber. His children were also put to death, though his daughter had to be raped first – it was against the law in Rome to execute a virgin. Livilla was spared, even though Sejanus's first wife confirmed that Drusus had been poisoned by the ambitious couple.

This was done out of consideration for Livilla's mother Antonia, who had warned Tiberius of Sejanus's plot. Antonia was not so forgiving, however, and starved her daughter to death.

Throughout all of this, Tiberius had not stirred from the fun and frolics on Capri. However, Sejanus's plotting made Tiberius fear that there might be other conspiracies against him. He soon became paranoid and started to seek out treason everywhere, questioning those accused under torture. It became a capital offence to change your clothes near a statue of the emperor or to carry a coin bearing his head into a brothel or a lavatory. Such disrespect was considered proof of treason. There were informers everywhere and endless show trials that could only have one outcome.

On a personal level, Tiberius turned into a brutal sadist; people were flogged mercilessly for simply crossing his path. When a fisherman offered him a large mullet he had caught and hauled up the cliff at the rear of the palace, Tiberius became so afraid that he ordered that the man's face be scrubbed raw with the fish's scales. The poor man cried out in agony: "Thank heavens, I did not offer Caesar the lobster I caught." Hearing this, Tiberius ordered that his face be scrubbed with the lobster, too. And, when his litter was held up by bushes obstructing the road, he ordered the centurion who was supposed to make sure that the road was clear to lie on the ground and had him flogged to the point of death. Tiberius took a sadistic pleasure in watching these punishments.

Not a day went by without someone being sentenced to death; the wives and children of the victims shared the same fate. Young girls were deflowered before being strangled, and anyone who showed a willingness to die was forced to live. He would send friendly letters to people, inviting them to Capri. When they arrived, he would torture them to death. People were flung off the cliffs into the sea where sailors from the fleet waited with poles and oars to beat to death anyone who had survived the fall. One particularly nasty torture Tiberius devised was to tie a cord tightly around a man's penis and then force him to drink huge draughts of wine. Many killed themselves rather than visit him on Capri.

Despite Tiberius's fear of people plotting against him in Rome, the danger was rather closer to home. Although his astrologers had curbed some of his worst excesses by telling Tiberius that he still had a long time to live, he was killed in his bed by Gaius Germanicus, the very man he had chosen to be his successor. His last wish was for his corpse to be buggered by a well-endowed slave. No one could be found to perform the task, despite the large amount of cash on offer.

CHAPTER 5

Born Gaius Julius Caesar Germanicus, Caligula was brought up in the military camps of his father Germanicus Caesar and got his nickname – which means "Little Boots" – from the scaled-down army footwear he wore as a youth.

His father died in AD 19, and his mother and two elder brothers were then executed by the Emperor Tiberius during his paranoid purges. However, after being summoned to Capri, Caligula managed to ingratiate himself with Tiberius, by constantly being at the emperor's beck and call. It was said of Caligula that no one ever made a better slave or a worse master. Not only did he have to tolerate the whims of the man who had killed half of his family, he also had to witness the old man's sexual depravity and his delight in both torture and mass executions. As Tiberius's favourite, he also got to indulge in sadistic whims of his own. Suetonius wrote:

> Even at that time he could not control his natural cruelty and viciousness. He was a most eager witness of the tortures and executions of those who suffered punishment, revelling at night in gluttony and adultery, disguised in a wig and a long robe, passionately devoted besides to the theatrical arts of dancing and singing, in which Tiberius very willingly indulged him, in the hope that, through these, his savage nature might be softened. This last was so clearly evident to the shrewd old man, that he used to say now and then that to allow Gaius to live would prove the ruin of himself and of all men, and that he was rearing a viper for the Roman people and a Phaethon for the world.

Phaethon was the son of Helios, the sun god, who was allowed to drive the chariot of the sun through the sky for a single day, but lost control of the horses. As a result, the sun came too close to the earth and scorched it. To prevent further damage, Zeus hurled a thunderbolt at Phaethon, who fell to earth at the mouth of the River Eridanus – later identified as the River Po, which runs across the north of Italy.

Caligula married the daughter of a nobleman in the hope that it would improve his chances of succeeding Tiberius, but after losing his first wife in childbirth, he married a rich woman called Pollia simply for her money. Then he seduced the wife of Naevius Setorius Macro, prefect of the Praetorian Guard, even promising to marry her if he became emperor. At the same time, he wormed his way into Macro's favour. It was said that he then poisoned Tiberius. According to Suetonius, he did this little by little so that Tiberius, fearing that he was dying, would take the ring from his finger and hand it over, thus transferring power. Tiberius did take the ring off, but did not hand it over. He held on to it, so Caligula put a pillow over his face and smothered him. In other versions of the story it is said that he strangled him. A freeman had seen what had happened and cried out. Now, with the imperial ring on his finger, Caligula immediately ordered his crucifixion.

Suetonius, for one, believed this version of events.

"This is likely enough," he said, "for some writers say that Caligula himself later admitted, not that he had committed parricide, but that he had at least meditated on it at one time. They say that he constantly boasted, in speaking of his filial piety, that he had entered the bedchamber of the sleeping Tiberius with a dagger in his hand, intending to avenge the death of his mother and brothers, but that when the moment came, he was seized with pity, threw down the dagger and fled. Though Tiberius knew of this, he had never dared to make any inquiry or take any action."

The Romans were delighted that Tiberius was dead, and Caligula was a popular figure. His father was remembered with great affection and Caligula was widely pitied because of the destruction Tiberius had wreaked on his family. When he accompanied the dead emperor's funeral cortège on its journey to Rome, the crowds along the way turned out to cheer him.

When the procession reached the capital, Tiberius's will, which named his grandson Tiberius Gemellus as his successor, was voided and, as a direct descendant of Augustus through both parents, absolute power was placed in Caligula's hands by the unanimous consent of the Senate and the acclamation of the mob outside. According to Suetonius: "So great was the public rejoicing that within the next three months, or less than that, more than a hundred and sixty thousand victims are said to have been slain in sacrifice."

Initially, Caligula was a popular leader, largely because Tiberius was so hated. Even so, he gave Tiberius a magnificent funeral and a fawning eulogy, during which he cried copiously. He then restored the honour of his mother and brothers, collecting their ashes and moving them into Augustus's mausoleum. He renamed the month September Germanicus after his father and declared a general amnesty for all Romans who had been imprisoned or exiled by Tiberius. He promised to dismantle the old emperor's system of informers and stopped all treason trials. All of the documents concerning these cases were burned. In not so popular a move, he expelled all the *spintriae* from Rome.

To boost his popularity, the vast coffers that the miserly Tiberius had amassed were squandered on magnificent games. Caligula set a trend with this action. While Julius Caesar liked to affect disdain and read some administrative document during gladiatorial contests, the dour Augustus showed little interest and Tiberius rarely attended, in contrast, Caligula – and several of the emperors who followed him – liked to run the spectacle himself.

He also liked to make a spectacle of himself. He was particularly proud of the size of his penis and liked to show it off in public; he used the games as an opportunity to expose himself to the crowds. All the emperors that followed him knew that it was important to be seen masturbating while watching the slaughter, or being attended to by the most beautiful and skilled prostitutes the empire had to offer.

Caligula would often have to remove his thumb hurriedly, or perhaps his whole fist, from the anus of a catamite from Mesopotamia – a part of the world where anal elasticity was particularly prized – before making the life-or-death decision. Usually the crowd below bayed: *"Jugula! Jugula!"* – "Cut his throat! Cut his throat!" In some cases, though, they called for a reprieve. Caligula always went along with the crowd. To defy the mob was to invite a riot that might end with Caligula himself floating down the Tiber minus his cherished body parts.

If the thumb went down, the defeated gladiator would calmly sit back on one heel, grip the winner's thigh and tilt back his head to expose his neck. He would then give a little nod indicating that he was ready for what would be, in the circumstances of the arena, a relatively painless death. His opponent would then quickly cut his throat. The dying man would then release his grip and fold his arms, waiting patiently to die as great spurts of blood gushed from his neck. At the sight of this, and somewhat hideously, bodily fluids of a different sort would be spurting in the stands.

Some champions were real showmen and took great pride in spelling out the emperor's name in their victim's blood, with a severed head dotting the "i". If a gladiatorial contest went on for too long and the audience got bored, Caligula would call a halt to the bout and order the two contestants to cut each other's throats simultaneously; at least two deaths an hour were required in the arena.

Even the victor of a bout was not safe. If he was not one of the emperor's favourites, protocol demanded that he would have to take on the next contender. As he was already tired, and possibly even injured, this was a match he would probably lose. However, Caligula did not like to waste gladiators who were as gifted in the bedroom as they were in the arena. If the winner was one of his favourites, or if he fancied him, he would break etiquette by suspending the rematch, and would appease the mob by hurling money into the audience.

If one of the combatants lost his nerve and ran away refusing to fight – on his first appearance in the arena, say – the crowd would hiss and cry: *"Hoc habet"* – "He's had it." At the emperor's nod, his opponent would step aside and an extremely ugly Armenian dwarf in a gold costume would enter the arena. Armed with a vast array of weapons, he would put the disgraced gladiator to death in the most painful way. The dwarf's lethal skill was so awesome that the crowd would fall silent and the screams of the victim would be heard echoing around not just the arena, but also the hills that surrounded it. Within ten minutes he would be chopped into tiny cubes of flesh, which the dwarf would then piss on before he left.

After each bout, the black-clad, bald-headed "carrion man" came into the arena carrying a red-hot poker and a silver hammer. He would apply the red-hot poker to the genitals of the fallen. If they did not react, he assumed that they were dead and struck them on the head with the hammer to release their soul. Anyone who was still alive, but too injured to continue, was dragged to the "finishing-off room" under the stadium, where a butcher who had taken time off from slaughtering horses would dispatch him with a few strokes of his cleaver. When the games were over for the day, the emperor would visit the victors in their changing rooms – so he could see them sweaty, blood-splattered and naked – and distribute a few coins.

For the first months of his reign, Caligula openly flaunted his incest with his favourite sister Drusilla. Nobody could tell him not to. They had had an incestuous relationship since childhood. Caligula was in the process of deflowering his sister when they were caught in bed together by their grandmother, Antonia. When he became emperor, they lived openly together as lovers, even though she was married.

Caligula was often seen riding round the seedier quarters of the city with Drusilla, masturbating with one hand and hurling gold coins into the crowds with the other. He was so proud of his relationship with her that he had a small amphitheatre built in celebration of it. For a small fee, the plebeian rabble could watch him bugger his sister on the solid gold stage. She was a willing, active participant in this. They even planned, at some point, to resort to vaginal sex and have a boy child to take over the empire.

To spice up the show, Caligula would employ his favourite gladiator, Superbus, who came from the mountains of Tingitana near modern Tangiers, some other studs from other corners of the empire or even a well-endowed senator to sodomise him while he was having anal sex with Drusilla. Valerius Catullus, the son of a consular family, openly proclaimed that he had buggered the emperor so many times that he had worn himself out.

While the plebeian mob enjoyed the spectacle of the emperor buggering his sister, oracles and soothsayers warned that such public incest would bring ruin on Rome. Caligula quickly recalled Tiberius's ring of spies, and harbingers of doom soon found themselves facing an unsporting death in the arena.

Seven months after his accession, Caligula fell ill. His fever soared and his face was covered with weeping orange pustules that seemed to give off the odour of death. He named Drusilla heir to the throne, but as no woman had ever ruled Rome, a struggle for the imperial ring developed.

Fearing the worst, the mob flocked to the palace. One sycophantic senator said that he would be willing to sacrifice his own life if Caligula's was spared. Caligula rallied and took him at his word. He was put to death on the spot. Caligula then ordered the execution of all those who had anticipated his death and had their severed heads piled on his sick bed, believing that he would draw strength from them.

As soon as he recuperated, he instigated a series of treason trials of his own. Tiberius's chosen heir, Gemellus, was disposed of extra-judicially by Caligula and Naevius Setorius Macro, the prefect of the Praetorian Guard, who took it in turns to force a red-hot poker up his anus. Gemellus's father-in-law Gaius Silanus was forced to commit suicide after being accused of treason. Others had to pay the full, gruesome penalty and their bodies were slowly mutilated before they were beheaded.

Increasingly paranoid, Caligula began to fear the growing power of Macro. He tricked him into believing that he was going to be made prefect of Egypt, then had him arrested for being his wife's pimp over the affair that she had had with Caligula himself and forced him to commit suicide.

While Drusilla remained in favour, Caligula's other two sisters, Agrippina the Younger* and Livilla, came under suspicion. He spared their lives, but ordered that they should be handed over to the mob. For five days, everyone including lepers, beggars and cripples were allowed to use them for any sexual act they desired, even though Agrippina was heavily pregnant at the time. A tent was erected in front of the palace to house the two unfortunate women and an imperial commission noted down the details and duration of each act. Queues formed and Caligula would drop by, when he could spare time from the arena, the amphitheatre and Drusilla's bed, to see how his other two sisters were getting on. The commission recorded a staggering seven thousand sex acts over the five days. That's nearly 30 an hour for each woman or almost one every two minutes – though it was, of course, possible that each was satisfying more than one gentleman at a time.

Although Caligula had promised philosophers their freedom to say or write anything they liked when he came to power, those who did not extol his policies had their mouths sewn up and their hands chopped off. And prisoners released in the first flush of the new regime who were too debilitated by incarceration to celebrate their new-found freedom or to heap praise on their liberator were sent to the arena.

When Drusilla died, suddenly, at the age of 23, the doctors diagnosed "a surfeit of buggery". She had just finished a marathon 24-hour session with Caligula and seven well-endowed lads freshly arrived from Caesariensis, modern-day Algeria. Caligula berated the doctors for not resuscitating her, even though she was stiff and cold. Although she was already dead, he sodomised her corpse one more time and declared her a goddess. Even after she was cremated, in the Roman way, he tried to revive her by masturbating into her ashes.

Temples were consecrated to her throughout Rome and the empire, and coins were minted in her honour. A season of public mourning was announced, during which it was a capital offence for anyone to laugh, bathe or dine with members of their own family.

Making Drusilla a goddess was not a universally popular move, however. A number of leading senators and philosophers insisted that deification should be reserved for outstanding figures, such as Julius Caesar and Augustus. As a result of their opinions, they found themselves being crucified upside down in the arena while being burnt alive.

After the period of mourning was over, Caligula took time off from running the empire and spent lavishly on games, banquets and public displays. The *spintriae* were allowed back into Rome and put on ever-more-spectacular displays of public copulation, and dancers, singers, actors and prostitutes were summoned from the four corners of the empire. As a demonstration of his power, Caligula built a three-mile-long pontoon bridge across the Bay of Naples and rode back and forth across it for two days. At the end of his spectacle, he invited the people who had massed along the shore to celebrate the event by joining him on the bridge. It collapsed under their weight and thousands drowned.

Caligula built vast galleys, villas and country houses regardless of the expense. Guests at banquets would find gold moulded in the shape of food on plates in front of them. He would dissolve valuable pearls in vinegar and drink down the mixture. He soon squandered the vast fortune that Tiberius had left.

To raise money, he started a fresh round of treason trials. Those condemned would forfeit their property. He named the amount of money that he sought to raise and kept signing death warrants until he had amassed that sum. He condemned as many as 40 men in one afternoon to raise the desired figure and boasted afterwards that it had been a particularly tiring day.

He revoked the Roman citizenship of many who had earned it and seized their estates. Others were forced to name him as their heir before he sent them poisoned sweetmeats. He also sold off the public properties left over after the games. One senator, who nodded off at an auction, woke up to discover that he had bought 13 gladiators at a massively inflated price. Others were simply forced to buy things at prices they could not afford. Bankrupted, many committed suicide afterwards.

He executed men for little or no reason. His own brother was put to death without warning. Senators were executed secretly and Caligula would continue to summon them as though they were still alive, only to announce some time later that they had committed suicide. His uncle Claudius, it was said, was spared only because his terrible stutter made him a laughing stock.

The arena was a public forum and, between bouts, all emperors joined in a little light-hearted banter with their subjects. Caligula, however – like Nero later – was quick to take offence, particularly if someone complained that their family fortune had just disappeared into the imperial coffers or if they raised some other grievance. Caligula would instantly order the speaker's death, along with the deaths of the hundred or so people sitting around him. Sword-wielding imperial guards would then hack their way into the audience who would scramble toward the exits, causing such a crush that sometimes thousands of innocent people were trampled to death.

Caligula's reign was full of such pointless brutality. Petty criminals were fed to his lions, on the grounds that they were cheaper than butcher's meat. After an oratory competition, he forced the losers to erase their wax tablets with their tongues, on pain of death. However, the story that he made his horse Incitatus a consul is probably without foundation, though his favourite mount was given a marble stall, an ivory manger with purple trappings and a jewelled necklace, along with a house replete with furniture and servants. And the entire neighbourhood was ordered to keep silent so that the horse could sleep undisturbed. It was even said that, after Drusilla's death, Caligula attempted to conceive a fitting heir to take over the empire with Incitatus.

Incest was Caligula's *vitium*. Denying his descent from his grandfather Agrippa, who was a commoner, he boasted instead that his mother had been conceived from Augustus's incest with his daughter Julia. He then took his two surviving sisters, Agrippina and Livilla, as his lovers – even though it was said that he did not love them as much as he had loved Drusilla and that he prostituted them to his catamites.

When he married them off, he attended the wedding and then took them back to his house, warning their new husbands "not to take liberties with my wife". He also openly had sex with them in front of their husbands. Later he banished them.

He ate and drank to excess and had sex with any man or woman that took his fancy. None dared refuse him. He would then publicly recount in detail the performance of his lover. He counted a beautiful young pantomime actor, Marcus Lepidus Mnester, among his gay lovers and kissed him in public, even – scandalously – in the theatre. He also had an affair with his own brother-in-law. Various hostages were also forced to have sex with him.

Caligula's passion for Pyrallis, a common prostitute, was even more notorious. And there was almost no woman of rank with whom he did not make free. He would invite a bunch of senators to dinner and would assess their wives as though he was purchasing a slave. If any dropped her head modestly, he would reach out and lift it again. Some were sent divorce papers in the name of their husbands, which were then filed in the public records.

At the wedding feast of Gaius Piso and Livia Ostella, Caligula abducted the bride. According to Suetonius, he simply said to Piso: "Hands off my wife," then had Livia taken to his home. The following day he issued a proclamation saying that he had "taken a wife in the way that Romulus and Augustus had done" – alluding to the rape of the Sabine women and the way in which Augustus had taken his wife, also called Livia, from her husband. However, Caligula tired of Livia after a few days and divorced her. Two years later, he banished her because he suspected that she had been seeing Piso again.

After that he summoned Lollia Paulina, the wife of one of his generals, from the provinces because he had heard that her grandmother had been a beautiful woman. He married her, but soon dumped her, leaving orders that no other man may make love to her. Sometimes it seemed that sex with ordinary women was not good enough for him. On nights when the moon was full, he invited the moon-goddess to his bed.

Caligula still aimed to find a suitable replacement for Drusilla. The only woman who fitted the bill was Caesonia, who was neither young nor beautiful. She was seven years older than him, the mother of three and had been married five times. However, she was known as one of the most lascivious women in Rome.

She would be seen riding beside him dressed in a cloak and helmet and carrying a shield. He also liked to display her naked to his friends. Apparently, even undressed, she appeared rather masculine, but that appealed to the somewhat effeminate Caligula. When Caesonia got pregnant, he made her his fourth wife.

Although Caesonia was notoriously promiscuous – she certainly did not stop screwing around because she was married to the emperor – Caligula was convinced that the child was his because of the violent way the little girl would scratch at the eyes of the children who played with her. He named his daughter Drusilla. Obsessed with incest, he intended that, when she was old enough, she should fulfil the plan that he had made with her namesake, his sister, and that the product of their incest would become the ruler of the empire. Fortunately, he did not live that long.

Caligula's behaviour became increasingly sadistic. He would close the granaries so that the people would go hungry, or he would scatter free tickets to the circus among crowds, causing stampedes in which many people died. He put on contests between mangy beasts and people who were crippled or infirm. When one contestant complained, he had his tongue cut out before being returned to the arena.

People were condemned to death in the arena without the case against them even being heard. A famous writer was burnt alive for writing a line that contained a *double entendre*. For some unspecified offence, the manager of the gladiators was chained up and beaten for days on end. He was only finally killed when Caligula could no longer stand the smell of his putrefying brains.

Parents were forced to watch the execution of their own children. One man was brought on a litter when he pleaded that he was too ill to attend. Another was invited to dinner after the execution so that Caligula could try to cheer him up. His son had been executed for being too well dressed and coiffed. Caligula was bald, so anyone who had a good head of hair risked, at the very least, having their head shaved. The grieving father was invited to dinner again on the day of his son's funeral. He attended because he had another son whom he did not want to lose.

Because Caligula was bald, no one was allowed to look down on him from above. The word "goat" was not to be used in his presence either, as he was thought to have very hairy legs.

Ptolemy was condemned to the arena for wearing a purple cloak that attracted admiration. Aesius Proculus, a particularly tall and handsome man, was dragged from his seat in the amphitheatre and forced to fight two gladiators. When he beat them both, Caligula ordered his death, after he had been displayed to the ladies bound and clad in rags.

Men of rank were branded on the face, shut up in cages like wild animals or sawn in half. The actor Apelles was asked who was greater, the king of the gods Jupiter or Caligula. When he hesitated to answer, Caligula had him cut to pieces with a lash, praising his voice as he pleaded for mercy and then remarking on the melodiousness of his groans.

Caligula told his torturers to take their time and to "strike a man so that he feels he is dying". He ordered one senator to be slit open before his eyes and for his internal organs to be removed with red-hot pincers in an order that would prolong his agony. Then the man was sawn in two and torn to pieces. Caligula's lust for cruelty was not sated until he saw the man's limbs, bowels and other body parts dragged through the streets and piled up in a heap before him.

He was so inured to the sight of pain and blood that he often ordered torture or decapitation as entertainment while he was eating, but then such gruesome entertainment was considered to be mere foreplay by some Romans. The senator Lucius Quintus was gay and kept a series of pretty young boys around him throughout his life. He took them on military campaigns with him and gave them more power and respect than he gave to his closest relatives and friends.

While handling the consular affairs of a Roman province, he was at a dinner party, lounging on a couch with his latest catamite. Lucius had been drinking and the youth began to flatter him.

"I love you so much," he said, "that one time when I attended my very first gladiator show, I rushed away early to meet you, although I wanted very badly to see a man get slaughtered."

Lucius was happy to accommodate the boy.

"Don't just lie there, holding it against me," he said. "I will make it up to you."

He ordered a condemned man to be brought to the dinner party, along with an officer with an axe. Lucius then asked his young lover if he wanted to see the man killed. The boy said he would like that very much. So Lucius gave the order and the man's head was chopped off. Later, when sanity had returned to the empire, Lucius Quintus was expelled from the Senate for this little gesture of love.

Caligula, however, lived a life without consequence. He took to the arena himself to face a gladiator who was armed with a wooden practice sword. Naturally Caligula carried a metal blade. He killed the man and claimed the victor's laurels.

At the dedication of a new bridge, he pushed a number of people into the water and, using a boat-hook, held them down under the water to make sure that they drowned. He killed people with a cudgel simply for disturbing him at the games and beat sacrificial victims to death in the temple with a hammer. A slave who was accused of stealing had his hands cut off and hung around his neck; he was then displayed at a party with a placard around his neck explaining what he had done.

At one dinner, two consuls asked why he was laughing. Caligula replied: "Why do you suppose? It's just that, at a single nod of my head, both of you could have your throats cut on the spot."

A famous actor was flogged savagely to see whether he could still speak so sweetly under torture. And when Caligula kissed the neck of a wife or lover, he would whisper tenderly: "Off comes his beautiful head whenever I give the word." Even Caesonia was threatened with torture, so that Caligula could discover why she loved him so.

Caligula was so reckless with other people's lives that he even bewailed the fact that his reign had not been beset by any great catastrophe; Augustus's rule, he said, had been made famous by the loss of three legions under Publius Quintilius Varus in the Teutoburg Forest in AD 9.

In AD 39, Caligula went to Germany. While he was there, he discovered a plot by the military commander Gaetulicus to kill him and have him replaced with Marcus Aemilius Lepidus, the son of the triumvir of the same name, the widower of his sister Drusilla, the lover of his other sister Agrippina the Younger and, in his youth, Caligula's own bum chum. The two men were executed and Agrippina was exiled along with her sister Livilla.

While he was in Germany, he wanted to take revenge on the Teutons for the loss of Varus's three legions in the Teutoburg Forest, after which the entrails of seventy thousand Roman soldiers were seen decorating the trees. Afterwards, Teutons had pickled the Romans' testicles and, though it was now 30 years on, they had only finished eating their stocks the year before.

Hearing that the emperor was in the area, the Teutons gathered on the far side of the Rhine and started to make obscene gestures. Caligula, however, was unwilling to risk his own life against these barbarians, whom he had only previously seen in the arena. There they were a favourite, as they could defend themselves against any man. They even knew how to finish off a bear by grabbing its tongue then pushing a fist down its throat, choking it to death. Consequently they were put up against animals that they had never seen before and died ravaged by Libyan lions or gored by Mediterranean bulls.

Instead of taking these wild men on, Caligula got some of his own men of Germanic background to dress up in skins like the Teutons. They were sent off into the forest. The rest of the army then pursued and captured them. The captives were brought back to camp where they swore allegiance to Caligula and kissed his boots before being summarily slaughtered. News of this great victory was sent back to Rome.

The following year, he invaded and plundered Gaul, heading a column that included prostitutes, cooks, actors, entertainers of every kind and well-endowed slaves to cater for his every whim. When he tired of riding up and down the column, urging his troops on with a whip, he would relax on a litter and was covered with swan's down. For sport, he would use a catapult to knock Gaulish peasants' heads off. When the army wintered in Lugdunum, now Lyon, he organised a speaking contest where the punishment for a poor performance was to be thrown in a sewer. This humiliation befell his uncle Claudius, who was visiting from Rome, because of his stutter.

To raise money from the rich burghers of Lyon, Caligula sold his own imperial excrement for an equal weight in gold. His exiled sister's possessions were then sold off. Then he ordered the possessions of Augustus and Tiberius to be brought from Rome so that they could be sold too.

He planned to invade Britain, and even had triremes carried overland from Rome, but when he reached the English Channel, he ordered his men to collect seashells from the beach. Each one, he said, represented a slaughtered Briton. He took the name Britannicus, meaning the conqueror of Britain, while rebuking the Senate. They were accused of indulging in revels, going to the theatre and living comfortably in their villas while he was risking his life in battle.

Before returning to Rome, he planned to slaughter his own legions, rather than pay them. He ordered them to assemble without their weapons. They realised what was going on, however, and he was forced to flee. Even so, he entered Rome in triumph. Three months of games were ordained to celebrate his victories, during which thousands of criminals and dissidents were slaughtered. This consumed almost all the money he had raised in Gaul.

To refill the treasury, he imposed new taxes on food, lawsuits, the wages of porters, marriage and the earnings of prostitutes – even those he forced into prostitution himself. He set up a brothel in his palace and forced Roman matrons and their sons and daughters into prostitution, displaying them naked for hire there. Patrons were lent money at extortionate rates. Details of his new taxes were not published. When he was forced to do so, the law appeared in tiny letters, posted up in a narrow corridor where it was impossible to copy. Later he took to straightforward confiscation, complaining that he was so poor that he could not afford a dowry for his baby daughter.

In the summer of AD 40, he retired to one of his many lavish villas outside Roman to complete his preparations for becoming a god. Magicians from every quarter of the empire gathered around his naked body in a darkened room and recited incantations that, they assured him, would allow him to blast jets of fire from every orifice.

Philosophers were then called to impart the great wisdom of the ages. They prattled out some platitudes, afraid that anything meaningful they said might offend him. He quickly grew tired of this charade and ordered red-hot pokers to be shoved up their backsides. Hearing the resulting screams, Caligula said: "Now that is true philosophy."

As the final part of his preparation for divinity, members of distant tribes known for their sexual ability – variously the Garamantes, Cietae and Quinquegentanei – were summoned to teach him the "seven secrets of sexual self-annihilation". These, unfortunately, have been lost in the mists of time, but they sound like the sort of thing that should be on the sex education curriculum of every secondary school. These lessons learnt, Caligula was now ready for deification.

He returned to Rome unannounced, went to the games and waded about in the glistening pools of blood that had collected in the arena. He smeared his body with it, drank some and then called for his favourite gladiator, Superbus, to bugger him in the arena in front of a crowd of a hundred thousand. While Superbus was doing this, a masked figure clad in black appeared behind him carrying a scimitar. At the exact moment the hapless gladiator came in Caligula's anus, the black figure lopped off his head with the scimitar, showering the emperor externally with blood while he was being bathed internally with semen. This depraved scene, Caligula believed, made him a living god.

He had temples and statues built. Statues of other noted Romans were destroyed and even those of Augustus were moved. The certificates of deification of Julius Caesar and Augustus were old and out of date, he said. There were to be no rivals. Nothing was to detract from his newfound status. He even thought of destroying the poems of Homer. Virgil's work was banned from libraries. He also ordered his statue to be placed in the Temple in Jerusalem so that the Jews could worship him too – though the procurator of Judaea procrastinated and the statue was not put in place by the time of Caligula's death.

However, attaining divinity left Caligula listless. How could he hope to experience anything so intense again? To console him, Caesonia plied Caligula with drugs designed to improve their love-making. These made him even more unstable. He often wore women's clothing or dressed as a god with a blond beard, or as Venus, or a triumphant general, wearing the breastplate of Alexander the Great, which he had had stolen from Alexander's sarcophagus in Alexandria. He also caused a scandal, singing and dancing in public and appearing on stage with lowly actors – a thing that no Roman of rank should do.

Caligula was already in danger from the legions in Germany who had turned against him. Then the legions that had accompanied him to the Channel backed a plot led by the senators Sextus Papinus, Betilienus Bassus and Anicius Cerialis, along with his son of the same name. Anicius Cerialis Jr betrayed the conspiracy, however. He was pardoned and, after he had publicly sodomised and strangled his father, he was awarded a provincial governorship. The other two senators, along with the commanders of the rebellious legions, were kebabbed on a skewer and roasted over an open fire, or burnt to death bit by bit as their flesh was torn away with red-hot pincers. Caligula watched while trying on the theatrical costumes of various gods and goddesses. As the executions reached a climax, Caligula looked on in flowing women's robes.

Then he deliberately alienated those who were closest to him, threatening to kill both them and himself if they thought he deserved to die. Omens told of his forthcoming death and a bunch of actors got so bold that they staged a play about the death of a king – in this case, Philip of Macedonia, the father of Alexander the Great. Caligula, though, was still riding high. When the gladiatorial games were interrupted by a thunderstorm, he ordered the god Jupiter to descend from the skies and fight a duel. When Jupiter failed to show, Caligula claimed victory by default, while the public kissed his boots.

The emperor also delighted the plebeians by returning to the arena himself. Dressed as a Thracian gladiator and wielding a razor-sharp sword, he faced gladiatorial opponents armed only with wooden daggers. Any attempt to defend themselves brought boos from the crowd, while imperial guards were poised to strike them down if they posed any threat. Knowing that if the emperor attacked they would be sliced to pieces, the only way out was for the gladiators to prostrate themselves and beg for imperial mercy. Few of them got it.

Meanwhile, Caligula continued to humiliate those of rank around him. He would insist on sleeping with their wives and, afterwards, would publicly tell the woman's husband that his wife was no good in bed or hire her out as a whore to any low-life who wanted her. The prefect of the Praetorian Guard Cornelius Sabinus was one of those humiliated in this way. The other prefect, Cassius Chaerea – there were always two – had distinguished himself as a soldier in the Rhine mutiny of AD 14, but he had a high squeaky voice and Caligula teased him unmercifully. The emperor taunted him for his effeminacy, giving as the daily password to the palace words like "Priapus" and "Venus" to provoke him further. And if Chaerea had to beg the emperor for a favour, Caligula would stick out his middle finger in an obscene gesture for the poor man to kiss. As a result, Sabinus and Chaerea organised a plot to rid themselves of their unruly emperor.

On 24 January AD 41, Caligula attended the Palatine Games, where he was stabbed at least 30 times by Sabinus, Chaerea and other high-ranking conspirators. As he lay writhing on the ground, he was dispatched with a sword thrust through his private parts. His wife Caesonia was stabbed to death by a centurion, while their daughter's brains were dashed out against a wall.

Caligula was just 29 years old and had ruled for less than four years when he died. His body was taken secretly to the garden of the Lamian family, partially burnt in a hastily constructed funeral pyre and then buried. When his sisters returned from exile, they had his body dug up and cremated properly; Caligula's ashes were then placed in the family tomb. His stuttering uncle Claudius, whom Caligula had spared as a laughing stock, succeeded him.

That, at least, is the conventional tale. However, documents recently unearthed in Albania tell a different story. They say that Caligula planned his own end, so that his deification would be complete and he could rejoin his sister Drusilla in celestial incest. First he went on holiday to Lake Nemi in the Alban Hills, 15 miles southeast of Rome.

The engineers who had built the pontoon bridge across the Bay of Naples provided a fleet of luxurious galleys, with jewelled prows, gold-plated bulkheads and mosaic floors. On board they had running water, a steam bath and a crew of a thousand. Caesonia and daughter Drusilla each had one to themselves, while Caligula had a second galley alongside his outsized vessel, manned – or rather unmanned – by eunuchs who sang while he lay on a bed of swan's down on the upper deck, contemplating the stars – soon to be his new heavenly home.

On 10 January AD 41, he ordered one final week-long sex extravaganza. He pleasured himself in every way imaginable. As slaves performed acts of quadruple buggery, Caligula ordered the opulent ships to be set on fire. They sank in flames as the orgy continued.

Back in Rome, Caligula had built a new amphitheatre, whose stage was held together with gold nails and was lit by silver reflecting panels. It had a capacity of only twenty thousand and was much smaller than the gladiatorial arena, where the crush to get in when the gates opened often left many dead. An elaborate bejewelled altar was built to Caligula's own cult. When it was finished, it was said, there were only two gold coins left in the imperial coffers. These were to cover the eyes of Caligula's corpse when he had risen to become the emperor of heaven.

The story suggests that Caligula had colluded with his disgruntled prefect of the Praetorian Guard Chaerea, who was to deliver the *coup de grâce* and allow his divine spirit to escape its corporeal body. The rest of the Guard, under Sabinus, were to slaughter the remaining senators and destroy the Senate building. That would leave the empire in the hands of Claudius, whom Caligula considered a bumbling idiot. That would bring the whole of Roman civilisation crashing down, leaving Caligula as the last and greatest Caesar on earth, while he then directed human affairs, in incestuous union with his sister Drusilla, from above.

This was to happen on 24 January AD 41. When the doors to the small amphitheatre were thrown open, there was such a crush that hundreds perished. The day's entertainment began with a flamingo – a bird that had never been seen in Rome before. Caligula stepped forward and, with an emerald-encrusted dagger, slaughtered it.

He then led a dance that he himself had choreographed. Called the *Cinyras*, it told of epic deeds of incest. However, it was tame stuff for an audience used to seeing the real thing and there was disquiet. A second piece, called the *Laureolus*, was a bizarre "snuff" ballet that included ritual slaughter. At the end of the performance, only three of the dancers were still alive and the stage was glistening with blood.

While the corpses were being dragged off, the survivors – two men and one woman – made their way into one of the tunnels that led out of the amphitheatre. Caligula stopped them to congratulate them and, in rapid succession, sodomised all three. Just as he was about to come, he withdrew and stepped back out into the amphitheatre so that the audience could witness the last gush of imperial semen spurt from his penis.

Caligula looked up to where the deified Drusilla awaited him and shouted: "Testicles!" This was the signal for Chaerea and the Guard to advance on him. The first blow hit him on the shoulder, slicing six inches into his upper body. Chaerea had obviously decided not to make it a painless end. He took his sword and stuck it into Caligula's stomach until it came out of his back and then twisted.

Chaerea then pulled out the blade, raised it and with one stroke neatly decapitated Caligula. It was said that Caligula's head flew up into the air and landed on the altar still mouthing obscenities. His body crumpled, and the rest of the Praetorian Guard closed in on him. They cut him to pieces, paying special attention to the mutilation of his genitals.

CHAPTER 6

Claudius has often been portrayed as a stuttering buffoon. In fact, he was enormously well read and an accomplished writer. He was the first Roman emperor since Augustus to extend the bounds of the Roman Empire, making Britain a Roman colony and extending Roman rule in North Africa. On the sexual front, though, he was a bit of a flop.

Born Tiberius Claudius Nero Germanicus on 1 August 10 BC in Lugdunum, modern Lyon, in Gaul, he was the son of the general Nero Claudius Drusus, who himself was the son Livia gave birth to three months after marrying Augustus. Although Livia was still married to Tiberius Claudius Nero at the time of the conception, Drusus was thought to be the son of Augustus, who was already *in futueres cum* Livia at that time. After Drusus's birth, a popular rhyme did the rounds. It translated variously:

> Nine months for common births the fates decree;
> But, for the great, reduce this to three.

Or:

> How fortunate those parents are for whom
> Their child is only three months in the womb.

Drusus was killed when Claudius was one, but Claudius had other claims to fame. He was the nephew of Emperor Tiberius and the grandson of

Mark Antony. An ugly, sickly and clumsy child, he was left to his own devices. He spent his time reading and writing books in Greek. These were mainly about Etruscan and Carthaginian history, and, in all, he produced some 30 books. He also spent time eating, drinking, gambling – even writing a book on how to beat the system – and, of course, chasing women. Although Charles Laughton* portrayed him as gay in the unfinished von Sternberg* movie classic *I, Claudius*, he was one of the very few Roman emperors who did not indulge himself freely with other men. Suetonius said: "He was immoderate in his passion for women, but wholly free from the love of males."

The historian Edward Gibbon, author of *The Decline and Fall of the Roman Empire*, concurred, saying: "Of the first 15 emperors, Claudius was the only one whose taste in love was entirely correct."

While this is probably not entirely true, he was certainly a good deal straighter than most of his predecessors.

As a boy he was engaged to Augustus's great-granddaughter, Aemila Lepida, but the engagement was broken off when her parents offended Augustus. After that he married five times. His first wife was Plautia Urgulanilla, who produced two children. He divorced her in AD 24 on the grounds of adultery, scandalous behaviour, "filthy conduct" and suspicion of murder. Their second child, a daughter called Claudia, was born five months after the divorce. Her real father was a freedman called Boter. Claudius disowned the child and ordered her to be hurled naked at her mother's door.

Claudius was no luckier with his second wife. She died on their wedding day; a necrophiliac's wet dream, I suppose. Things did not get any better with his third wife. Tiberius had picked out a relative of Sejanus, called Aelia Paetina, for him. It was during the downfall of Sejanus that Claudius developed his idiot act; it helped him survive Tiberius's treason trials and the reign of the murderous Caligula. He divorced her later for "slight offences".

During the reign of Tiberius, Claudius found himself increasingly marginalised. Much of his branch of the family was destroyed in the struggles for succession, but when Caligula came to power in the spring of AD 37 he was seen as an ally – or, at least, he was not seen as a threat. It is plain that Caligula considered his uncle Claudius to be a bumbling fool. On 1 July Caligula appointed Claudius consul and he took public office for the first time at the age of 46. Unfortunately, his new position now made him the sexual target of dangerous women. First came Messalina Valeria, the great-great-granddaughter of Augustus's sister, the virtuous Octavia, making her Claudius's first cousin once removed. When they married in AD 39, she was 17 years old; he was 48. They had two children – a daughter called Octavia, who later married Nero,* and a son called Tiberius Claudius Caesar Germanicus, who was later renamed Britannicus after his father invaded Britain.

The young Messalina* was too hot for Claudius to handle. She was so horny that, at night, she would visit Rome's brothels and hire herself out as a whore.

Her over-active libido may be explained by Roman dental hygiene practices. According to her dentist Scribonius Largus, who wrote *De compositione medicamentorium*, Messalina cleaned her teeth with a common tooth powder containing calcined stags' horn. This was probably added for its abrasive property, but stags' horn has an ancient reputation as an aphrodisiac. So while this dentifrice was saving the empire from its oral decay, it was adding to its moral decay. It prevented some cavities, while filling others.

Juvenal told the tale:

> Once Messalina sensed that the Emperor Claudius was asleep, this royal whore was brazen enough to prefer a command mat to her marriage bed in the palace, and she slipped on a night-cowl and departed, accompanied by only one female slave. She hid her black hair beneath a blonde wig and entered a brothel that smelt dank from old bedspreads, heading straight to her own empty little cell. With her nipples exposed and gilded, she prostituted herself under the name of Lycisca, and she displayed the womb that bore you, O highborn Britannicus. Here she passionately took on all comers and demanded the coins due from each, and when finally the brothel-keeper sent his girls home, she went away depressed – the last to close her cell. Lust still flared in her throbbing loins. Exhausted by men, but not satisfied, her cheeks darkened from the smoke of the lamps, Messalina carried the stink of the brothel back to the imperial bed.

Even that did not satisfy her and it was said that she sent out emissaries to find "men capable of assuaging her insatiable lubricity", but, in the end, "none were able to conquer her in amorous combat". She later challenged the most famous courtesan in Rome to a contest to see who could have the most men in a single night.

Messalina was not the only high-born married woman to hire herself out as a prostitute. Many Roman matrons found it a creative way around the strict laws on adultery, which forbade them from having sex with anyone but their husbands. The punishment was banishment or the forfeit of their property. However, for girls who wanted to play around, the remedy was simple. Suetonius said: "Married women from well-known families were registering as prostitutes, and were escaping punishment for their adulteries by renouncing the privileges of their rank in society."

By tradition it was said that, when Caligula was assassinated on 24 January AD 41, Claudius was found trembling behind a curtain and, as the only surviving member of the dynasty old enough to rule, was reluctantly proclaimed emperor by the Praetorian Guard. However, Claudius went on to prove that he was an astute politician and there are indications that he had a hand in the plot to assassinate Caligula.

The Albanian documents tell a different story entirely. They say that, after the ritual assassination of Caligula, Sabinus and the Praetorian Guard were about to move on the terrified senators when they heard a stentorian voice telling them to stop. It was Claudius. Once Caligula was dead, he threw aside the pretence of being a fool, lost his stutter and seized control, with grateful senators falling over themselves to pledge their allegiance to him.

Chaerea, Sabinus and others who had been in on the assassination of Caligula were taken away and garrotted. Caesonia and baby Drusilla were disposed of and the allegiance of the army was assured by the distribution of Claudius's considerable wealth. He had the decency to have Caligula's body cremated, under the cover of darkness. When Agrippina and Livilla returned from exile, they did not dig up his remains to rebury them in the family tomb, but rather pissed on them and fed them to wild dogs.

He reigned as Tiberius Claudius Caesar Augustus Germanicus, though he had no legal right to the name Caesar. By taking the name Caesar, Claudius began the process of changing it from being a family name to being a title – which eventually developed into the appellation

Kaiser and Czar. Claudius also established the pre-eminence of the army. No future emperor could rule without its support.

Despite saving the senators' lives, his elevation was far from popular with the Senate, whose members conspired several times to take his life. Nevertheless, he was maintained in power by the army and he forced many of those who opposed him in the Senate to commit suicide. He won the allegiance of the masses by staging some bloodthirsty games. He impressed them by eating a hearty dinner while the killing was going on. Not once did he raise his thumb to spare a defeated gladiator. Instead he ordered the condemned man to remove his helmet, so that the spectators could witness the full horror of his death. Great scrolls were unfurled from the top of the columns surrounding the arena offering money to all those who supported the new regime and, by the end of the games, the masses belonged to the emperor.

Claudius also had an ally in Messalina who, though she comprehensively cuckolded him, had one mission in life – to put her son on the throne. To do that, she had to keep her husband alive and began a murderous campaign against all of her potential rivals. First she bumped off Caligula's sister Livilla. She had married the powerful Marcus Vinicus, who had been consul in AD 30. Next she denounced Julia, the daughter of Tiberius's dead son Drusus, for immorality. In the process, Messalina destroyed the reputation of the prefect of the Praetorian Guard, who was about to report her own sexual shenanigans to Claudius. This had the added advantage of creating a palace vacancy for one of her own amours.

Almost as soon as Claudius took power, preparations for the invasion of Britain began. It was to be spearheaded by four legions. Claudius himself took part, arriving in the war zone in the late summer of AD 43. After a parade at Camulodunum, modern Colchester, he returned to Rome in triumph in AD 44, his military credentials now firmly established.

As a judge, he was castigated for allowing the testimony of common prostitutes. He also censured a notorious seducer of young girls and married women, telling him: "Restrain your passions, or at least go more carefully in future." No further action was taken against him. As Claudius himself admitted: "Why should it be any of my business who your mistress may be?"

He broke with convention in the arena, too. When the gladiators let out the standard cry, "Hail Caesar, we who are about to die salute you," Claudius replied: "Or not, as the case may be."

And, in some of the strangest legislation ever planned, he considered publishing an edict legalising the breaking of wind at table, either silently or noisily, after hearing of a man whose modesty caused him to restrain himself to the point where the build-up of gas endangered his health.

While Claudius was away conquering Britain, the murderous Messalina had been attempting a few conquests of her own. However, the imperious Appius Silanus had turned her down and, when Claudius returned, she took her revenge with the help of Claudius's freedman, Narcissus. Claudius later told the Senate that Narcissus had burst into his bedroom one night and told him that he had had a dream that Silanus was plotting to assassinate him. The dream was presented as *prima facie* evidence against Silanus. Messalina had already sent a messenger to Silanus, summoning him to the emperor. She then told Claudius that she had dreamt the same dream for several nights running. Then, lo and behold, Silanus turned up at the imperial quarters in the middle of the night. Case closed. Silanus was arrested and executed.

Silanus's execution prompted the governor of Dalmatia to revolt. The rebellion was put down in just five days. During that time, Messalina seized the opportunity to rid herself of other rivals or unwanted ex-lovers. She also got rid of her stepson-in-law, Gnaeus Pompeius, who had married Claudius's daughter, and was, therefore, a potential rival to Britannicus as Claudius's heir. He was dispatched *in flagrante delicto* with his male lover.

Her next target was Valerius Asiaticus, a wealthy and ambitious Gaul who had married into the Roman aristocracy. His wife had had a brief affair with Caligula and her sister had briefly married him, but he also owned the gardens of the general Lucullus, well known for his taste, which Messalina wanted. She gave a prefect half a million sesterces – equivalent to about $20,000 – and the promise of a promotion if he arrested Asiaticus for sodomy. He was brought to the palace in chains and tried behind closed doors. The evidence against him was pitiful and Claudius had a mind to acquit, but Messalina was adamant. They compromised. Asiaticus was to die, but he could choose the method of execution.

Messalina could curb neither her ambition, nor her sexual appetite. Still in her mid-20s and married to a man in his late 50s, she fell for the young consul-designate Gaius Silius. She bombarded him with presents and, while Claudius was away in Ostia in AD 48, she married him in a Bacchic ceremony.

Along with the senators she had sent to their deaths, she had also been responsible for the death of Claudius's freedman secretary Polybius. The other freedmen turned against her. Narcissus informed Claudius of Messalina's marriage. Unlike her other fooling around, this was a political threat. Claudius rushed back from Ostia and Narcissus convinced him that Messalina and Silius aimed to seize power. Claudius gave him command of the Praetorian Guard and they set out for Silius's house. Messalina stopped them on their way and begged for mercy for the sake of their children. Claudius countered this by flourishing a list of her lovers, which Narcissus had thoughtfully provided.

The chief Vestal Virgin stopped them next and demanded that the empress be given a hearing. She was pushed to one side with promises; the more immediate task was to get to Silius. He was arrested and taken to the barracks of the Praetorian Guard, where he was given a drumhead court-martial. He asked only for a swift and painless death. Messalina was later found in Lucullus's garden. She had been stabbed to death.

Having been so unlucky in love, Claudius ordered the Praetorian Guard to kill him if he tried to get married again. However, the death of Messalina created a vacancy which every ambitious woman – and every ambitious family – in Rome wanted to fill. Therefore, to maintain political stability, it was necessary for him to marry. Narcissus suggested that he remarry Aelia Paetina. The influential freedman Callistus, another of the conspirators behind the downfall of Caligula, suggested Lollia Paulina, a wealthy woman who had briefly been another of Caligula's wives; but the rising star among Claudius's freedmen, Pallas, proposed a much more politically advantageous match. He said that Claudius should marry Caligula's sister Agrippina, who also happened to be Claudius's niece.

Agrippina, it seems, had much the same idea.

"She had a niece's privilege of kissing and caressing Claudius," said Suetonius, "and exercised it with a noticeable effect on his passions." And she made full use of kisses and endearments to "draw him into love with her ... and he was completely won".

Claudius was assured that the marriage would be popular among the people and his friend Vitellius canvassed the Senate. At their next meeting, the senators passed a motion that "obliged the emperor to marry Agrippina as a measure highly conducive to the public interest". They then passed a second motion, allowing uncles to marry their nieces, which had previously been considered incest. Without a day's delay, Claudius married Agrippina on 1 January AD 49, after being a widower for just three months. Claudius was now 58; his wife was 33. That day he executed 35 senators and 300 knights who had opposed the match.

Once again, Claudius had made a disastrously bad choice. Agrippina was the granddaughter of the promiscuous Julia. She had seen her mother, Agrippina the Elder, beaten up by a centurion and starved to death on the orders of Tiberius. Then she had been *futuendus stultus* and prostituted by her brother, Caligula. None of this was designed to leave her terribly stable emotionally.

Agrippina was also an ambitious woman. She had a son called Nero by her first husband, Gnaeus Domitius Ahenobarbus, whom she was determined to see succeed Claudius as emperor. She was also ruthless. She had been accused of poisoning her second husband, Passienus Crispus, to facilitate the match with Claudius.

Within a year, she had assumed the title "Augusta", meaning empress. Claudius had adopted the ten-year-old Nero and named him co-heir, along with seven-year-old Britannicus. Agrippina got Nero betrothed to Claudius's daughter Octavia, his own cousin and step-sister, breaking off the girl's previous engagement to Lucius Silanus on the grounds of incest. Lucius was stripped of office and was forced to commit suicide four days later.

By now Agrippina's face appeared on coins. She wore a military cloak trimmed with gold and entertained ambassadors when they visited the palace. And she was no more faithful to Claudius than Messalina had been. Toward the end of his life, he regretted marrying her. When congratulated on condemning a woman accused of adultery, he remarked ruefully: "Destiny has ordained that my wives should be unfaithful to my bed." He seemed fated, he said, to marry women who were "unchaste but remained unchastened".

When Nero was 16 and old enough to rule, Claudius became mysteriously ill; it is thought that Agrippina had fed him poisoned mushrooms. He lingered for a while and, ostensibly to make him vomit, she tickled his throat with a poisoned feather. This seems to have done the trick, for Claudius finally passed away on 13 October AD 54. At noon that day, the youthful Nero was acclaimed emperor. Already well known to the army and the public, he faced no serious challenges to his succession. Britannicus was poisoned the following year and Nero married his sister, Octavia.

CHAPTER 7

Nero is popularly portrayed as the mad emperor who played the fiddle while Rome burned. This is not true. The violin was not invented until the sixteenth century and its bowed forerunner did not reach Europe from Central Asia until the tenth century. Nero was a dab hand with the lyre, though. Mind you, he was not above a little fiddling about, either.

Whether he burnt down Rome or not, it was easy to predict that the reign of Nero was going to be *stercus* – and it was not all Agrippina's fault. When congratulated on the birth of his son, his father, Gnaeus Domitius Ahenobarbus, said that any fruit of their union would turn out to be a disaster.

It was in the genes, or at least the *gens*. For over two hundred years the *gens Domitia* had given to Rome generals and consuls renowned for their brutality, and Gnaeus Domitius Ahenobarbus was as bad as the rest of the bunch. The Emperor Augustus actually reprimanded him for the bloodthirsty games he put on and prosecuted him. He ran over a child on the Appian Way for fun, killed one of his freedmen for not drinking as much as he was told to and ripped out another man's eye in the Forum. Under Tiberius he was charged with treason, adultery and incest with his sister – and was only saved by the accession of his brother-in-law, the like-minded Caligula. Fortunately Ahenobarbus died when Nero was three, leaving the child to learn everything he needed to know about murder, cruelty and sexual perversion from his monstrous mother. Given the family background, the chances that he was going to turn out well adjusted were slim.

With no father around, Nero developed an incestuous passion for his own mother. Her enemies tried to discourage this, fearing that she would become even more powerful. It seems that they failed. Mother and son often rode together in the same litter and the stains on his clothes afterwards seemed to indicate that something sexual had been going on. Later, he included a prostitute among his concubines who looked conspicuously like Agrippina. He had little time for the noble and virtuous Octavia, who was his wife. As Tacitus puts it: "Stolen joys are sweeter."

Nero was 17 when Claudius died in AD 54, but his mother ruled as regent. She sought to control her son by putting him under the control of Sextus Afranius Burrus, who owed his position as prefect of the Praetorian Guard to Agrippina, and the Stoic philosopher Lucius Annaeus Seneca, who was also a protégé of Agrippina, even though Caligula had wanted to kill him. Irritated by his oratory, Caligula had tried to frame Seneca in a conspiracy, but one of his mistresses persuaded Caligula to banish him to Corsica, claiming that as he came from a family with a history of bronchial disorders, he did not have long to live. After eight years of exile, Agrippina recalled him to be Nero's tutor. However, Seneca's Stoic philosophy did little to temper Nero. It did little to temper Seneca either. Although the Stoics insisted that man should not be moved by earthly passions, Seneca had an eye for see-through women's fashions, was an expert on Roman sex toys and loved describing the sale of naked slave-girls, as we have seen. He also made himself a rich man by lending money.

Although both Burrus and Seneca owed their positions to Agrippina, according to Tacitus: "They both waged a crusade against Agrippina's ferocity."

At first she sought to exercise her authority by sitting beside Nero on the imperial dais during public sessions, but he got wise to this and, when she entered, he would rise to greet her and then escort her to another seat. After that, she hid behind a curtain so that she could hear what was going on.

Burrus and Seneca both feared that Agrippina's power would cause disaffection in the army; Roman soldiers did not like to be ordered around by a woman. So, in an attempt to increase their influence with the young Nero, they furnished him with a mistress, a freedwoman called Acte Claudia. Nero promptly got carried away and tried to take Acte as his wife. Although it was against the law for him to marry a former slave, he had men of consular rank swear falsely that she was of royal blood.

According to Tacitus: "Agrippina raged with womanly jealousy that she had a freedwoman for a rival and a maid for a daughter-in-law. She could not wait for her son's repentance or satiety. The more scandalous her accusations, the hotter his passion, until at last he gave way completely to his love and, throwing off allegiance to his mother, put himself in the hands of Seneca."

Nero fired Pallas, the man Agrippina had made financial controller, and stripped her of her Praetorian Guard. However, when Agrippina poisoned Britannicus – still a potential rival – at a children's party, mother and son were reconciled.

Another story has it that, after using him regularly as a catamite, Nero poisoned the 14-year-old Britannicus himself. Nero certainly had interests in that quarter because Seneca provided him with handsome male slaves. According to Catullus, it was common for a young Roman to have sex with such a *concubinus* until he was married. Seneca's preference also lay that way.

Whichever way it happened, mother and son found a common cause in the murder of Britannicus. However, Nero was not willing to drop Acte, even though it would have seemed politic to have feigned a separation. So Seneca got his friend Annaeus Serenus to pretend that he was passionately in love with Acte, though actually he acted as a go-between between Acte and Nero, and made a show of showering her with gifts that actually came from the young emperor. Eventually Agrippina mellowed. Acte was no threat and she offered Nero the use of her own rooms to carry on the affair "which, after all, his youth and high position fully excused".

Despite his background, Nero was a model emperor – at first. He hated the brutality of the gladiatorial arena and, being an admirer of all things Greek, began poetry competitions, theatrical performances and athletic events as rival attractions. Even the Vestal Virgins were invited to watch the athletics – though this may have been sadistic in its way. It must have been agony for these six girls, who had to forswear sex for 30 years, to watch fit, young, male athletes performing Greek-style in the nude.

A glutton, Nero's major pleasure at this point seems to have been having enemas to keep his weight down. He also took to playing the lyre. No one was allowed to leave the theatre during his recitals. This rule was so strictly enforced that one woman actually had to give birth in the audience. A *pulchellus puer*, he also fancied himself as a new Hercules and it is said that he tried to have a lion tamed to such a degree that he could face it naked in the arena.

Conservative elements in Roman society criticised him for introducing too many Greek things and for encouraging youths from patrician families to exhibit themselves on the stage. Tacitus wrote:

> Our fathers' manners, disused by degrees, were now being entirely thrown over by licence imported from abroad, whereby everything that was corrupt and corrupting was exhibited within the city. These foreign pursuits were ruining our young men, who were giving themselves up to the indolent and shameful homosexual practices of the gymnasium. In this the emperor and the Senate led the way, having not only given a free rein to vice, but even compelled Roman nobles, in the name of oratory and poetry, to degrade themselves on stage. What was left for them was to strip themselves naked, put on boxing gloves and practise fighting thus, instead of with the weapons of a soldier.

And one thing did lead to another. Tacitus was soon bewailing: "Whole nights were now given up to debauchery. What was left for virtue? Every debauchee in these promiscuous crowds could practise by night the lusts he had conceived as fantasy during the day."

Nero removed the guard from the Pons Milvius, a celebrated sexual resort within two miles of the city, "to allow full freedom to lust and debauchery of every sort there". He also instituted the festival of the Juvenalia, celebrating the arrival of puberty when the first down or beard was shaved from a boy's face. "This festival gave occasion for great licentiousness and debauchery, especially of a pederastic nature, and the fullest opportunity taken thereof, for gratifying such tastes."

Nero's darker side gradually took over. He would go out at night in disguise, robbing shops and attacking passers-by. If his victims offered any resistance, he would stab them and drop their bodies down the sewer. It was risky behaviour as some of his victims fought back. On one occasion he was almost beaten to death by a senator whose wife he had molested.

He would slum it in the taverns and brothels of the Subura on these nocturnal trips, and would violate both women and boys. He was soon indulging himself sexually with married women and freeborn boys. Then he raped the Vestal Virgin Rubria; a very serious matter – they attended to the sacred fire of the goddess Vesta. When Hannibal marched into Italy in 216 BC and beat the Romans at the Battle of Cannae, the defeat was blamed on the unchastity of the Vestal Virgins. The offenders were punished in the traditional way: they were scourged and then buried alive.

After that Nero saw no reason to keep his vices private. He held huge public feasts inviting all the prostitutes and nude dancing girls in the city. When he sailed down the Tiber to Ostia or when he cruised around the Gulf of Pozzuoli to the west of Naples, he would have temporary brothels erected along the shore. These would be staffed by married women who would try and lure him ashore.

According to Suetonius, Nero practised every kind of obscenity.

"As for his own body, it is known that he dishonoured it to such a degree that after he had defiled every part of it with unnatural pollution, he at last devised a new kind of sport."

He had men, women and children tied to stakes naked. Then, dressed in skins, he would attack their private parts as if he was a wild animal.

"After working up sufficient excitement by this means, he was dispatched – shall we say – by his freedman Doryphorus," said Suetonius.

Nero did not believe that he was alone in his sexual cravings. According to Suetonius's informants, Nero "firmly believed that no man or woman could remain chaste or pure in any part of their body, and that most people hypocritically concealed their secret vices under a pretence of virtue". So if anyone owned up to obscene practices that matched his own, he pardoned them for any other crime they committed.

He also set about squandering the vast fortune that had been left by Claudius and praised Caligula for the speed at which he had emptied Tiberius's huge coffers. Nero spent eight hundred thousand sesterces – the equivalent of $32,000 – a day entertaining the exiled Parthian King Tiridates and then gave him a parting gift of a hundred million – $4 million. Tacitus said that, in all, he gave away over 2,200 million sesterces, or $88 million. He was just as extravagant on his own account. He never wore the same clothes twice and would bet four thousand gold pieces per spot on a winning throw at dice. Low-lifes, such as Spiculus the gladiator and Menecrates the lyre-player, were given houses and estates worthy of a triumphant general. Paneros the moneylender was given a funeral worthy of royalty.

When he travelled, it was always in a convoy of more than a thousand carriages. The mules were shod with silver and the escort jangled with bracelets and medallions. When he went fishing, he used a golden net strung with purple and scarlet thread.

His extravagance also stretched to architecture. He built a palace that stretched between two of Rome's seven hills called The Passageway. Its pillared arcade ran for a whole mile and the entrance hall was so large that it could house a statue of Nero 120 feet high. This was a measure of his vanity. Nero was so vain that he changed the name of April to Neroneus and planned to rename Rome Neropolis.

Suetonius said that the lake in the palace courtyard looked like a sea and that the surrounding buildings looked like a whole city. The walls were overlaid with gold and studded with precious jewels and mother of pearl. All the dining rooms had ceilings made from carved ivory, with panels that slid back so that the guests could be showered with flowers or perfume. The main dining room was round and its ceiling revolved in time with the sky; the bathrooms had fresh water, seawater and sulphur water on tap.

"Now at least I can live like a human being," said Nero when he moved in.

He decided to build huge baths near his summer residence at Baiae near Naples. It would be fed by all the hot springs in the district. Baiae was another loose-living resort like Pons Milvius, and Cicero, the foremost orator of the era, left a description of what went on there during a courtroom attack on the self-willed Clodia Metella, the wife of the politician Metellus Celer, the lover of the erotic poet Catullus and the seducer of a young trainee lawyer who was Cicero's client:

> Baiae does not simply tell us a tale, but rings with the report that there
> is one woman so deeply sunk in her vicious depravities that she no

longer even bothers to seek privacy and darkness and the usual veil of discretion to cover her lusts. On the contrary, she actually exults in displaying the most foully lecherous goings-on amid the widest publicity and in the glaring light of day ... If a woman who has no husband throws open her home to every debauchee and publicly leads the life of a whore, if she makes a habit of being entertained by men who are total strangers, or if she pursues this mode of existence in the city, in her own gardens, among the crowds at Baiae, if in fact she behaves in such a way that not only her general demeanour but also her dress and associates, her hot eyes and uninhibited language, her embraces and kisses, her beach parties, all show that she is not only a prostitute, but a lewd and depraved prostitute at that; if a young man should happen to be found in the company of such a woman, then surely, you would agree that this was not so much adultery as just plain sex – not an outrage of chastity, but mere satisfaction of the appetite.

Nero then planned to build a canal from Rome to Baiae. It would be 160 miles long and wide enough for two quinqueremes – ships with five rows of oars – to pass. The advantage would be that he could sail to his summer palace without going out to sea. Prisoners from every part of the empire were brought to Italy to work on it. It was to be paid for by the fabled treasure of Queen Dido, which she took with her when she fled from the Phoenician port of Tyre – modern Sur in Lebanon – to found Carthage in North Africa in the ninth century BC. The treasure was supposed to be hidden in caves somewhere in the Sahara. Search parties were sent, but the treasure failed to materialise and soon Nero could not even pay his soldiers.

To raise the money he resorted to robbery, blackmail and punitive taxes. He even had to sell some expensive dyes that he had forbidden anyone else to use. When he saw a woman wearing the forbidden colour at one of his recitals, he had her stripped of her clothes – and then her entire property.

A man of diverse tastes, Nero had long fallen out of love with Octavia and quit her bed. When friends criticised him for his treatment of her, he said: "Just having the trappings of an empress ought to make her happy."

He tried to strangle her on several occasions, then declared that she was barren and divorced her. This was an unpopular move, so he banished her. Finding that was even more unpopular, he charged her with numerous cases of adultery, but the people called refused to testify against her, even under torture. So he bribed his old tutor Anicetus, the freedman who was now commanding the fleet at Misenum in the Gulf of Pozzuoli, to say that he had debauched her. She was banished to the island of Pandataria, where she was later murdered.

The reason that Nero wanted to get rid of Octavia was that he had fallen in love with the daughter of a quaestor, or treasurer, named Poppaea Sabina.* She was a rich girl from Pompeii, where the family sponsored the games. Tacitus wrote:

> This woman had every quality – except virtue. Her mother had been the great beauty of her day, and had bequeathed her daughter both her distinction and her looks. Her wealth was equal to her rank. In conversation she was charming and witty, and she had a lively mind. Outwardly she was modest and discreet, but in private she was depraved. She seldom appeared in public and when she did she had her face veiled. But this was merely a ploy to increase the interest in her beauty. She cared nothing for her reputation, sharing her affections between her husband and lovers, and transferring her favours when she saw advantage in it.

She was also a little older than Nero and famously said that she would "rather die than see my beauty fade". She had also been a *pessima puella*. At various times she was married to two of Nero's friends, Rufrius Crispinus and the future emperor Otho. Nero had her current husband, Atticus Vestinus, a consul, murdered so that he could have her.

Although she was beautiful and enchanting, she was not nearly as wicked as Messalina or Agrippina. However, *mater carus* was jealous again and disapproved of the affair; this time, though, she was not going to get her own way. When Nero tried to conceal their affair by marrying her off to his best friend Otho, Poppaea accused him of being "a mother's boy, who was bound to obey orders". This stung.

Having outgrown their incestuous relationship, Nero had become weary of his mother's interference in his sex life and threatened to abdicate and go into retirement in Rhodes; an act that would have deprived her of power, too. He stripped her of all her honours and privileges. Refusing to live with her any more, he ejected her from the palace and took away her guards. Then he harassed her with lawsuits until she left Rome and moved to her riverside estate. He did not even leave her alone there: he sent people to drive or sail past, jeering at her as they went.

Knowing his mother's murderous nature, Nero became afraid. Encouraged by Poppaea, he decided that she must die. He tried to poison her three times, but on each occasion she had been one step ahead and taken an antidote. Then he had a machine rigged up that would dislodge the panels of her bedroom ceiling so that they would fall on her while she was sleeping, but one of the men involved in the plot could not keep a secret. Plainly some more sophisticated method was going to be needed.

Nero pretended to make peace with Agrippina and invited her to celebrate the Feast of Minerva with him at Baiae. As her ship was coming into the jetty, he had one of his captains ram her, damaging her boat. After the feast was over and Agrippina was ready to go home, Nero offered to lend her one of his boats. He walked down to the quay with her and, according to Suetonius, in a filial display of affection, even kissed her breasts before seeing her on board.

The boat had been built by Nero's old friend Anicetus and was designed to collapse when it got out at sea. Nero sat up all night for news that his mother had drowned. The boat had indeed collapsed, but Agrippina was a strong swimmer and had swum ashore. Her freedman Lucius Agerinus came running to Nero with the good news that his mother was safe and sound. Nero seized the opportunity, dropped a dagger near Lucius and accused him of trying to assassinate him on his mother's orders. Lucius was quickly dispatched and a military tribune was then sent to kill Agrippina. The story was to be put about that, when Agrippina's plot to kill Nero had failed, she had committed suicide. This would hardly have fooled a doctor at the postmortem, as Nero ordered that the first stab should be to her "womb" – that is, "the place where the emperor first entered the world". It is impossible to imagine any woman trying to commit suicide by stabbing herself in the *cunnus*.

Once the deed was done, Nero dashed off to examine her corpse, "handling every part of it, finding fault with some, commending others" as if he was assessing the body of a lover – which indeed he was. He performed this gruesome survey joyously, drink in hand. Then he had Seneca dash off a letter to the Senate explaining the discovery of the supposed plot. There were no repercussions. Either everybody was glad to see the back of Agrippina, or they were so afraid of Nero that they kept quiet. The only person at all unsettled was Nero himself, who later complained that he was haunted by Agrippina's ghost. That did not stop him from murdering his aunt, though. The old lady, confined to bed with severe constipation, stroked the bum-fluff on his chin and said: "May I but live to touch this soft hair when it is first shaved, I shall die content."

"In that case, I must shave at once," he said.

Then he prepared her a laxative of lethal strength and seized her property before she was quite dead.

Meanwhile in Britain, Boudicca, Queen of the Iceni, had revolted after her daughters had been raped and she herself had been stripped and flogged. Nero ordered the revolt to be put down with the utmost brutality.

"Every kind of atrocity was inflicted upon their captives," said second-century historian Cassius Dio. "They hung up the noblest and best-looking women naked, cutting off their breasts and stitching them to their mouths, so that the women appeared to be eating them, and after this they impaled them on sharp stakes, run up the body."

In AD 62, Nero married his mistress Poppaea, just 12 days after he was rid of Octavia, and made her Augusta. From then on she required the milk of five hundred wild asses for her daily bath to keep her complexion just the way the emperor liked it. That same year, the prefect of the Praetorian Guard, Sextus Afranius Burrus, died and Seneca retired. The two restraining influences in his life were now gone. Poppaea later had Seneca killed because he favoured Nero's previous mistress, Acte Claudia, over her.

Burrus was replaced by the infamous Gaius Ofonius Tigellinus, who had been exiled in AD 39 by Caligula for adultery with Agrippina, his sister and a number of other Roman matrons. He encouraged Nero to new heights of debauchery and Tacitus left a vivid description of a feast, including entertainment, laid on by Tigellinus in Nero's honour.

The most notorious and profligate of these entertainments were those given in Rome by Tigellinus. A banquet was set out upon a barge built for the purpose on a lake, and this barge was towed about by a vessel picked out in gold and ivory and rowed by naked, debauched youths who were assorted according to their age and proficiency in libidinous practices ... On the banks of the lake were brothels, filled with women of rank, and opposite them naked prostitutes, indulging in indecent gestures and lewd posturings. At nightfall, the nearby woods and houses echoed with songs and were ablaze with lights and Nero disgraced himself with every kind of abomination, natural and unnatural, leaving no further depths of debauchery into which he could sink.

At Tigellinus's instigation, a series of treason laws removed anyone who was considered to be a threat. Meanwhile, military setbacks spawned an economic recession, but Nero and Poppaea continued to live in lavish style; a style that they maintained even after fire left much of Rome in ruins in AD 64.

Although Nero himself commanded the fire fighting and did all he could to save the city, someone had to be blamed. He was already unpopular. His artistic inclinations were well known, hence the rumour that he sang or played the lyre – or more popularly the fiddle – as he watched the city burn. There was another even more damaging rumour that he had started the fire himself to clear the way for an even more extravagant palace called the Golden House, which he built on the burnt-out ruins of The Passageway. This further fanned resentment, as the new palace was built at a time when public reconstruction should have been a priority.

Nero was not about to take the blame for the fire. He wanted to blame the Jews, but Poppaea liked the Jews at court so, instead, she suggested blaming the Christians. They were a new cult in town and could carry the can, for once, "on account of their sullen hatred of the whole human race". They were rounded up and, with typical cruelty, Nero ordered that they be "lighted up, when the day declined, to serve as torches during the night". They were tied to stakes, smeared with tar and set alight so that they illuminated the gardens where the newly homeless sought refuge. However, this was a bit of an own goal.

Tacitus reported that the Christians behaved so bravely that "humanity relented in their favour".

A plot to assassinate Nero and to replace him with Gaius Calpurnius Piso was uncovered in AD 65. Among the conspirators forced to commit suicide was the poet Lucan. The plot left Nero grumpy and paranoid.

Although he doted on Poppaea, when she nagged him after he had come back late from the races, he kicked her to death. She was ill and pregnant at the time. Their only daughter, Claudia Augusta, died in infancy.

Nero was upset by Poppaea's death, but he did not mend his ways. Instead, he took up a young boy called Sporus – who looked like her – and had him castrated. All other signs of his masculinity were also removed. An incision was made where his scrotum had been in an attempt to turn him into a woman, and Nero called him Sabina.

On a trip to Greece, they went through a wedding ceremony with Sporus wearing a rose-tinted bridal veil. There was even a marriage settlement and the reception was well attended. Indeed, the joke circulated that the world would have been a better place if Nero's father, Domitius, had married such a wife. They travelled together in Nero's litter, with Sporus dressed in the fine robes of an empress. They attended Greek events and fairs together, and were seen kissing openly in the streets when they returned to Rome. Despite his mutilation, Sporus seems to have been genuinely fond of Nero and he stuck by him after he had been deserted by nearly everyone else.

While Nero was a husband to Sporus, he also wanted to be the wife of his freedman Doryphorus. He balked at the idea of taking the route he had forced Sporus to take and forwent the castration, but he did have another big wedding. Suetonius said: "Nero put on the bridal veil, soothsayers were in attendance, the dowry, the marriage bed, the nuptial torch, were all there. Everything was in public and exposed to view – even those things which are usually performed in darkness when the bride is a woman." And on the wedding night he "imitated the moans and cries of a virgin being deflowered".

Nero was fond of appearing dressed as a woman and "his costume and head-dress were both effeminate and indecent". He would surround himself with "troops of slaves and freedmen, and players and dancers lost to all sense of decency themselves, minions and whores, seeking only their own advancement through ministering to their master's most depraved desires".

Shortly before his death, Petronius, the author of the wild and pornographic *Satyricon*, wrote "a list of Nero's acts of lechery, with the names of the youths and the women whom he had debauched, detailing all the lustful novelties of each case" and sent it to the emperor. It must have made a good read, but Nero was in no mood for such a work. When he broke the seal, he imagined that he would find another one of the usual flattering letters or deathbed bequests that he usually received. Nero was livid, particularly because by this time Petronius was dead and could not be punished. Even so, a victim had to be found.

What puzzled Nero was how such a detailed list of his depravities could be compiled. Then he thought of Silia, the wife of a senator, who "had been a partner in every lubricity, and had also been an intimate of Petronius," according to Tacitus. "She was sent into exile for not keeping her mouth shut about all she had seen and known." If that was the case, she got off lightly.

Although Nero now had a husband and a wife, a proper female replacement for Poppaea had yet to be found. So he decided to marry Claudius's daughter Antonia. When she refused him, he claimed that she was part of a conspiracy against him and had her executed. The rest of the family, including those related by marriage, were also killed. During this purge, Nero anally raped the young Aulus Plautius, crying out as he did so: "Now mother come and kiss my successor." He claimed that Aulus had been Agrippina's lover and that she had encouraged him to make a bid for the throne. After he had come, he killed him. As an afterthought, he married Statilia Messalina, the great-great-granddaughter of Taurus, who had twice been consul and who had won a triumph.

Poppaea's son by her first husband, also called Rufrius Crispinus, although still a child was also perceived as a threat. He was drowned by his own slaves while on a fishing expedition on the grounds that the boy had played at being a general and an emperor. But although he happily murdered all the children of those accused of conspiring against him, Nero knew how to take a joke. Numerous songs and lampoons circulated about him – especially about his relationship with his mother and his subsequent murder of her – but he did nothing about it. However, for other offences, he introduced "ancient-style" executions. The victim would be stripped naked, his head would be held by a wooden fork and he would be beaten to death with rods. Nero began signing so many death warrants that he regretted he had ever learnt to write.

In AD 67, with Rome in crisis, Nero left for an extravagant tour of Greece. Increasingly paranoid, he ordered the popular and successful general Gnaeus Domitius Corbulo to commit suicide. Fearing for their own lives, the governors of the Roman provinces went into open revolt. Their leader, Gaius Julius Vindex, said contemptuously of Nero: "I have seen him on stage playing pregnant women and slaves about to be executed."

Nero, though, was more interested in watching young men in the gymnasium. His response to the rebellion was reportedly: "I have only to appear and sing to have peace once more in Gaul." Graffiti daubed on columns in Rome answered this by saying that his crowing had even awoken the *Galli* – which means both "cocks" and "Gauls".

The legions proclaimed Servius Sulpicius Galba, the governor of Spain, emperor. The Senate then condemned Nero to die a slave's death – first whipped, then crucified. The Praetorian Guard turned against him and he fled with Sporus to Antium, modern Anzio in southern Italy. There are two versions of his death. In one told by Suetonius, with the help of a servant, he stabbed himself in the throat with a dagger on 9 June AD 68, at the age of 31. His last words were said to be: "What an artist dies with me."

Nero was terrified that his body would be mutilated after his death, but he was buried by faithful Acte, who put flowers on his grave for years to come.

However, according to Tacitus, he escaped and reached the Greek islands, where he turned up in the guise of a red-haired prophet and the leader of the poor, but the governor of Cythnos recognised him, had him arrested and carried out the sentence passed by the Senate.

Nymphidius Sabinus, the prefect of the Praetorian Guard, took over power in Rome, on the grounds that Galba, now aged 73, was too old to be emperor. Sabinus sought the backing of the mob by giving way to their murderous instincts.

"As a gesture to the crowd he did not prevent them beating to death anyone they came across associated with Nero," said Plutarch. "They killed Spiculus the gladiator in the forum by throwing him under statues of Nero as they were being dragged away; they spread-eagled the informer Aponius and drove cartloads of rocks over him; and they tore a considerable number of people to pieces, some of them completely innocent."

Sabinus did not discourage the rumour that he was the son of Caligula. It seems that when Caligula was in his teens he had had an affair with Sabinus's mother Nymphidia – "a not unattractive woman, who was the daughter of a seamstress by the emperor's freedman Callisus," says Plutarch. However, the affair had apparently occurred after the birth of Sabinus and a less flattering report circulated saying that he was the son of the gladiator Martianus, whose reputation proved irresistible to seamstress Nymphidia. It was said that Sabinus bore a close physical resemblance to Martianus.

However, as prefect of the Praetorian Guard, Sabinus claimed sole credit for Nero's downfall. He sent for Nero's lover, Sporus. Plutarch said that he had Sporus brought from Nero's funeral pyre while the corpse was still burning, "used him as his wife and called him Poppaea". He also angled for supreme power "with the covert support of ... certain women".

Sporus did not have to put up with Sabinus long, though. Galba was on his way with another couple of imperial hopefuls. Sporus went on to become the lover of the Emperor Otho, who had been a companion of Nero in his debaucheries. After Otho's death, Sporus began appearing on stage as a girl in what was said to be a very degrading show. The humiliation finally became too much for him and he committed suicide.

CHAPTER 8

Nero was the last emperor of the Caesarean dynasty which could trace its lineage back to Julius Caesar's father. After Nero came AD 69 – the "year of four Emperors". In rapid succession came the rebel provincial chiefs Galba, Otho and Vitellius, all of whom reigned for only a few months each and all of whom met violent ends.

Gladius Languidus

The first of these was Servius Sulpicius Galba, who, unlike other Caesars, fancied mature – even old – men, as long as they were strong and well proportioned. As a general in Germany and North Africa, he was in a good position to indulge his passion. As a youth he had been one of Tiberius's "minnows" on Capri and he was very thin, a characteristic attributed to his sexual practices. He had three noted lovers – Titus Vinius, Conelius Laco and his freedman, Icelus.

According to Plutarch, Vinius had a "profound, in fact, unparalleled craving for money and he was also prone to acts of vice with women". When he was young and serving in his first campaign under Calvisius Sabinius, he had smuggled Calvisius's wife – "a slut", Plutarch notes – into the camp disguised as a soldier and "enjoyed her in the general's headquarters". Caligula had him jailed for this, but he was set free when Caligula died.

While a dinner guest of Claudius, he had stolen a silver goblet. From then on Claudius ordered that no silver should be put within his reach, only earthenware. Laco was almost as money grabbing, and Vinius and he used Galba as their puppet to get cash.

Galba's relationship with Icelus was more of a love match. The ex-slave had a notorious reputation for homosexual activity. He was the one who brought the news of Nero's death to Galba in Spain. The new emperor greeted Icelus, it was said, "with the fondest kisses and lewd embraces in public". Then he ordered Icelus to go and get himself depilated immediately, so he could take him to his private apartments and *pedicado* him – though one classical author points out that it would have been more in keeping for Galba to have had him there and then in front of everyone.

Galba's father was the hunchbacked consul Gaius Sulpicius Galba and his mother Mummia Achaica, the granddaughter of Catalus and the great-granddaughter of Lucius Mummius, who had sacked Corinth and finally put paid to any Greek threat to Roman hegemony. She bore him two children. Then, the rich and beautiful Livia Ocellina, attracted by his noble lineage, set her cap at him. One day when they were alone together, he stripped off his shirt to reveal a humped back – saying that he wanted to show that he had nothing to hide from her. His frankness, apparently, made her even more *fervidus* for him and the two married.

Galba himself had also married, but when his wife Lepida and the two sons she had borne him died, he remained resolutely single. He even resisted the advances of Nero's mother Agrippina the Younger, who pursued him after her first husband Domitius had died. Even though his wife was still alive at the time, Agrippina made such shameless advances to him that, in front of a crowd of married women, Lepida's mother slapped her.

When the newly renamed Galba Caesar Augustus arrived in Rome, he executed a number of highly placed Romans, including Nymphidius Sabinus, leaving Nero's ex-"wife" Sporus without his new mentor. Tigellinus, who had laid on such extravagant entertainments for Nero, survived the bloodletting – even though the mob was calling for his execution – by staging a similarly lavish banquet for Vinius. After the banquet, Vinius went to Tigellinus's house with his widowed daughter Crispina and Tigellinus ordered his number one concubine to take off her necklace – worth a cool six hundred thousand sesterces, or $24,000 – and put it on Crispina's neck.

Vinius suggested to Galba that he make Otho – the *collusor* of Nero's ex, Poppaea, and the former governor of Lusitania (Portugal and southwest Spain) – his successor. The deal was that Otho was to marry Vinius's daughter Crispina if Galba succeeded in making him Caesar. Galba agreed, but then had second thoughts.

However, at this point, the legions in Germany proclaimed their leader Aulus Vitellius emperor. Otho turned to the Praetorian Guard for support. They killed Galba and his chosen successor Lucius Piso Licianus in the Forum, along with Laco and Vinius – despite Vinius's protests that he was on Otho's side. The money-grubbing Vinius's head was then sold to his daughter for ten thousand sesterces.

Flos Juventutis

According to Plutarch, Marcus Salvius Otho "was a man not undistinguished by birth, but hedonistic self-indulgence had corrupted him from childhood to a degree few Romans have equalled" – which is saying something. In stark contrast to Galba, he preferred young boys. It is also thought that, as a youth, he had been a catamite and that he kept his body depilated. However, he pretended to have a passion for a freedwoman at court, even though she was old and on her last legs. This won him an entrée with Nero and he was soon accompanying the young emperor on his nocturnal forays into the brothels of Subura. It was also said that Otho had "entered into immoral relations with Nero, with whom he practised reciprocal bodily pollution".

Otho and Nero also had a love triangle with Poppaea Sabina,* though classical sources disagree on the details. Some say that Otho had her first and boasted of her beauty. This piqued Nero's vanity and he had to have her, too. Plutarch said that Otho seduced her on Nero's behalf on the understanding that they would share her. Tacitus maintained that Nero had her first, then parked her with Otho until he could rid himself of Octavia, though in another book Tacitius said that she was Otho's wife and that he was willing to share her. Cassius Dio, on the other hand, said that Nero gave her to Otho and that they shared her. There was also, of course, the possibility that Poppaea orchestrated the whole thing.

Whatever the case, the relationship was, predictably, disastrous. Despite his proclivities, Otho enjoyed Poppaea physically, and soon developed such a deep passion for her that he could not bear to share her with Nero. He was tormented by the fact that Poppaea would spend a night or two in the palace and then return claiming that she valued their "marriage".

"Nor was Poppaea herself ... displeased at his jealousy," said Plutarch.

"*Amantium irae amoris integratiost,*" according to Terence.

"I am devoted to Otho," Poppaea protested to Nero. "No one else lives in such style. Wealth and culture are united in him; he is equal to any fortune."

Nero nihil est.

According to Plutarch, she felt that "marriage to Caesar would be an inconvenience, but that she was not averse to it, due to her penchant for stolen fruits, and because she enjoyed him as a lover".

Her rapid transition between being compliant lover and untouchable married woman plainly turned Nero on. Meanwhile, she derided Nero because he had a slave-girl – Acte – for a mistress and scoffed at him for being a mama's boy because he was under the thumb of the voracious Agrippina.

Things came to a head when Otho turned away Nero's messengers when they came to fetch her for an assignation. Then he left Nero cooling his heels outside a locked bedroom door, "pleading for the return of the love he had entrusted to Otho's keeping". Otho was lucky to escape with his life, but although it was early in Nero's reign, he was still afraid of scandal. Soon after Otho had helped him kill Agrippina – at Poppaea's behest, it is generally agreed – Nero merely annulled their marriage, such as it may have been, and, at Seneca's suggestion, sent Otho to Lusitania as governor. As a result the following lampoon did the rounds:

> Why's Otho banished? Know the cause,
> Comes not with the reign of laws.
> Against all rules of fashionable life,
> He dared commit adultery with his own wife.

Plutarch noted that: "It is paradoxical that he should have been spared by the emperor who murdered his own wife and sister to marry Poppaea."

The "wife and sister" was Octavia. Since Claudius had adopted Nero, Octavia was legally Nero's sister until she was adopted by another family so he could marry her. "*Sunt superis sua jura*," as Ovid said.

The governorship of far-flung Lusitania kept Otho out of harm's way for ten years; during this time, Nero progressively lost the plot, but Otho continued to harbour a grudge. As soon as the opportunity to revenge himself for the loss of Poppaea presented itself, he joined Galba in revolt. On entering Rome as Emperor Marcus Otho Caesar Augustus, he took one of Nero's wives for himself – the doubly widowed castrato Sporus. He also intended to marry Nero's widow Statilia Messalina, but failed to impress her as he was a notable effeminate, wore an ill-fitting toupee perched on his bald pate and rode around Rome in the type of closed sedan chair that was normally used by women.

However, Otho was popular with the mob for his treatment of Nero's orgy impresario Tigellinus, who was now terminally ill. Plutarch noted in high moral dudgeon: "While right-thinking men regarded his filthy, unspeakable bedsports with whores and vile women (which his incorrigible lust still hungered for and clutched after as he died by slow degrees) as the ultimate retribution and worse than a thousand deaths, nonetheless it was generally considered an outrage that he still looked on the light of day after he had quenched it for so many noble Romans."

Otho summoned Tigellinus, who offered the messenger a huge bribe if he would let him go. When it was refused, Tigellinus gave the messenger's intended gifts away and then asked him to wait while he shaved. The messenger agreed and Tigellinus cut his own throat. However, it may not have been such a sorrowful suicide. Tacitus said that Tigellinus died "among the embraces and kisses of his concubines".

Otho's popularity with the people was not going to save him, though. Before Galba had died, the legions in Germany declared their leader, Aulus Vitellius, as emperor. They promptly marched on Italy. Otho and his army went out to meet them. Of the two opposing generals, Plutarch said: "It would be difficult to say which of them was more profligate, effeminate, ignorant of warfare and ridden with debt."

Tacitus said that, of all mortals, these two "were the worst in debauchery, cowardice and extravagance" – and, among the Roman emperors, they were up against some stiff opposition.

Otho wrote to Vitellius, offering to share the empire if Vitellius would become his son-in-law. Plainly Vitellius did not fancy Otho's daughter. The result was a battle outside Cremona. Although Otho's men taunted Vitellius's soldiers, calling them "actors and ballet dancers", they were soundly thrashed. Bodies were piled so high that they reached the top of the pillars at the ancient temple there. Otho committed suicide after his defeat and Vitellius rode in triumph into Rome, where he and his men pulled off their trousers – that is, their "barbaric Gallic riding breeches" – and donned the togas of senators.

Vitellius, Vitellus

Vitellius's family, though old and noble, was said to have been founded by a freedman – a cobbler who had married a prostitute. Vitellius's father, Lucius Vitellius, had advanced himself by prostrating himself in front of Caligula and begging Claudius's wife Messalina to allow him to take off her shoes. He carried these around under his toga, and took them out periodically to kiss them.

It was said that Vitellius's greatest vice in later life was gourmandising. He would eat massive meals, dose himself with emetics, throw it all up and begin all over again. He was also addicted to pederasty and "in his youth had gained much skill and experience in the passive art". Indeed, he boasted that he had secured his father's first promotion at the expense of his own chastity. This act of prostitution, he said, was his first step on the way to becoming emperor.

He gained further advancement on Capri among Tiberius's male prostitutes, where he had earned the nickname *Spintria* – "from the fertility of his mind in inventing fresh forms of groups for pederasty and the agility of his body in carrying them out".

Suetonius wrote that he was "stained with every kind of lascivious debauchery" and, consequently, he became a favourite at court. It was said that he "became the wanton of four emperors before attaining that position himself". This implies that he was also a catamite to Caligula, Claudius and Nero – though it is the only reference to Claudius being a sodomite.

Vitellius married Petronia, a consul's daughter. They had a son called

Petronianus, who was blind in one eye. Petronia wanted a divorce and said that she would name Vitellius her heir in her will, providing that he renounce all rights to the child. He agreed to this. Apparently, Petronianus disliked Vitellius as much his mother did. The story goes that Petronianus planned to poison his father but, overcome with guilt, took the poison himself. Others said that Vitellius simply murdered him. He then married Galeria Fundana, the daughter of a magistrate. She bore him one daughter and a son who had such a bad stammer that he could hardly get a word out. Meanwhile, Petronia married Dolabella, whom Vitellius had put to death when he came to power.

After defeating Otho's army, Vitellius gleefully allowed his men to whip, wound and murder captured slaves. Then he addressed his comrades over the unburied corpses, saying: "Only one thing smells better to me than a dead enemy and that is a dead fellow-citizen." Following that he took a large slug of wine to staunch the stench.

When he arrived in Rome and saw Otho's simple headstone, he said: "That's all the mausoleum he deserved." He then sent the dagger Otho had used to kill himself to the Temple of Mars and staged an all-night orgy on the Apennine hills.

It was also said that Vitellius was responsible for the death of Sporus, the catamite of Nero, Sabinus and Otho. Apparently, Vitellius ordered him to appear on stage playing the part of a girl who had been raped. For a Roman, this was the ultimate humiliation, and Sporus committed suicide.

Once in power, Vitellius indulged himself in monumental gluttony, eating four times a day at other people's expense with massive drinking binges between meals. Each day he would send out messengers ordering various households to prepare meals for him, none of which was to cost less than four hundred thousand sesterces – $8,000. At a famous feast his brother gave for him when he entered Rome, two thousand fish and seven thousand game birds were served. His favourite dish was a huge concoction called the "Shield of Minerva". The recipe called for pike's livers, peacock's brains, pheasant's brains, flamingos' tongues and the entrails of lampreys. Ingredients had to be brought by warship from as far afield as the Black Sea and the Strait of Gibraltar. He also snacked between meals, grabbing half-burnt sacrificial offerings from the flames and stuffing them into his mouth.

When he travelled, he would stop at every inn on the way, grab piping-hot meat from roadside stalls and stuff himself with half-eaten leftovers. His court favourite was the man who invented the meat pie. As a consequence he was massively fat and found it hard to walk; doubly hard, in fact, as he had a crippled thigh after being run down by a chariot Caligula had been driving.

He liked torture for entertainment. People would be invited to the palace and killed for no reason. One man who had merely paid a courtesy call was sent off to be executed. When Vitellius withdrew the order at the last moment, he was praised for his clemency, but the emperor explained that he had decided that, instead of having the man sent away for execution, he would rather have the treat of seeing him killed before his eyes. Then, when the man's two sons came to plead for their father's life, he had all three of them executed together.

A knight who had been condemned cried out "You are my heir" as he was being led away. Vitellius ordered that his will be brought. It showed that Vitellius was only a joint-heir, so he had the knight and the other beneficiary killed. To maintain his lifestyle, Vitellius borrowed from numerous people. Naturally, anyone who asked for their money back did not survive.

At the circus he had some spectators killed for supporting the rival team. He particularly disliked satirists and astrologers. Any who came up before him were condemned without the case for the defence being heard. He then issued an edict that all astrologers must leave Italy by 1 October AD 69. An imitation edict was then posted up around Rome saying that the astrologers had decreed that Vitellius would be no more by that date. The poster got it wrong. Vitellius lived until 20 December. Even so, Vitellius was a believer. A German soothsayer said that he would have a long and secure reign if he outlived his mother. So, when she fell ill, he starved her to death. In another version of the story, he poisoned her.

Once he was in power, Vitellius indulged his passion for rough trade, and publicly showed his affection for actors and chariot drivers. His deepest affection was reserved for his freedman Asiaticus, who had been his lover since his youth. Asiaticus had run away from him more than once, but each time they had been reunited they had kissed and made up. As emperor, Vitellius showered favours on him, but the good times were short-lived.

Before Vitellius had even entered Rome, the legions in the east had proclaimed Vespasian emperor. When Vespasian's forces defeated his own, Vitellius considered abdication, but the Praetorian Guard forbade this. He sent the Vestal Virgins to Vespasian to try and arrange an armistice. When this failed, he hid in a janitor's cupboard. Dragged from his hiding place, he was marched half-naked to the Forum, where crowds threw dung at him and mocked his huge paunch. Then he was executed by the death of a thousand cuts and his body was thrown in the Tiber. Titus Flavius Vespasianus then became the fourth emperor of AD 69 as Caesar Vespasianus Augustus.

CHAPTER 9

Caesar Vespasianus Augustus – or, as he was known more simply, Vespasian – was the first emperor of the Flavian dynasty. He was the son of Flavius Sabinus, a tax collector. Vespasian ingratiated himself with the Emperor Caligula, though not as a *pathice*. Comparing himself to the notorious passive pederast Licinius Mucianus, he said: "At least I am a *man*."

Under Claudius, he found favour through the freedman Narcissus and was sent to Britain where he occupied the Isle of Wight and conquered Devon. "*Crepito fatigo totus rotundus,*" as Livy remarked. Vespasian survived Nero's reign by being out of Rome, largely in North Africa and Judaea. Even so, he was undiplomatic enough to fall asleep during one of Nero's performances in Greece. He had to flee for his life and hid in an out-of-the way town in the East until he was finally forgiven and was made a provincial army commander.

Vespasian was a well-known womaniser. Even though he was of humble birth, he was known for his ability to quote Greek. He once quoted a line from the *Iliad* to a tall man with an enormous penis. The line ran: "Striding along and waving a lance that casts a long shadow."

While he was a provincial governor, Vespasian married Flavia Domitilla, the former mistress of Statilus Capella, an African knight from Tripoli. She was not even a Roman citizen. They had three children – Titus, Domitian and Domitilla. However, Domitilla and Flavia both died before Vespasian became emperor. He then took up again with Antonia Caenis, his former mistress. She was a secretary to

Antonia, Tiberius's sister-in-law. As she was a freedwoman, they could not marry, but she was his wife in all but name, even when he became emperor; there was a lifelong love between them. Vespasian eventually replaced her with a handful of mistresses, but he built an inscribed marble altar, honouring her.

Although life in Rome was as debauched as ever, Vespasian tried to curb the people's lust. He issued a decree that any woman who took another person's slave as a lover should become a slave herself.

His great failing was greed, and he upped taxes. He was the first emperor to tax public lavatories – hence the French word for a public urinal, *vespasienne*. His son objected to this measure, thinking it vulgar. So when the first money came in, Vespasian held the coins up to his nose and asked him whether he could detect any offensive odour. Money, he said, had no smell. Vespasian could also be generous, though. Money was spent on literary prizes and on restoring the Venus of Cos.

When a woman told Vespasian that she was in love with him, he took her to bed. Afterwards, his accountant discovered that, in post-coital rapture, Vespasian had given the woman four hundred thousand sesterces – $8,000 – and asked him: "How shall I enter this in your expenses' ledger?"

Vespasian replied: "Just put it down as 'For Vespasian's being seduced'."

His other weakness was for a regular massage at the baths.

As a result of drinking tainted spring water, Vespasian was struck down with unquenchable diarrhoea. On his deathbed he said: "*Vae, puto deus fio*" – "Oh dear, I think I'm becoming a god." He was right. Immediately after his death on 24 June AD 79, he was deified.

Two of Vespasian's sons succeeded him. After the relative sexual continence of the founder of the dynasty, these two boys quickly showed the Roman Empire that the Flavians could be just as kinky as the Caesars had been before them.

Culus Strictus

The first of the two sons to succeed was Titus Flavius Vespasianus. This was the same name as his father, so to avoid confusion he ruled under the name Titus Vespasianus Augustus – or just plain Titus. Born on 30 December AD 41, the year Caligula was assassinated, he was a close friend of Britannicus, Nero's catamite. When he came of age, he was both graceful and handsome, except for a certain paunchiness. Like Nero, he liked to write and sing and he mastered the harp. According to Tacitus, his youth was "enlivened by pleasure".

His first wife was Arrecina Tertulla, daughter of the prefect of the Praetorian Guard. When she died, he married the well-connected Marcia Furnilla, but divorced her after she gave birth to a daughter. It has to be said that he was happier when he was surrounded by rough soldiers. In command of one of his father's legions in Judaea when the province rebelled, he had his horse killed under him, but mounted another belonging to a man he had just slain.

When Galba became emperor, Vespasian, who was in the East, sent Titus to congratulate him. It was widely believed that Galba was going to adopt him and make him his heir to the throne, but when Titus found Italy torn between the competing forces of Galba, Otho and Vitellius, he turned back. However, on his way back to Judaea, he stopped off to see the oracle of Venus on Paphos, who told him that soon he would be wearing the emperor's purple.

Back in Judaea, Titus led the final assault on Jerusalem, killing 12 of the garrison with successive arrows and taking the city on his daughter's birthday. His men then saluted him as their emperor and begged him to take them with him to Italy. This spawned the suspicion that he planned to rebel against his father, which was further fuelled when he attended the consecration of a sacred Apis bull at Memphis in Egypt wearing a crown. However, he sailed quickly from Alexandria to Reggio on navy transport and then rushed to Rome to quash the rumour. Arriving before his father expected him, he said simply: "Here I am, father, here I am."

Titus then became one of his father's most trusted lieutenants, drafting his speeches and murdering his enemies. As well as being cruel, he was profligate, holding wild, all-night orgies for his companions. Criticised and hated, he became famous for the troops of catamites and castrated boys he kept around him. He was especially fond of beautiful, young, male dancers and kept the most charmed and androgynous of them as pampered pages and attendants. It was also said that he kept eunuchs for the sole purpose of drinking his sperm.

Sent out East to retake Jerusalem once again, he fell in love with Queen Berenice, who was dubbed the Jewish Cleopatra. Twelve years older than him, she was the twice-widowed daughter of Herod Agrippa I and, according to Juvenal, the incestuous lover of her brother Herod Agrippa II, with whom she jointly ruled the kingdom of Chalcis in southern Lebanon. First married when she was 13 to one of her father's political allies, her bridegroom died shortly after the marriage, perhaps due to the sudden onset of old age. Then she married her uncle Herod, King of Chalcis. She bore him two sons before he died in around AD 48 or 49 when she was 20 years old.

Her sons were not old enough to take power and Berenice realised that the Chalcisians would not tolerate a woman ruling as regent, so she brought in her brother Herod Agrippa II, then King of Judaea, as her co-ruler. However, ugly rumours about their incestuous relationship damaged them both politically, so Berenice married King Polemo of Cilcicia. Polemo even underwent the pain of circumcision to marry into the family of Herod, but it seems his *cucumis circumcidere* was not up to the job. The first-century Jewish historian Flavius Josephus said that she left Polemo out of "sheer licentiousness" and returned to live with Agrippa. In AD 65, she risked her life to intercede for the Jews who were being massacred by the Romans. When Titus turned up to recapture Jerusalem in AD 70, he was enchanted by her. Even though, as had been the case with Cleopatra, she was no looker – plump with unexciting classical features – he fell for her energy and erudition and she became his mistress. For her, though, the affair may well have been a cynical political calculation. Claudius had reduced Chalcis to provincial status; with Vespasian on the throne, it might be possible to win back her kingdom.

They lived together openly in Rome; some sources even said that they were man and wife. It was also said that he promised to marry her, but this would have been out of the question as Romans still remembered Cleopatra and wanted no truck with a foreign queen. Dallying with an oriental babe in Judaea was one thing; marrying her in Rome was quite another. Vespasian was against the match, too. He could not understand what his son saw in a woman who was neither beautiful nor young enough to bear him any children. Eventually the Senate insisted that Titus choose between his beloved Berenice and the throne. He chose the throne.

In the meantime, Titus subsidised his extravagant lifestyle with Berenice by taking bribes, and it was generally thought that he was going to be another Nero when he became emperor. In fact, when he took office, the wild orgies he had enjoyed as heir were toned down to the point where they became civilised dinner parties. He also sent Berenice away, which was painful for both of them. She went back to her beloved brother Agrippa and, in a very un-Nero-like way, Titus "ceased ... favouring too lavishly certain of his most pleasing young men". Some of his rejected favourites found fame as dancers on the public stage, attracting a particular notoriety for having been the lovers of the emperor, although Titus refused to go and watch them, even at public events.

According to Suetonius, he "lost no opportunity to court popularity, sometimes he would use the new public baths with the common people". However, he enjoyed nudity and, as there was a virulent gay bathhouse scene going on, it seems that he merely used the occasion as an excuse to pick up new lovers.

He pardoned those who conspired against him. The chief conspirator was his brother Domitian, but he did not have the heart to execute him, or even dismiss him from his court. Instead he took Domitian aside, reminding him tearfully: "You are my partner and chosen successor."

As he lay dying of malaria at the age of 41 on 1 September AD 81, Titus said that he had only a single sin lying on his conscience. This remark was thought to be a reference to an incestuous affair that he had had with his brother's wife, Domitia, which might have explained the enmity between him and his brother. Titus also awarded a consulship to Domitia's first husband, Aelius Lamia, to annoy the young Domitian.

Domitia herself denied the rumour, although she was a notoriously promiscuous woman who was quite capable of such a thing. Suetonius, however, dismissed the idea.

"Had the allegation been true," he said, "she would surely never have denied it, but rather have boasted of it, as she did with all of her other misdeeds."

A fresco from the House of the Centurion, 1st Century, Pompeii.

A marble head of Caesar Augustus.

The decadence of the Romans, as imagined by Thomas Couture, 1847.

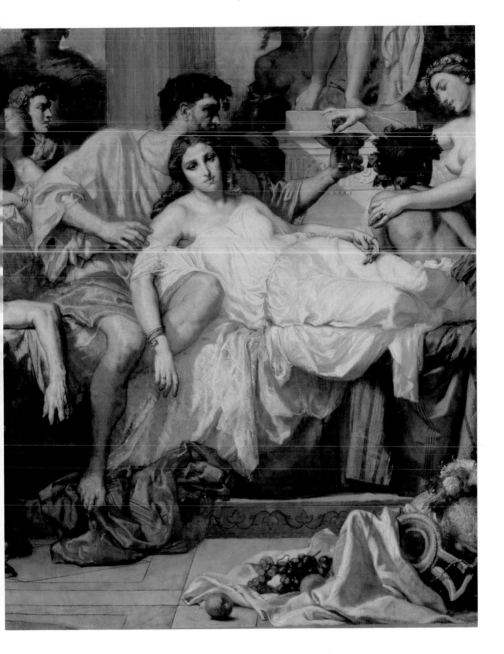

Agrippina the Elder, wife of Tiberius and mother of Caligula.

Tiberius, Emperor of Rome AD 14–37.

An early 20th-Century illustration shows a banquet in Nero's palace.

C · GALIGVLA · CÆS · AVG · IIII · RO · IMP·

Ant' temp figuriat 1596

A 16th-Century Italian engraving of Caligula.

The Rape of Lucretia by Giulio Cesare Procaccini (d.1625).

Whatever his motivation, it seems that Domitian had a hand in Titus's death. It was said that he helped ease his brother out of the world by packing his deathbed with ice and snow.

CHAPTER 10

Whonen Domitian came to the throne he began his reign with a brutal purge of the Senate and his name became a byword for cruelty. A handsome boy, he passed his youth and adolescence in great debauchery and was publicly condemned for his homosexuality. He was not above prostituting himself. A man of Praetorian rank called Claudius Pollio liked to show off a letter he had in Domitian's handwriting in which the future emperor, while he was still a youth, promised him a night of passion. Also while still a youth, it was said that he was debauched by Nerva, who, although considerably older than him, succeeded him as emperor.

He later changed his ways. According to Suetonius, Domitian carried off his wife Domitia Longina from her husband Aelius Lamia "after seducing many other wives". To show his gratitude, or to ensure his lovers' husbands' compliance, he distributed government jobs. One day, he gave away more then 20 lucrative appointments, causing Vespasian to remark: "I am amazed that he did not name my successor while he was at it."

According to Juvenal, Domitia was seduced as a child by the nobleman Rubrius Gallus. Then she married into the blue-blooded family of Aelius Lamia. It was thought that Lamia sought advancement through his young wife, presenting her at the court of the new Caesar for his perusal. Domitian must have been struck by her extraordinary beauty, which is plain from the coins depicting her and a bust that has survived from that time.

Domitia was reluctant to leave her husband at first in case the emperor, having seduced her, cast her aside, but when he made it clear that he wanted to marry her, there was no contest and Lamia meekly relinquished his lovely wife. Taking another man's wife is often seen as one more misdemeanour on Domitian's roster of sin, but this was commonplace in imperial circles. Octavian had taken Livia from Tiberius Claudius Nero when she was pregnant. The cuckolded husband even attended their wedding. Caligula had taken Lollia Paulina and Caesonia from their husbands, and Nero took Poppaea from Otho. A husband often regarded it as a chance of advancement if the emperor wanted his wife, and gave in gracefully. Lamia, though, must have regretted the move. He lost his wife and there is no record of him being awarded a command in the army or the governorship of a province. In fact, his compliance got him killed. One day, Domitian praised his singing voice and Lamia replied innocently: "I have given up sex and gone into training."

There was an ancient myth that said that abstaining from sex improved your singing. Domitian, famously, had no sense of humour and the remark was enough to get Lamia executed for treason.

Domitian and Domitia had a son, but he died in infancy. Domitian later divorced Domitia for having an affair with the actor Paris, but took her back afterwards because, according to Suetonius, "he could not bear to be separated from her". Domitian called his decision to take Domitia back "a recall to my divine bed" – or, at least, the sacred couch where the gods got their jollies. The reconciliation was not without its casualties, though. It was said that Domitian loved Paris himself, but he still had him murdered because of his affair with Domitia. Despite the reconciliation with Domitia, Domitian took his plump and ungainly niece Julia, Titus's daughter, as his mistress and she lived in a *ménage à trois* with them.

Both Vespasian and Titus had urged him to make a dynastic marriage to Julia when she was still a virgin, but Domitian refused because he was so hung up on Domitia at the time. Now Titus again asked Domitian to marry the girl. Marriages between uncles and nieces had been legalised under Claudius, although Claudius's marriage to Agrippina did not set a very happy precedent. When Domitian refused, Titus, who was after Domitia himself, advised him to take another wife. Domitian pointed out that the unmarried Titus had a vacancy, too. It was one that would not be filled. Julia, meanwhile, married her cousin Flavius Sabinus, although Domitian still continued shagging her, and Titus continued making advances on Domitia, though she later swore on oath that she did not commit adultery with him.

Domitian got another chance to demonstrate his singular lack of a sense of humour when Helvidius Priscus wrote a farce called *Paris and Oenone*. Oenone was the lover of the Greek hero Paris, who deserted her for the beautiful Helen, starting the Trojan War. Then, when Paris was wounded, she refused to come to his help, even though she was the only one who could cure him. Helvidius used this story as a vehicle to satirise the emperor's marital difficulties. A tough critic, Domitian had Helvidius executed.

Despite the reconciliation, Domitia does not appear on coins at this time. Domitian was a deeply religious man. His wife was an adulteress and her representation as a goddess on the coinage would have constituted blasphemy. However, to keep her out of trouble, he made sure that she had a more active social life. She presided at the games with him and, when she entered the amphitheatre, was hailed as *domina* – "mistress". The propaganda was put out that their original affection had been restored because their happy marriage had been ordained by Venus herself.

Domitian may have forgiven her for indulging in Venus's wrestling match with Paris, but the Senate did not. She remained uncrowned. This must have been doubly galling as Titus had named Julia *Augusta* in the hope that she would have a son whom he could name as his successor. He also honoured his daughter Julia as Venus – which is understandable – and Vesta – which is not.

As emperor, Domitian revived the old law banning homosexual intercourse with boys of free birth along with many other vices, even though he continued to practise most of them himself. He also prohibited the castration of boys. It was said that he did this because of his brother Titus's fondness for eunuchs. Castrated boys were no longer to be sold to brothels or used for the purposes of prostitution and a maximum price was fixed for those remaining in the hands of slave-dealers in an attempt to discourage the practice. The emperor, however, was above the law. He kept a number for himself and he used them for sex.

While praising Domitian for introducing these restrictions, Martial also sang the praises of Earinus, a beautiful castrato who was kept as a catamite by Domitian.

"He banished eunuchs from Rome and kept them in his palace," said Martial. "He waged war against vice in all forms and practised it in all forms."

Domitian's clean-up campaign also extended to women of notoriously bad character. They were forbidden to use litters and were not allowed to benefit from inheritances and legacies, even if they had gained their infamous reputation by being debauched by Domitian himself. A knight was struck from the jury-roll because he had taken back a wife whom he had previously divorced for adultery – even though, of course, Domitian had done the same thing himself. He also reintroduced the old law levying a ten-thousand-sesterce fine – $200 – for sodomising a freeborn boy and then upped the penalty to death, even though that did not stop him from doing it himself.

The Vestal Virgins who had let their standards slip also suffered in Domitian's crusade for family values. Ex-virgin Vestals were punished, but instead of being buried alive – the traditional penalty – the unmaidenly Oculata sisters and hymen-less Varronilla were allowed to choose how they died, while their lovers were sent into exile. However, when the Virgin-in-Chief Cornelia, who had been acquitted first time around, came up on the same charge again, she was buried alive and her boyfriend was flogged to death.

On the other hand, Domitian allowed female gladiators into the arena for the first time since Nero. They were, of course, to perform topless. Even better, for the first time he allowed female athletes, who had to perform nude. Domitian quickly became an athletics fan and turned up in his finest Greek tunic.

He also had a thing about dwarfs and other physical freaks. In the arena, topless female gladiators were pitted against armies of midgets, and he took a gibbering pinhead in soiled imperial robes with him to the games. His passion for the deformed was not uncommon among Romans. Women hunchbacks and other cripples were much sought after as concubines and were a staple in many harems. Great phallic power was attributed to male dwarfs because of their proportionately outsized genitals, and the finest matrons in Rome would turn out to see Domitian's dwarf gladiators training in the nude.

Augustus had kept a pet dwarf called Lucius, and Caligula's retinue of little people were given the power of life and death over their full-grown compatriots. Deformed people were so much in demand in Rome that poor parents would deliberately twist or snap their offspring's limbs. Ironically, this could ensure the child had a healthy living; on the other hand, it could also result in an excruciating death. Magicians and soothsayers liked to disembowel deformed people while they were alive in an attempt to read the future in their uncoiled intestines.

At first, Suetonius said of Domitian that "his vices were balanced by his virtues; but later he transformed his virtues into vices, too ... and fear of assassination made him cruel".

When it came to out-and-out sadism, Domitian seems to have been in two minds. In the beginning, Suetonius said, he shrank away from any form of bloodshed. He reprieved criminals sentenced to the old punishment of being flogged do death as he "shrank from the atrocious punishment".

He did, however, invent some pretty nasty tortures himself. Burning the sexual organs of his victims was one of his favourites, though he also enjoyed shoving red-hot embers up their backsides. What was worse, you could never tell when such discomfort was coming your way. A government official might be invited to dine with Domitian and leave happy and carefree. The next day, out of the blue, he would find himself being crucified. Just for added creepiness, Domitian loved killing flies.

As emperor, he was particularly tough on the Christians. He liked to insert a burning reed into their glans or burn their testicles off. One way or another, a slow and painful death was ensured for all. Christians were hacked to pieces, burnt to death, or a stake would be inserted up their anus to pierce their entrails. Spikes, pincers and iron claws would be used to tear the flesh from the bones, or honey would be spread on their genitals and the victim would be left to be stung, or bitten, to death by insects.

The faithful would be hung up by one leg, by their thumbs or by their hair. Women would have their breasts cut off. Machines would be employed to crush victims or they would be pulverised with hammers, whips or cudgels. Martyrs were smeared with honey and milk, then nailed into barrels and force-fed. As a result they would be devoured by parasites from both the inside and outside or they would simply rot away. It could take two weeks for them to die.

Victims were also skinned alive or roasted to death. Sewn inside an animal's carcass, they would be left to die in the hot sun, unless vultures got to them first. People were boiled in oil or had molten lead poured over them. Eyes were torn out. Limbs were severed. Genitals were crushed. Or a hapless Christian could be buggered to death with a giant, saw-toothed, metal dildo.

St Cyrilla had her belly slit open and filled with red-hot coals. St Euphemia was forced to watch as her severed limbs were fried in a large pan. St Laurence was roasted to death on a griddle, while St Antipas was cooked inside a bronze horse.

St Prisca's belly was opened and filled with grain so that she could be eaten by wild pigs. St Laurus was given a quicklime enema that dissolved her entrails. St Eucratia's liver was torn out and eaten, while St Febronia's tongue was fed to mastiffs. And St Fausta was sawn in half lengthways, using the cleft of her vulva as a starting groove. There were endless ways you could meet an excruciating death under Domitian.

And it was not just the Christians who suffered. Later he persecuted the Stoic philosophers who, he said, abused him and "preached doctrines contrary to the regime".

Given his reputation for cruelty and his murderous reputation with the Senate, Domitian loved to put the wind up people. Cassius Dio recorded an incident when the emperor invited a number of notable Romans to dinner one night. His guests were shown into a room hung entirely in black and furnished with black benches without cushions. Their places were marked with tombstones, each with one of the guest's names on it.

"Then there appeared beautiful boys, naked, and painted black like spectres," said Cassius Dio. "They moved around the guests in an uncanny dance, and then stood at the feet of each of them. Now food and drink were brought in, as for the banquet of the dead – all black and in black dishes."

The guests shook in terror, each expecting the death blow to fall any minute. The room was as silent as the grave. Only Domitian spoke – and he talked of murder and sudden death.

When the meal was over he let them go, but, beforehand, he had dismissed all their servants so that they had to be driven home by strangers, all of which increased their terror. When they got home, a messenger arrived from Domitian and, again, each of the guests thought that their time had come. Instead, each was given their tombstone place card, which was made out of silver. They were also presented with the valuable dishes they had eaten out of, plus the nude boy who had waited on them, now washed and beautifully dressed.

"These were their compensations for the death agony they had suffered all the preceding night," said Cassius Dio. "Such were the feasts that Domitian gave to celebrate his victories [as he said] – or rather [as the people said] in honour of those who had lost their lives, both in Dacia [Romania] and Rome."

Cassius Dio also said that Domitian "never had a genuine affection for any human being, except one or two women". However, he was, according to Suetonius, "extremely lustful" and called his relentless sexual activities "bed-wrestling" as if it were a sport. He liked to depilate his concubines himself with tweezers before entering them, and enjoyed swimming with prostitutes.

Eventually Domitian found some excuse to execute Julia's husband, Flavius Sabinus, and took her openly as his mistress again. They lived together and he "demonstrated his love for her so openly and so ardently that she became pregnant by him". She died, however, after he forced her to have an abortion. Grief-stricken, he had her deified; though Domitian himself, when he died, was not made a god.

Domitian's love for Julia and his deification of her may have annoyed his beloved wife Domitia. There are indications that she was behind his assassination on 18 September AD 96. He was just 44 years old, but was already paunchy and bald. He even wrote a manual called *Preservation of the Hair*; it is dedicated to a friend and begins with a quotation from Homer: "Cannot you see that I, too, have a tall and beautiful person?"

In the book he rues the loss of his hair, but adds: "I am resigned to having an old man's head before my time. How pleasant it is to have good looks, but nothing is more fleeting than beauty."

Domitian's assassination did not come as much of a surprise. He knew that he was in danger and had his apartments lined with polished marble so that he could see if anyone was creeping up on him from behind. He could not stay awake forever, though, and was stabbed to death in his bedroom. The fatal blow was a thrust to the groin. The body was then cut into pieces, but it is said that Domitia collected the bits and had them sewn together again so that a sculptor could use the corpse as a model for a statue.

Amare Juveni Fructus Est, Crimen Seni

Domitian was succeeded by Marcus Cocceius Nerva, who had been his lover when he was young. Despite this lapse, Nerva Caesar Augustus was known as one of the "Five Good Emperors" – largely because he renounced the terror tactics that Domitian had used to maintain his tyranny.

Like Domitian before him, he outlawed castration. Possibly with Claudius and Agrippina or Domitian and Julia in mind, he also banned men marrying their own nieces. He was a handsome man, but had an exceedingly large nose, possibly due to his excessive drinking. Already 65 years old when he came to power, he was so ill and weak that he threw up his food – so he did not have much energy for *iter caeli* when he got into office.

His reign lasted for little over a year. During that time, the Praetorian Guard forced him to punish Domitian's assassins and adopt Marcus Ulpius Trajan.

Quod Aetas Vitium Posuit, Aetius Auferet

Trajan became one of Rome's greatest emperors, a great soldier and leader of men who both enlarged and strengthened the empire. He was also an ardent pederast. One day, when he entered the sacred enclosure, the whisper was heard: "Now it is time for Zeus, our master, to look out if he wants to keep Ganymede for himself."

Ganymede was the son of the King of Troy whom Zeus, disguised as an eagle, kidnapped because of his great beauty. Or, in the Cretan version, he was abducted by the legendary King Minos to serve as a cupbearer. The Latin version of the Greek name Ganymede is *Catamitus*, giving us the word catamite, which means "bum boy". Ganymede is also the largest moon of Jupiter, but the Romans did not know about that: it was only discovered by Galileo in 1610.

After Domitian had died, Trajan entered the palace and greeted the Senators with a kiss. His wife, the matronly Pompeia Plotina, was not so forthcoming. She said: "I enter here such a woman as I would wish to be when I leave." It seems that she got her wish: they had no children.

Plotina had originally been picked out as wife for Trajan's father, but he had handed her over to his son when Nerva adopted him, as he thought that she might be a helpmate when he became emperor. Consequently, Trajan and Plotina were around the same age, which was unusual for Roman nobles, who tended to marry much younger women. This would not have mattered to Trajan, though, because he had no interest in women at all. He left her at home in seclusion in Rome while he went about his business campaigning as a soldier.

A bust of her in the Vatican Museum shows her to be hard and rather masculine, which may have been her appeal, but there was no way that she could match the previous Empress Domitia for poise or looks. Pliny commended her for her modesty and obedience, for want of anything else to praise.

After Trajan finally beat the Dacians in AD 106, he held games that lasted for 123 days. During that time, eleven thousand animals, both wild and tame, were slain and ten thousand gladiators fought. In celebration, he also built a new baths with a gym attached and attended regularly. And he liked watching young boys do a "barbarian dance".

Trajan modelled himself on Alexander the Great, who had been *fructus* in his youth, though he eventually went straight, married three times and took on the entire harem of Darius III, the Persian king he defeated. When Trajan reached the Persian Gulf in AD 115, he wept because, at the age of 62, he was too old to repeat Alexander the Great's feat and go on to conquer India. Besides, Alexander was just 25 when he had fought his way to the Gulf.

Although Trajan was a rough soldier he liked to surround himself with a troop of pretty young boys. They would accompany him on his campaigns and he would refer to them as his *paedagogium* – that is, a place where pages are trained. They were, in fact, his harem. Some were castrated; others were allowed to develop – but he used both kinds to satisfy his lusts. He was not condemned for this. The only disgrace was to be seen as the passive partner – *machismo* was all that counted to the Romans.

One of the boys he loved became his successor. He was called Hadrian.

CHAPTER 11

S uetonius published his deliciously saucy *Lives of the Caesars* during the reign of Hadrian. Unfortunately, Suetonius died early in Hadrian's reign and so did not include him in his book, which is a shame because, for once, he could have included some intimate first-hand knowledge. While Hadrian was away building his famous wall, Suetonius, it was said, was "over familiar" with the emperor's wife Sabina. As a result, he was sacked from his post as the secretary of the imperial correspondence.

There has been a great deal of speculation about what this "over familiarity" could have been. It was plainly a serious matter, though, because along with Suetonius his patron Septicus Clarus, the prefect of the Praetorian Guard to whom *Lives of the Caesars* was dedicated, also got the boot.

The *Historia Augusta*, a collection of biographies of Roman emperors written in the third century, has an entry on Hadrian. This seems to be based on an older document, the *Vita Hadrian* by Marius Maximus, which has been lost. Anyway, the *Historia Augusta* entry says that Suetonius and Septicus were given the chop "because they had at that time, in their relations with his wife Sabina, behaved with greater familiarity than the etiquette of the court required".

Perhaps Suetonius had read aloud from his early book *Lives of the Famous Whores*. Or had he titillated the empress with saucy tales from his researches into Tiberius's times on Capri? The offence seems to have been a great deal more serious than that, in Hadrian's eyes at least, as the tale of Suetonius's sacking in the *Historia Augusta* is followed by the remark:

"Hadrian would have dismissed his wife too ... if he had been a private citizen." Maybe Suetonius was simply practising what he preached.

Whatever he, Septicus and Sabina got up to, after Suetonius was sacked he found the time to complete his *Vitae Caesarum*, which has provided much of the gossip for this book so far. So I guess we should be grateful.

Not that Hadrian cared much for Sabina as he was very much batting for the other team. A handsome youth, he could not help but come to the attention of his Uncle Trajan and was certainly one of the old man's catamites. This was not against his nature. He had been educated in Athens and was greatly enamoured of all things Greek – so much so that he was nicknamed "The Greekling". Throughout his life he was a great lover of the youthful Greek masculine ideal.

He also had a close relationship with Trajan's wife, the matronly Pompeia Plotina – so close, in fact, it was rumoured that they were lovers. It was Plotina who persuaded Trajan to adopt Hadrian, hence putting him on the throne – though, inevitably, his gay relationship with Trajan led to the accusation that he had come to power by prostituting himself. A contemporary historian said: "Widespread rumours asserted that he had bribed Trajan's freedmen, had cultivated his favourites and had had frequent sexual relations with them during the periods when he was an inner member of the court."

As a young man at court, it was well known that Hadrian enjoyed depilating Trajan's favourites. He did not go for the smooth look himself, though. Hadrian was the first Roman emperor to wear a beard – a Greek style – which set the fashion for the emperors who followed him. He was certainly well disposed to Trajan's lovers. When he became emperor, he increased support payments to the old emperor's redundant catamites.

When Hadrian was 24 years old, Plotina urged him to marry Trajan's grandniece and nearest blood relative, 14-year-old Sabina, after a squabble over some pageboys had caused bad blood between the two men. Trajan opposed the match. Sabina was a lively, vivacious and sexy young woman, hardly suited to being the kind of dutiful wife to a homosexual emperor that Plotina had been. However, Plotina talked Trajan around in the vain hope that the alluring Sabina might turn Hadrian straight.

The circumstances of their wedding were hardly propitious. There was nothing Sabina could do to beguile her new husband and the marriage was a disaster. He was not cruel to her, but, her romantic needs unsatisfied, she felt cruelly done by. Just as had been the case between Trajan and Plotina, they produced no children; unlike Trajan and Plotina, though, they grew to hate each other.

Inured to the charms of the nubile young Sabina, Hadrian preferred older women, the motherly sort, and he was more emotionally bound up with Sabina's mother Matidia, who had been widowed at a young age. The childless Trajan treated her as a daughter, even though she was, in fact, his niece, and called her Augusta. When Matidia died, Hadrian was distraught. He managed to pull himself together enough to give a funeral oration, though, in which he praised her gentleness, gravity, loyalty, amiability, tenderness, modesty, great beauty and chastity. Sabina hardly got a look in. He even built a temple in Matidia's honour, even though this had never been done before for a woman who had not been formally deified.

Hadrian continued to nurture his close relationship with motherly Plotina and, because she had no children, she indulged him. They dined together on his birthday, when Sabina was out of town, and they were in Syria together when Trajan died.

Although Hadrian made no pretence of loving Sabina, she must have been miffed when rumours circulated that, when he was away with the army, he was suspected of seducing the wives of his fellow officers – as well as indulging himself with his fellow officers, too. Sabina had interests of her own, though. Her travelling companion, the writer Julia Balbilla, praised Sabina's beauty in poems that leave a distinct impression that something was going on between the two of them. Balbilla was teasingly known as "the new Sappho".*

One of Hadrian's first acts in office was to segregate the baths. For some time, women had had the choice of either taking a bath naked with the men or staying away. Hadrian encouraged men to work in the morning and reserved the baths for the exclusive use of the women then. It was said that he did this for the sake of the women, but it may have been because he wanted to hang out with all the boys.

He reproached a man who spent too much time at the baths, after his wife wrote to him complaining that her husband was so preoccupied with his pleasures in the hot tubs and steam rooms that he did not want to come home to her. However, Hadrian's biographer, Aelius Spartianus, pointed out that the emperor was guilty of the same offence. It was also said that Hadrian was "a most ostentatious lover of the common people". He would volunteer to rub other men down if they could not afford to have a slave do it for them. Spartianus also remarked that "added to this are the assertions about his passion for adult males and the adulteries with married women in which he is said to have been involved".

Hadrian tried to make peace with the Parthians in Iran by returning to King Osroes the daughter Trajan had captured. However, he enraged the Jews by banning circumcision, as part of a general edict forbidding genital mutilation. He also prohibited the selling of slaves, of either sex, to pimps. Hadrian was also well known for his wit. He had already refused the petition of a grey-haired man, and when the man petitioned him again after having dyed his hair, he dismissed him by saying: "I have already refused this to your father."

Hadrian always had a keen eye for male beauty and wrote a great many love poems to his favourites. Then, on a trip to Greece, the 50-year-old Hadrian met a teenage shepherd from Bithynia, northern Turkey, called Antinous. Their meeting was commemorated in verse:

> Sing to me of that odorous
> Green eve when couching by the marge [margin]
> You heard from Hadrian's gilded barge
> The laughter of Antonius.

> And lapped the stream and fed your drouth [dryness]
> And watched with hot and hungry stare
> The ivory body of that rare
> Young slave with his pomegranate mouth.

"*Si vis me flere, dolendum est Primum ipsi tibi*," as Horace said.

According to the historian Charles Reginald Dawes, Hadrian was immediately fascinated by the extraordinary beauty of both the shepherd boy's face and form. Under the aegis of the emperor, Antinous came "to be regarded as the supreme example of male adolescent loveliness, his boyish beauty being almost indefinably mingled with an effeminate Graeco-Oriental sensuousness, thus producing the true ideal of the boy lover". *Totum dependeat*, Charles.

Antinous's influence on sculpture was immense. During the reign of Hadrian, the image of the Antinous-type eclipsed the female figure almost entirely. Over five hundred busts of him still survive today. According to the distinguished art historian Lord Kenneth Clark* (of *Civilisation* fame, and father of bad-boy Tory minister Alan), the likeness of a nude Antinous reappears in the Renaissance, particularly in Donatello's* David. Antonius also became the ideal for the gay "uranist" movement of the nineteenth century, which boasted Oscar Wilde* among its ranks. Leading uranist John Addington Symonds* raved about him in a long essay describing the physical appearance of Antinous derived from statues and portraits.

"Antinous, as he appears in sculpture, is a young man of 18 or 19 years, almost faultless in form," frothed Symonds. "His beauty is not of the pure Greek type. Though perfectly proportioned and developed by gymnastic exercise to the true athletic fullness, his limbs are round and florid, suggesting the possibility of early over-ripeness. The muscles are not trained to sinewy firmness, but are yielding and elastic; the chest is broad and singularly swelling; and the shoulders are placed so far back from the thorax that the breasts project beyond them in a massive arch. The legs and arms are modelled with exquisite grace of outline, yet they do not show that readiness for active service..."

This panegyric gushes on almost endlessly. His "whole body combines the Greek beauty of structure with something of Oriental temperament voluptuousness". The head is "not too large..."; the throat "massive". The hair lies "thick in clusters, which only form curls at the tips". The nose is "straight, but blunter than is consistent with the Greek ideal". The cheeks and chin are "delicately formed, but fuller than severe taste approves..." The mouth is "one of the loveliest ever carved". The lips "pout".

Symonds drools on and on about the deep-set, half-closed eyes, the thick eyebrows, the low, square forehead, the face's innocence and immaturity and sense of "rapidly approaching over-bloom", concluding that "a prevailing melancholy and sweetness of temperament is overshadowed by resignation, brooding, the innocence of youth

touched and saddened by a calm resolve or an accepted doom..."
Symonds is plainly in love. It is safe to assume that Hadrian felt the
same way.

Antinous was called Hadrian's Ganymede, thus making it pretty
plain what they were getting up to. They were an item for seven years.
Aelius Spartianus, Hadrian's biographer, also raved about the beauty of
his shape and form and of the pleasure that Hadrian experienced with
him, saying: "He was one of nature's masterpieces, a youth of
incomparable beauty, a fit object for an emperor's passion, especially an
emperor of so cultured and artistic a temperament as Hadrian."

Of Hadrian himself, Spartianus said: "He was at once serious and
gay, friendly and dignified, wanton and irresolute, thrifty and generous;
he could affect emotion or conceal it, he was both cruel and gentle, in
fact at all times and in all things he was versatile and varied."

Hadrian's gay goings-on with Antinous and other youths did attract
criticism in some quarters – largely because he neglected the running of
the empire. When he was not building walls, Hadrian would leave the
boring business of administration in the hands of Lucius Aelius Caesar
and retire to Tibur, modern Tivoli, 14 miles to the east of Rome.
According to Sextus Aurelius Victor, author of *History of the Emperors*:
"In Tibur he built palaces and gave himself up to banquets, sculpture
and painting, as is the way of rich men with their fortunes. He paid
great attention to all luxuries and sensual delights. This gave rise to
scandals. It was said that he had sexual connections with youths and had
been ardently devoted to Antinous."

But Victor was not one to be judgemental.

"I shall leave the matter undecided," he said, "although in my
opinion a friendship between two persons of a different age is always
suspicious when one of them has a lascivious temperament."

And Hadrian was certainly known for that.

On a trip to Egypt, Antinous drowned in the Nile and, according to
Spartianus, Hadrian wept like a woman. This can hardly have impressed
Sabina, who had also come along for the ride. It is not clear how he
drowned. According to Hadrian's own account, Antinous "fell in the
Nile".

"Teneris heu lubrica moribus aetas," as Claudian put it.

But as Hadrian's favourite he would have been surrounded by guards and courtiers, so it is unlikely that he simply slipped and fell in. He may well have been pushed, as court favourites rarely have any friends. Some have suggested that he committed suicide because he was ashamed of the shameful life he was leading. Others have said that he sacrificed himself to propitiate the gods for the deeply superstitious Hadrian.

Sextus Aurelius Victor said: "Hadrian, they say, had wished to prolong his own life, and had been asked by magicians for a substitute who was willing to die for him. All others refused, but Antinous gave himself up."

Another story suggests that Hadrian sacrificed the boy himself. There may be an ulterior motive here. The third-century Christian writer Oregenes Adamantius – aka Origen – wrote that "Even the life of the favourite of Hadrian could not keep Antinous from a morbid lust for women." Maybe Hadrian was just a jealous as gay men are when their boyfriends start going with women. (See *Sex Lives of the Famous Gays*.)

Hadrian named a new city after Antinous, calling it Antinoöpolis – modern Sheikh Abade – on the eastern bank of the Nile some 160 miles south of Cairo (which the Romans, somewhat confusingly, called Babylon) near to the spot where Antinous had died. Hadrian also deified Antinous and statues and busts of him were erected in every city in the empire – the reason why so many of them survive today. Sextus Aurelius Victor suggests that this was done out of love and gratitude.

A gay cult soon sprang up around the dead Antinous. The "priests" of the new divinity were chosen from the best-looking boys and pederasty was part of the cult's rituals. A feast, known as the "sacred nights" of Antinous, was observed for a century after his death, until it was condemned by the Christian missionary St Clement of Alexandria. At that time, the worship of Antinous was seen as a serious rival to Christianity.

Hadrian's love for Antinous can hardly have made things any easier between him and Sabina, but even after Plotina died in AD 121, they stuck together, despite their mutual loathing. Sabina later boasted that she had ensured that she would never have a child "lest she should put another monster on the throne". One early biography, the *Epitome de Caesaribus*, said that "she had taken steps to make sure that she did not become pregnant by him, as offspring of his would harm the human race".

It was not hard for Sabina to avoid having children. Both contraception and abortion were freely available at the time. Soranos, a doctor from Ephesus, a Greek town in Asia Minor, was practising in Rome then and wrote extensively on these matters:

A contraceptive device differs from an abortion. The former prevents conception, the latter destroys what has already been conceived. Let us be clear in distinguishing between what destroys and what prevents conception.

As for abortions, some people call them "expulsions" and do not use any special drug, but rather induce them by physical means, such as getting the patient to make violent movements or jump up and down. Hippocrates, in his *On the Nature of a Child*, mentions jumping combined with a hard spanking, using the hand and fingernails to facilitate expulsion.

On the other hand, some doctors reject abortion entirely, quoting another line of Hippocrates: "I have never given a single abortion to one single woman." Supporters of that belief add that the role of medicine is to protect and safeguard that which nature gives life to...

There were pro-life campaigners even then.

... Still other doctors introduce a distinction: they refuse to give an abortion to women wanting one as a result of adultery or to preserve their beauty, but they will authorise it when it provides a way to eliminate a health risk during pregnancy. Perhaps the womb is too small to handle going to full term or fistulas block the mouth of the vagina; or some other illness ravages the woman. These doctors say, though, that they prefer contraceptives, since it is less dangerous to prevent pregnancy than it is to induce an abortion.

The abortion methods Soranos recommended were taking a bumpy wagon ride, carrying heavy weights, taking hot baths or administering caustic douches. However, there is one method he absolutely forbids.

"One should never detach the embryo with a sharp instrument," he said. "There's too much risk of wounding the surrounding regions."

Soranos of Ephesus was also pretty good when it came to female sexual anatomy:

The vagina of a woman is described as follows: the visible external parts of this organ are called the "wings", constituting the so-called "lips" of the vagina. They are thick and fleshy. Downwards, they end at the thighs and are separated from each other by a slit. Toward the top, they reach up to what is called the *nympha*. This latter, which stands right at the start of the two lips, consists of a fleshy little button, which resembles the masculine organ. It is called the *nympha*, because it is hidden away just as a newly-wed bride [*nympha* in Greek] is hidden away behind her veil.

Soranos could find it two thousand years ago. *"Nil sine magno Vita labore dedit mortalibus,"* as Horace said in his *Satires*.

On the subject of contraception, Soranos recommended avoiding sexual intercourse at the fertile times of the month. He also suggested inserting a woollen tampon, soaked in vinegar or a mixture of honey, oil and resin, into the vagina. The astringent properties of the vinegar would pucker the uterus around the plug and would prevent the semen from getting through. On the other hand, the glutinous mixture of honey, oil and resin would slow the sperm. Soranos dismissed the use of amulets and prescriptions taken by mouth – on the grounds that, apart from anything else, the oral contraceptives of the ancient world ruined the digestion.

Five hundred years earlier, Aristotle had recommended a pre-sex douche of olive oil, which would have helped. However, the famous prostitutes of Ancient Greece, the *hetairai*, usually insisted on the foolproof method of anal intercourse, unless the client strongly objected to it.

The first-century Roman poet Lucretius had other ideas. He recommended that women undulate their hips during intercourse, which apart from giving their partner pleasure would, he thought, direct the seminal fluid away from the danger zone. It may not have been effective, but it would certainly have increased the pleasure.

Pliny was less sanguine. He thought that the most effective way to avoid pregnancy was to have less sex, and the methods of contraception he recommended certainly reflect that. He prescribed "mouse dung ... applied in the form of a liniment", which would have made cunnilingus out of the question. Otherwise you could swallow snail excrement or pigeon droppings mixed with oil and wine, something that would certainly have cut down on the kissing. Or you could put the testicles and blood of a dunghill cock under the bed. According to Pliny, one way to guarantee a woman's "aversion to sexual intercourse" was to rub her loins with "blood taken from the ticks on a wild black bull". Rubbing a woman's loins is seldom a good way to put her off sex. However, trying to collect parasites from an already ticked-crazed wild black bull might well prove fatal. Besides, as Ovid said: *"Quod juvat, invitae saepe dedisse volunt."*

Pliny's contemporary, Dioscorides, whose works were still being used in the sixteenth century, recommended inserting pepper into the mouth of the uterus; that must have made the woman's eyes water. This was sympathetic medicine, as sneezing is not a bad way of expelling semen from the vagina: Dioscorides sought to induce the cough a little closer to the source of the problem. Otherwise he recommended only having sex during the first five days after menstruation, a method now known as "Vatican roulette".

"Contra felicem vix deus vires habet," said Publilicus Syrus.

The real problem with all of these methods, Soranos concluded, was that they made no allowance for unpremeditated intercourse. A kiss can lead to consummation quicker than you can find your condiments. In that case, he advised, when the man is just about to ejaculate, "the woman should ... hold her breath and draw her body back a little so that the semen cannot reach the mouth of the uterus, then immediately get up and sit down with bent knees, and in this position provoke sneezing".

A post-coital cuddle was out of the question in Roman times, it seems. But then, *"Ad supervacua sudatur,"* according to Seneca. Soranos also recommends a thorough douche, though, which might have helped.

History does not record whether Sabina used any of these methods. Given Hadrian's preferences, it would hardly have seemed worth consulting Soranos of Ephesus or any other of these learned gentlemen. However, it was thought that she got pregnant by another man and had the foetus aborted in case Hadrian claimed the child and raised it as his own. We do not know who the father of the child was, but it would be nice to think that it was Suetonius. He was just 17 years older than Sabina – seven years older than Hadrian and, judging by the vivid descriptions of sex in his writings, a bit of an old goat. Perhaps he was having a threesome with the handsome prefect of the Praetorian Guard, Septicus Clarus, or even the Sapphic Julia Balbilla. But as Suetonius drew a veil over own sex life, we shall never know.

Despite everything, Sabina stuck with Hadrian. She liked being empress and Hadrian insisted that she was treated as one. And even though he had no interest in Sabina sexually, Hadrian had her watched by his secret police. That's how he got to know about Suetonius's "over-familiarity" with Sabina. With that level of surveillance, it would have been difficult for any other lover to have got to her. As a trusted courtier, Suetonius had privileged access, so to speak.

Otherwise Hadrian was an inattentive husband, always putting other people first. He built a huge temple in Nemausus, now Nîmes in France, to commemorate Plotina. He also composed a memorial hymn and wore black for nine days. Hadrian used to say that although Plotina had asked much of him, he never refused her anything, as her requests had been so wise and modest. It was not something he said of Sabina, who was both feckless and demanding. When Sabina died in her mid-50s, Hadrian was suspected of poisoning her.

After the death of Antinous, Hadrian fell for the handsome Lucius Ceionius Commodus Verus Aelius, who was described as a "most depraved and licentious youth". He adopted him as his heir and named him as his successor, and – as if the man did not have enough names already – Hadrian tacked Caesar onto the end of his name. It was said that Hadrian adopted Verus "for his debauchery". Gibbon said that he was "a gay and voluptuous nobleman, recommended by his uncommon beauty to the lover of Antinous", while other commentators simply called him "the second Antinous".

According to the *Historia Augusta*, Verus's great beauty was the only thing that commended him to Hadrian. Other sources say that his manners were charming, his conversation sparkling and witty and his morals utterly depraved. "The sensuous charm of personality and the exotic licentiousness" of his lifestyle were said to have fascinated the ageing emperor and they were bound together by a secret oath.

Verus's major claim to fame was the special bed he had made. It had four high cushions and was enclosed with a fine net. The bed would be filled with rose petals with the white tips removed. He would lie on the petals with his lovers, smothered in Persian perfumes, under a coverlet made of lilies. When his wife Lucilla complained about this, he said: "Suffer me to engage in my desires with other women, for 'wife' is the name of a duty, not a pleasure."

There is no record of Verus ever doing anything else but *futui* and, it was said, he "gave himself up entirely to debauchery". He liked to dress his pageboys up like Cupids with wings. He knew Ovid's *Art of Love* by heart. A great gourmet, he kept a famous cookery book beside his bed. I don't know when he found time to read it as his famous bed saw so much action that Spartianus was moved to remark: "Never was a man such a slave to infamous pleasures; for not content with ordinary ones, he invented new kinds of vice…" – maybe that's where the cookbook came in – "… and outdid the most depraved princes in effeminacy."

The problem was, with all that *capulus*, Verus died before Hadrian – as Gibbon put it, he was "ravished from his embraces by an untimely death". However, he had done his duty – that's to say his wife – and they had a young son, also called Lucius Verus, and a daughter called Ceionia Fabia.

Hadrian was then on his last legs. As the young Lucius Verus was too young to take over, Hadrian adopted the senator Antoninus Pius as his heir, on the provision that he adopt Lucius Verus and Marcus Aurelius, who was engaged to Ceionia Fabia. These two were to become co-emperors on Pius's death. However, when Hadrian drank himself to death in AD 138, Marcus Aurelius broke off his engagement to Ceionia Fabia and married Antoninus Pius's daughter, his own first cousin Annia Galeria Faustina, instead. It was an inspired political move.

Pius Stolidus

Sadly, for our purposes, Antoninus Pius was another of the "Five Good Emperors" and it has been said that he was "the one ruler against whom history has no reproach". However, Marcus Aurelius mentioned that Antoninus had "overcome all passion for boys" – implying that at one stage he had had a passion for boys to overcome. Historians generally remark that Antoninus was one of the emperors who broke the Scantinian Law – the law that stated that it was an offence to have sex with boys of free birth – and it was said that Antoninus was a temperate man "in affairs of state, not love affairs".

He was also good to the girls. After the death of his wife, Faustina the Elder, he gave state support to a number of young women who were called the Faustinians. He also took a mistress.

Chapter 12

Caesar Marcus Aurelius Antoninus Augustus ruled Rome in what is thought of as its golden age. He was serious and high-minded and is largely remembered now as a philosopher thanks to his *Meditations*. He was, however, surrounded by others who were not so earnest – notably his co-emperor, Lucius Verus, and his wife Faustina the Younger.

Lucius Verus followed in his father's footsteps. He was tall, handsome and blond – he even sprinkled gold dust in his blond hair to make it, well, blonder. According to Gibbon: "Among the many vices of this younger Verus, he possessed one virtue – a due reverence for his wiser colleague to whom he willingly abandoned the ruder cares of the empire."

While Marcus Aurelius remained in Rome to run things, Verus went out to the East and took command in Syria. There, according to the contemporary biographer Julius Capitolinus, he "acquired a bad reputation, not only for the looseness of his rather free living, but for adulteries and love affairs with youths as well". It is said that he rivalled Caligula, Nero and Vitellius in his vices. He would roam the streets at night in disguise and visit brothels and taverns, where he would drink with crooks and get into brawls.

He gave lavish banquets where the handsome serving boys would be presented to the guests. They would eat and drink so much that Verus often fell asleep on his couch – the Romans, of course, reclined on couches to eat. Although the chair had been invented by the Egyptians in the third millennium BC, it did not become popular for everyday use until the Middle Ages. Verus's guests would be given the gold and silver goblets and dishes that they had eaten from, along with other expensive presents, to take home with them and they would play dice all night. When Marcus Aurelius heard of this, he groaned.

Verus was to marry Marcus Aurelius's daughter Lucilla, but Marcus Aurelius would only accompany her as far as Ephesus in modern Turkey, so that he did not have to witness what Verus was up to in Syria. When Verus appeared to take possession of his bride he was clean-shaven, after being persuaded to shave his beard off in Syria by one of his mistresses. The fashion now was for beards and being clean-shaven was considered to be positively poofy. Even so, Marcus Aurelius conferred all of his many names on Verus so that they would truly be brothers, and asked the Senate to honour them equally. However, Marcus Aurelius tried to keep Verus under control by sending a legate called Lido to Syria. Lido mysteriously died, though, probably poisoned by Verus, who then married off Lido's widow to one of his own freedmen.

When Verus returned to Rome, he brought a troop of actors with him. One of them was called Paris. This, as we have seen, was a very popular name for a leading man. The Trojan hero Paris was reputed to have been the most handsome man in the ancient world. Verus filled his palace with young boys "with whom he wildly indulged in Eastern depravity". He had one room fitted out like a tavern and he held pederastic orgies in it with his freedmen and the friends of Paris. These would last for days on end and Verus's villa on the Clodian Way became the most notorious house in Rome.

According to Capitolinus, Verus knew no shame. He even invited Marcus Aurelius to these bashes. There were rumours that he even had sex with his mother-in-law, Marcus Aurelius's wife Faustina – she was much nearer his age than that of the staid Marcus Aurelius – and his own sister, Marcus Aurelius's former fiancée, Ceionia Fabia. Just as had been the case with his father, though, Verus had a weak constitution and his excesses led to an early death at the age of 42. After 11 years of joint power, Marcus Aurelius was now in sole command of the empire.

The even-handed Capitolinus then reported a "well-known tale that Marcus's life did not warrant". He said the story circulated that, growing tired of Verus's wicked, wicked ways, Marcus Aurelius had handed him a sow's womb that he had smeared with poison. After relating this tale, Capitolinus then rejected it out of hand, calling it sacrilege. Capitolinus was, of course, writing after the death of Marcus Aurelius, after the old man had been deified.

Marcus Aurelius was so well loved – "except by voluptuaries" – that, in many houses, a statue of him stood among the household gods. While it might be safely assumed that he was a bit of a Goody Two-shoes, in his famous book of philosophy, *Meditations*, Marcus Aurelius does hint that he was exposed to great temptations while living in the same house as his grandfather's predatory mistress. He did not succumb, though.

"I preserved the flower of my manhood and did not make proof of my virility until the right time, but even deferred the time," he said.

Although breaking off his engagement to Ceionia Fabia so that he could marry Faustina instead had been a good political move, it also had its downside. Ceionia Fabia was a good deal older than Faustina, who was only about eight at the time of her engagement. That meant that they would have had to wait at least four years until they could marry. In fact, they waited seven years, eventually marrying in AD 145 when Faustina was 15. It was not a good idea to keep a woman like Faustina waiting. From what we know of her, she would have been overheating, and the passionless Marcus Aurelius was clearly not up to the job of scratching her itch. There were plenty who were, however.

Marcus Aurelius's son and successor Commodus* was such a brute that there is every indication that he was not his son at all. It was said that the Empress Faustina the Younger's passion had been inflamed by a passing gladiator, who was Commodus's real father. When she fell ill, she confessed this to Marcus Aurelius. He consulted the high priests. Their advice was to have the gladiator killed. Faustina was to bathe herself in his blood, then sleep with Marcus Aurelius in that state.

This story was widely believed because Faustina the Younger, although the daughter of the goodly Antoninus Pius, was built more along the lines of Verus, thought to have been one of her many lovers. Her high-minded husband plainly bored her in the bedroom, so she chose to satisfy herself with numerous soldiers, sailors and gladiators. Legions of potential lovers were paraded before her nude so that she could assess their sexual endowments. This went on at her country home at Caieta, modern Gaeta, to the south of Rome. When Marcus heard about this, he was philosophical about it. He decided not to divorce her, saying: "If we send our wife away, we must give her back her dowry, too."

"Faustina, the daughter of Pius and the wife of Marcus, has been celebrated as much for her gallantries as for her beauty," said Gibbon. Like some eighteenth-century family therapist, he immediately spotted the mismatch.

> The grave simplicity of the philosopher was all calculated to engage her wanton levity, or to fix that unbounded passion for variety, which often discovered personal merit in the meanest of mankind. The Cupid of the ancients was, in general, a very sensual deity; and the amours of an empress, as they exact on her side the plainest advances, are seldom susceptible of much sentimental delicacy. Marcus was the only man in the empire who seemed ignorant or insensible of the irregularities of Faustina; which, according to the prejudices of every age, reflected some disgrace on the injured husband. He promoted several of her lovers to posts of honour and profit, and during a connection of 30 years, invariably gave her proofs of the most tender confidence, and of a respect which ended not with her life. In his *Meditations*, he thanks the gods, who had bestowed on him a wife, so faithful, so gentle, and of such wonderful simplicity of manners. The obsequious Senate, at his earnest request, declared her a goddess. She was represented in her temples with the attributes of Juno, Venus and Ceres; and it was decreed that, on the day of their nuptials, the youth of either sex should pay their vows before the altar of their chaste patroness.

Marcus might have been a philosopher, but he was not very worldly. After all Plautus said: *"Mulieri nimio male facere melius est onus, quan bene."*

Even at the time Marcus Aurelius was widely condemned for promoting Faustina's lovers – Tutilius, Orfitus, Moderatus and Tertullus – to high office, even though, for one, he had caught Tertullus having breakfast with Faustina. Just in case Marcus had missed it, the situation was lampooned on stage. When an actor playing the Fool asked the Slave the name of his wife's lover, the Slave answered three times "Tullus". When the Fool asked once again, the Slave replied: "I have told you three times" – *ter* in Latin – "Tullus." But then as Juvenal said: "*Si tibi simplicitas uxoria, deditus uni Est animus, summitte caput cervice parata Ferre jugum.*"

Even though he was married to a *Nympharum torrendus*, Marcus Aurelius was the jealous guardian of his own reputation, and the antics of his co-emperor, his wife and, later, his son did not seem to tarnish it. The man was positively innocent when it came to sex. He married off his younger daughter Lucilla, still not out of mourning for Verus, to an elderly knight from Antioch, despite the protests of both Faustina and the girl herself. She later managed to marry the leading politician Claudius Pompeianus, whose career she then proceeded to ruin.

Marcus Aurelius refuted rumours that Faustina was having an affair with an actor and, according to Julius Capitolinus, sought to "reform the morals of married women and of young noblemen, which were growing lax". He also cleaned up the worship of the Graeco-Egyptian god Serapis, whose rites on 20 March had got mixed up with those of the lewd Egyptian fertility cult of Pelusia.

Not only was Faustina *in concubueris cum omnes* behind his back, she also seems to have had a hand in the rebellion of Avidius Cassius, who called himself "Caesar", in the East. Even so, when Marcus Aurelius went out on campaign he took Faustina with him and gave her the title "Mother of Camp". Avidius Cassius, it was said, was a contradictory character who was "sometimes devout, sometimes irreligious; sometimes rough and truculent, sometimes placid and mild; sometimes a drunkard, sometimes abstemious; sometimes a lover of chastity, sometimes a devotee of Venus".

He was, however, always very cruel, crucifying his own men if they had stolen anything from the provincials, in the very place that they had committed the offence. He also devised a new type of punishment. He would erect a pole 180 feet high and tie condemned men to it from top to bottom. Then he would light a fire under it. Men at the bottom would be burnt to death; those who were higher up would have died from smoke inhalation or out of sheer fright.

He would order ten men at a time to be chained together and then flung into a river or the sea. He also cut off the hands of deserters, or broke their legs, saying that, living in misery as a cripple, they were a better example to others than if they had been executed. And when his men mutinied, he emerged from his tent dressed only in a loincloth and said: "Strike me if you dare, and add that crime to your breach of discipline." No one dared. This added immensely to his reputation, not just in the Roman army, but among barbarians as well.

Avidius Cassius had been a favourite of Marcus Aurelius. The emperor put him in command of the legions in Syria when they were "abandoned to luxury and behaving with the morals of Daphne" – not the Greek goddess who was turned into a laurel bush to escape being ravished by Apollo, but a steamy coastal resort near Antioch, then in Syria and now in modern Turkey. Apparently, the naughty legionnaires were bathing in hot water and wearing flowers in their hair. Avidius Cassius soon put a stop to that and instilled a bit of old-fashioned discipline. All pleasures were banned from camp and anyone found in uniform in Daphne would be stripped of it. When Avidius Cassius rebelled, possibly at the behest of Faustina who let it slip that Marcus Aurelius was not well, he found that he was not as popular as he thought he was. He was murdered by his own men. They also killed his son, who was in charge in Alexandria, for good measure. However, Marcus Aurelius spared the women of the family and gave them gold, silver and jewellery.

When Faustina died, Marcus Aurelius got the Senate to deify her and he built a temple to her, "even though she had a reputation for a lack of chastity," said Capitolinus. A new order of Faustinian girls was established.

With Faustina in her grave, Marcus Aurelius's former fiancée Ceionia Fabia made new overtures, but Marcus said that he did not want to get married again because he did not want to place a stepmother over his troublesome brood. This was not a very good excuse, as all but two of the 14 children the fecund Faustina had provided were now married. Instead he took the daughter of his dead wife's procurator, or financial manager, as his concubine. Let's hope that she gave him some *pectus*. Marcus Aurelius was definitely a *mammeata* man. In his *Meditations*, written in Greek towards the end of his life, Marcus Aurelius says: "I follow the way of nature until I lie down, lying down on the earth from which my father drew his vital seed, my mother her blood, my nurse her milk."

His wet nurse would almost certainly have been Greek. Greek women were often employed in that role because it was vital for any educated Roman to master Greek from an early age, even though there was a danger that a Roman child might grow up speaking Latin with a Greek accent.

Marcus Aurelius's remark seems to have sparked a philosophical debate on the subject of mammaries. Even more confused about these matters than Marcus Aurelius himself, fellow philosopher Flavorinus, a hermaphrodite, mused: "Do you think that nature provided women with nipples as a kind of beauty spot?"

Such was the level of Roman intellectual enquiry. The Greeks would have despaired.

It has to be said that the image of Marcus Aurelius's father drawing his vital seed from the earth is rather odd – though young men, like the Old Testament's Onan, are often said to have spilled it on the ground – but then, a lot of Marcus Aurelius's *Meditations* are rather odd. He spent too much time thinking about it. Here, for example, is Marcus Aurelius on self-control: "Dissolve fantasies; check desire; extinguish cravings; let your governing self retain her power." This is not much of a recipe for a good sex life.

Here he is on moral cultivation: "The perfection of character consists in living each day as if it were the last and being neither violently excited, nor apathetic, nor insincere."

Merae fabulae sunt, et eas esse tales scis.

And here he is on reason and virtue: "In the make-up of the reasonable person I find no virtue that opposes justice; but I see a virtue that opposes love of pleasure, and that is self-restraint."

Coleus.

And there was no excuse for it. Although Marcus Aurelius fancied himself as a great philosopher, there was plenty of cracking competition for the ear of the empire. The great rhetorician Achilles Tatius was around at the time. He shunned Marcus Aurelius's stoicism.

"Love is handy and resourceful, a clever philosopher, who can turn any place into a temple of mystical thought," he said.

Then again: "The casual in sex is far more sweet than the carefully prepared. For its pleasure is natural and simple."

Tatius knew what he was talking about and introduced a note of romanticism into sex that had not been seen before in literature. He was, for example, a great devotee of kissing:

I could feel her kiss still resting on my lips like an alien thing, and I guarded it carefully as a secret source of pleasure. For a kiss is the greatest of pleasures. It is the lovechild of the mouth. And the mouth is the loveliest organ of the body. It is the source of speech, and speech is the shadow of the soul itself. The union and commingling of two mouths radiates pleasure downwards into the body and draws the soul up towards the kissing lips.

He also noted the reaction of his partner and the profound physical effect his kisses were having on her.

A woman's body is moist in embrace and her lips are tender and soft for kissing. She holds a man's body totally and pleasantly wedged in her embraces, into her flesh, and the man is completely surrounded by pleasure. She plants kisses on your lips like a seal touching warm wax. She kisses with art and makes her kiss sweeter, for she wants to kiss not only with her lips but also with her teeth, grazing around the mouth of the kisser, nipping with her kiss. Her breasts too, when fondled, have their own special pleasure. And when the height of Aphrodite's act is reached, she is frenzied with pleasure. She kisses with her mouth wide open and goes frantic. Tongues caress each other fiercely, fighting to kiss as much as possible. The pleasure is heightened when you open your mouth to kiss. When a woman reaches the very peak of lovemaking, she gasps with burning pleasure. The gasp reaches the lips with the breath of love. There it meets a wandering kiss looking for a way down. This kiss turns back with the gasp, follows it down and strikes at the very heart. Confused by the kiss, the heart throbs. If it were not firmly tethered in the chest, it could rip itself free and drag itself upwards towards the kisses.

This is a million miles away from Ovid's direct approach a century and a half earlier. The quasi-rape that characterised Roman sexuality had disappeared. Slaves and prostitutes were still there for the taking but, in the aptly named *The Golden Ass*, written at about the same time,

Lucius Apuleius describes the tender seduction of a young slave-girl called Fotis:

I said: "Behold, Fotis, I am yours, and shall presently die unless you take pity on me." Which when I had said, she eftsoons kissed me, and bid me be of good courage, and "I will," quoth she, "satisfy your whole desire, and it shall be no longer delayed than until night, when assure yourself I will come and lie with you; wherefore go your ways and prepare yourself, for I intend valiantly and courageously to encounter with you this night."

And when I was entering into the bed, behold my Fotis came in and gave me roses and flowers which she had in her apron, and tied a garland about my head, and bespread the chamber with the residue. Which when she had done, she took a cup of wine and delayed it with hot water, and proffered it to me to drink; and before I had drunk it all, she pulled it from my mouth, and then gave it to me again, and in this manner we emptied the pot twice or thrice together.

Thus when I had well replenished myself with wine, and was now ready unto venery not only in my mind but also in body, I removed my clothes, and showing to Fotis my great impatience, I said, "O my sweetheart, take pity on me and help me, for as you see I am now prepared unto the battle which you yourself did appoint – for after that I felt the first arrow of cruel Cupid within my breast, I bent my bow very strong, and now fear (because it is bended so hard) lest my string should break; but thou mayest the better please me, undress thy hair and come and embrace me lovingly."

Whereupon she made no long delay, but set aside all the meat and wine, and then she unapparelled herself and unattired her hair, presenting her amiable body unto me in the manner of fair Venus when she goeth under the waves of the sea.

"Now," quoth she, "is come the hour of jousting; now is come the time of war; wherefore show thyself like unto a man, for I will not retire, I will not fly the field. See then thou be valiant, see thou be courageous, since there is no time appointed when our skirmish shall cease."

In saying these words, she came to me to bed and embraced me sweetly, and so we passed all the night in pastime and pleasure, and never slept until it was the day; but we would eftsoons refresh our weariness and provoke our pleasure, and renew our venery by drinking wine. In which sort we pleasantly passed away many other nights following.

All of the human warmth in these words seems to have passed Marcus Aurelius by, however. He dismissed this new-found romanticism. The man had no soul.

"Copulation," he said, "is the friction of the members and an ejaculatory discharge."

With such a cold fish, one can sympathise with Faustina playing around. What she needed was less thought on his part and more action, but Marcus Aurelius had other concerns. A sickly man throughout his life, he was plagued by a chronic ulcer. He dosed himself with drugs, and some of the more apocalyptic passages of the priggish *Meditations* – still thought by some to be one of the greatest books of all time – have a distinctly Sixties' feel, indicating that Marus Aurelius was a *tiro in exercitu stellarum*.

Meditations? *Masturbatus*, more like.

CHAPTER 13

Marcus Aurelius's son Lucius Aelius Aurelius Commodus, who reigned as Caesar Marcus Aurelius Commodus Antoninus Augustus, was a bit of, if not a commode, certainly what you do in one. Ostensibly the son of the saintly Marcus Aurelius and the profligate Faustina, he took after his mother and not at all after his putative father. As we have seen, his real father was probably a gladiator. Commodus certainly had a yen for the arena, putting on over a thousand gladiatorial contests when he was emperor. And it was inscribed in the public record that he had entered the arena as a gladiator himself 735 times. This alienated him from the Senate, but endeared him to the masses.

Commodus was the first emperor "born to the purple"; his father, Marcus Aurelius, was already emperor when he was born. He did have a rival, though. He was one of twins. When his mother Faustina was pregnant, she dreamt that she was giving birth to snakes that were fighting inside her, and one of them was fiercer than the other. So it was to be that Commodus's twin, Antoninius, died at the age of four, leaving Commodus as the undisputed heir. Marcus Aurelius tried to teach him the principles of a good and worthwhile life outlined in his *Meditations*. Commodus, no doubt, was bored senseless.

"Straight from his earliest boyhood, he was base, shameless, cruel, lecherous, defiled of mouth too and lewd ... a glutton and a libertine who gave himself up to every type of debauchery," said his not-overly-sympathetic biographer, Aelius Lampridius.

Gibbon said: "The monstrous vices of the son have cast a shade on the purity of the father's virtue." And he had no doubt about who was to blame – Marcus Aurelius himself. "His excessive indulgence to his brother, wife and his son, exceeded the bounds of private virtue, and became a public injury, by the example and consequences of their vices."

By "his brother" here, I guess Gibbon means Lucius Verus, as both he and Marcus Aurelius had been adopted by Antoninus Pius.

Commodus's cruel streak first showed itself at the age of 12 when he found that his bath water was tepid; he ordered the bath-keeper to be thrown into the furnace. Fortunately, the man in charge of the slaves was a little more compassionate. He chucked a sheepskin into the furnace and the smell it gave off was enough to convince the young Commodus that his order had been carried out.

All the good teachers that Marcus Aurelius provided were soon driven away, while Commodus managed to keep hold of any evil ones that came his way. If a bad teacher was dismissed, Commodus would pretend to be ill until his soft-hearted father reinstated the man. Commodus kept a low dive in the palace for these men and "never spared any decency or expense". He played dice there and drove chariots wearing the dress of a lowly charioteer.

"Women of particular beauty of appearance, he gathered together like bought harlots, creating a brothel to make sport of their chastity," said Aelius Lampridius. "He conducted himself like a procurer's attendant, so that you would have thought him born for shameful things rather than the station to which fortune had advanced him."

A pretty youth with bright eyes and curly golden hair, he committed incest with his sisters before he even came to power. He married Bruttia Crispina, the granddaughter of a friend of Hadrian, though he does not seem to have had much time for her.

In AD 177, at the age of 16, Marcus Aurelius made Commodus his co-ruler. His accession was marked by the martyrdom of St Blandina. Her offence was to celebrate Easter in competition with the orgiastic rites of the cult of Cybele. Blandina and her followers were rounded up and subjected to a six-day death in the arena. They were stripped naked and tied to stakes, then attacked by wild animals. Many of the creatures were trained to violate the victims sexually or to sodomise them before eating them. Women were covered in grease made from the musk organs of the civet and were then raped half to death by packs of wild dogs or were buggered by baboons while spectators looked on. Victims were then consumed alive. Blandina herself was bundled up in a net and thrown in front of maddened bulls. Once she had been trampled to a bloody pulp, she had her head hacked off.

Commodus went with his father to fight invading German tribes along the Danube in AD 180. At 59, Marcus Aurelius, already worn out by years of campaigning, came down with the plague. From his sickbed, he begged Commodus to listen to the Senate and to shun the masses, but the 19-year-old Commodus knew that the sons of every other emperor had been poisoned, stabbed or strangled by their own family so that some ambitious senator could come to power. If he was to survive the succession, there was no time to lose. Marcus Aurelius was, by this time, a mass of pustulating boils. Commodus ordered everyone from his tent, donned a pair of protective gloves and strangled his father. He then quickly made peace with the marauding Teutons. The deal was that, if they offered obeisance to Rome, they could keep their lands. Each chieftain expected Commodus to bugger them to seal the deal. Then there were the deputy chieftains and sub-chieftains. It was five months before Commodus could return to Italy in triumph – exhausted, no doubt.

Entering Rome to the cheers of the crowds, he rode with his catamite Saoteros beside him in the chariot and showered kisses on the boy. They continued their "immodest caresses" throughout the following ceremony in the full gaze of the spectators. Such a display made it clear that he would have no truck with the Senate. He quickly recalled all the "servile and profligate youths" that Marcus Aurelius had banished, to form the core of his new administration. Among his favourites was a young freedman whom he called *Onos* – which means "Ass" – on the grounds that he was hung like a donkey. He made the man rich and appointed him Grand Priest of Hercules as a reward for his obvious merits.

Marcus Aurelius had opposed the brutality of the arena. He had it closed and it had fallen into dereliction. Seeking to get the plebeians on his side, Commodus reinstated the games, much to the delight of the masses. Just as Caligula had done, he made public appearances at the games. His initial popularity depended partially on what appeared to be a huge penis, one that was permanently semi-erect, that seemed to dangle beneath his robes. In fact, he had a strange and rather revolting blue-veined growth in his groin which was over 12 inches long. Those who got to know him more intimately found, to their disappointment, a more modest sexual appendage underneath it. Meanwhile he flattered the Senate, but murdered anyone who opposed him.

Commodus's games were to be as bloodthirsty as anything that had been staged under Caligula. He extended his palace so that the balconies of his private apartment overlooked the arena. He watched the games by day and, by night, practised privately there by the light of braziers. Then, early in the morning, he would race his chariot around the streets of Rome, crushing any hapless pedestrians who happened to be about to a bloody pulp.

Finally, at the age of 26, he entered the arena, throwing off his imperial robes to reveal a gladiator's leather costume underneath. He faced ten of the greatest gladiators of the day – though, like Caligula, he took the simple precaution of arming them with wooden practice swords, while his was metal and razor sharp. As he cut them down, he was cheered by an ecstatic crowd who were rewarded with gold coins.

The next day he faced an arena full of wild animals. From behind a bunch of slaves, who formed a human shield, he threw spears at them and took just two hours to dispatch a hundred bears. Whenever he called for refreshments, a seven-foot, naked female Nubian slave brought chilled wine made from honey and served in a cup shaped like a cudgel. Growing tired, he repaired to the balcony of his palace. From there, he threw javelins, dispatching 18 rhinoceroses, five hippopotamuses, two elephants and one giraffe in a single hour. After a short lie down, he slaughtered one hundred leopards with one hundred spears, missing with a single one. Then a flock of terrified ostriches were released. Using a bejewelled bow, armed with broad, crescent-headed arrows, he neatly sliced off their heads one by one. All of them were dead in 20 minutes.

During Commodus's career in the arena, he clocked up twelve thousand kills. He also made a big show of following all the rules – with the exception of allowing his opponents to be properly armed, of course. He allowed the crowd to pick his opponents, and he demanded the huge fees that top gladiators were paid by their aristocratic sponsors. Such was his fame in the arena that statues were erected all over the empire recording his record number of wins and noting that he could wield a sword left-handed, something that was highly prized in those days. He also raced chariots, but any gladiator or charioteer whose fame threatened to eclipse his own was summarily executed.

Commodus came to believe that he was the god Hercules and took to dressing in the traditional lionskin when he entered the arena to club lions and humans to death. He brought random acts of cruelty and murder to religious rites, and would enter the temple covered in blood or "polluted with his adulteries".

A fat man was cut in half, just so that he could see his innards tumble out. Other men would find themselves called "one-eye" or "one foot", then have an eye gouged out or a foot lopped off. He even posed as a surgeon so that he could wield a scalpel to deadly effect. He would name his favourites after genital organs of either sex and would take particular delight in kissing them there. Otherwise, he spent his time buggering burly wrestlers in the imperial baths.

In the evenings, Commodus would flit through the taverns and brothels of Rome. He would drink until dawn and, in every way possible, he tried to squander the wealth of the empire he was supposed to command. The Senate responded by mocking him. They named him *Pius* – "dutiful" – after he raised his mother's lover to the consulship and *Felix* – "Fortunate" – when he handed his regent Tigidius Perennis over to the army to be lynched.

However, there was a sycophantic lobby who insisted on calling him Britannicus, after his generals put down a rebellion in Britain. They brought him statues, depicting him as Hercules, and worshipped him as a god. He had the head of Nero removed from a colossus and his own put in its place. The inscription was altered to give Commodus's gladiatorial honours and a number of titles that were normally given to women.

Commodus was so proud of his prowess in the arena that he seldom appeared in public without being covered in blood. To intimidate the Senate, he would stride in without warning, fresh from the arena, stinking of sweat, wearing a blood-soaked, purple and gold imperial robe, with a gold crown – inlaid with jewels from all over the empire – on his head and carrying an ostrich or flamingo's head in his blood-caked hand. He would look at the severed head in his hand, then look at the head of a senator. It worked. August was renamed Commodus, while September became Hercules and October *Invictus* – "Invincible". December became *Amazonius*, because of his passion for his mistress Marcia,* whom he liked to depict as an Amazon – one of the race of warrior women from Greek mythology who were said to have had their right breasts removed so that they could pull a bow or throw a javelin better. For her sake, he even entered the arena as a gladiator in Amazonian dress and sometimes even declared himself to be an Amazon – though it must have struck him that his left breast was also missing.

Marcia was the go-between between the emperor and Pope Victor I.* Like many unwanted Roman babies, Marcia had been exposed as an infant, but had been rescued by a Christian called Hyacinthus.* He was said to be a eunuch and may also have been a priest. He certainly brought Marcia up as a Christian.

Like other men who rescued exposed infants, Hyacinthus made his living by selling the children he rescued into harems or brothels, once they were old enough to serve in that capacity. Marcia was lucky, however. She was good looking and would fetch a higher price in a private sale. So when she reached puberty, she was sold as a sex slave to a Roman nobleman, who was a friend of Commodus's sister, Lucilla.

In AD 182, Lucilla fell out with Commodus's wife Crispina, who seems to have been pregnant at the time, though she never produced an heir. According to Cassius Dio, Lucilla was "no more modest or chaste than her brother Commodus and detested her husband, Claudius Pompeianus". She got her lover, Marcus Ummidius Quadratus, to persuade her daughter's fiancé, Claudius Pompeianus Quintianus, a young member of the Senate, to attack and kill Commodus. He bungled it.

Quintianus hid in the shadows at the entrance to the Flavian amphitheatre and leapt in front of Commodus. Drawing his dagger, he yelled: "See, this is what the Senate sends you…"

It was a bad move. This ominous announcement gave Commodus's bodyguards time to react. Both Quintianus and Ummidius Quadratus were executed – tortured to death using several excruciating methods, including unhurried emasculation. Claudius Pompeianus was dismissed, his career now in tatters, and Lucilla was banished to Capri, where she was later killed. Commodus also took great delight in having Maternus, a former soldier who had been in on the planning of the assassination, dragged into the arena where he was eaten by lions. Another to perish in the resulting purge was the nobleman who owned Marcia, and she, along with the rest of his property, was forfeit to the emperor.

Commodus never appeared in public again after this. He quickly killed off all those who opposed him and he turned over political power to his new mistress Marcia and a series of advisers.

The plot seems to have pushed Commodus over the edge and into erotomania. Marcia organised a harem for him in the palace, "recruiting both married women and whores". In all, he had a seraglio consisting of three hundred beautiful women and three hundred "ripe youths ... picked from every rank and every province, chosen for their beauty and their sexual accomplishments", in the vain hope that this would assuage his lust. Then, it was said, "he abandoned himself without interruption to the most shameless and beastly debauchery, and wallowed in every sensual filth". The orgies were stage-managed by Marcia, who loved to show off her opulent figure, wearing revealing clothing even when the Pope visited her.

It has to be said that even the most virile man is going to be exhausted by six hundred active young lovers – so he could not pay due sexual attention to the lovely Marcia. When Commodus *virilitas flaccidus est*, he would get the boys and girls to perform erotic tableaux for him – just as the elderly Tiberius had done on Capri – until he was sufficiently stimulated to join in again. Unfortunately, he found that this was subject to the law of diminishing returns, so he had recourse to "prostitution" – that is, play the pathic – "and the most strange artefacts".

On one occasion, he made the prefect of the Praetorian Guard strip and dance completely naked to the accompaniment of cymbals in front of his concubines and catamites, who applauded loudly.

Having slept with his sisters, Commodus began going through his cousins – though when he caught his wife Bruttia Crispina indulging in extracurricular activities, he banished her and then had her killed. And when his new regent, the ex-slave Cleander, had it off with a couple of his concubines and gave them children, he had Cleander, the women and the children executed.

"He used to order the concubines themselves to be debauched before his very eyes," said Aelius Lampridius. "And he was not free from the disgrace of submitting sexually to young men, being defiled in every part of his body, even his mouth, by both sexes."

As well as having fun at non-stop orgies, banquets and the baths, he fought in the arena as a gladiator and among his chamberlains with sword-points uncovered. He also developed some peculiar habits when it came to eating. He had two misshapen hunchbacks served up on a dish covered in mustard, and, it was said, mixed human excrement with the rich food and ate it.

He singed the hair from his face rather than be shaved, as he feared that a barber wielding a razor might kill him. However, he took particular pleasure in depilating his young wards and loved to have naked and hairless youths scampering around his apartments, the most beautiful of whom he would adorn with jewels. Having naked boys in his bedroom would lead to his downfall.

Growing rapidly insane, he renamed Rome Colonia Commodiana – "Commodus's Colony". He also claimed to be the new founder of Rome. Before Christianity took over the empire, the Romans numbered their years from the foundation of the city by Romulus in 738 BC. But, like Cambodia's Pol Pot,* Commodus turned the clock back to Year Zero. Everything took his name. The army became the Legions of Commodus. The ships that brought grain from North Africa became the Fleet of Commodus. Even the Senate became the Lucky Senate of Commodus. The lucky people of Colonia Commodiana were, of course, fortunate enough to be living through the Golden Age of Commodus.

Dressed as a gladiator, he announced that on 1 January AD 193 – or 1 January AC 2 (After Commodus) according to the new calendar – he was going to assume political power again as consul. This did not go down well. Gladiators were all very well in the arena, but they were at the lower end of the social scale and were definitely not of consular rank.

On 31 December AD 192 – 31 December AC 1 – Philocommodus, one of his favourite boys, was playing in Commodus's bedroom while the emperor was asleep and came across a tablet. On it were written the names of all the advisers that Commodus was planning to kill.

Philocommodus means, of course, "lover of Commodus", but he did not seem to love Commodus very much. He took the tablet and showed it to all of those named. Realising that they were in imminent danger, they turned to Commodus's sexually neglected mistress Marcia.* At night she fed him a piece of poisoned meat, but he had been drinking too much wine and threw it up. Then, while Commodus lay semi-unconscious in the palace steam room, she persuaded one of her lovers, a champion wrestler named Narcissus, to strangle him. It was said, rather fancifully, that while the strangulation was in progress, she, at last, got the satisfaction of seeing his penis grow hard and, for his terminal orgasm, let the emperor come in her mouth. She was, though, a good Christian and went on to marry one of the conspirators.

Commodus's body was dragged through the streets and thrown in the Tiber. His name was removed from public buildings. The names of the months were restored. Suddenly it was year 970 again and Rome was Rome once more.

Suge Meum Fides

After Commodus was dead, his successor, Publius Helvius Pertinax, auctioned off the Samite vases filled with rosin and pitch that were heated for use in depilation. As well as raising money, this exposed Commodus's vices to the public, and those who purchased them were exposed as people who were also into that sort of thing.

A former slave trader – and the son of a freed slave – Pertinax also sold Commodus's catamites and concubines, with the exception of those who had been forced into the emperor's service. Pertinax, however, was not above a bit of pleasure himself. His biographer, Julius Capitolinus, assures us: "Many of those who he ordered to be sold were subsequently brought back into service and ministered to the old man's pleasures."

He also had an affair with Marcus Aurelius's daughter, Cornificia, who was about 33 at the time. Meanwhile, his wife openly *amplexus coniugales* a lyre-player. Pertinax did put rigid restraints on the behaviour of freedmen in the court, however. This made him very unpopular and, after three months as emperor, he was murdered.

Sit Iucundus Tibi Dies

Pertinax's father-in-law, Flavius Sulpincianus, then tried to have himself proclaimed emperor, but a senator called Didius Julianus warned the Praetorian Guard not to make any man emperor who might seek to avenge Pertinax. So Julianus thought he would have a shot at the top job himself and wrote a statement on a tablet saying that he would not restore Commodus's good name. Then, after promising not to harm Sulpincianus for wanting to become emperor, Julianus outbid his rival in an auction for the throne and was proclaimed emperor himself.

The only accusations levelled at Julianus were that he was a glutton and a gambler – and that he was old. In his youth, it was said, he was never "disgraced by these vices". However, he was seen as complicit in the murder of Pertinax.

Two weeks after Julianus had come to power, the army on the Danube rebelled and proclaimed their leader, Lucius Septimius Severus Pertinax, emperor. Julianus was murdered by a soldier and his body was handed over to his wife, Manlia Scantilla, and their daughter.

CHAPTER 14

Septimius Severus was the first African to become emperor. He was born in Leptis Magna in Tripolitania – near Al-Khums in modern Libya – in AD 146. Educated in Latin and Greek, the only game he played as a boy was called "Judges", where the *fasces* and axes – the bundle of birch rods with an axe head protruding from it that was the symbol of power in Ancient Rome – were carried before him. The symbolism of the *fasces* was appropriated by the Italian dictator Benito Mussolini* in the 1920s and gives us the modern word Fascism.

At the age of 17, Severus made his first speech and then headed to Rome, where he was made a senator by Marcus Aurelius. Invited to an imperial banquet, he wore a Greek tunic, rather than the toga that was *de rigueur*, and was given the emperor's own official toga to change into. He then inadvertently sat on the imperial chair, unaware that this was not permitted. That night, he dreamt that he had sucked on the teat of a she-wolf, like Romulus and Remus. Another night, a snake wound itself around his head. Friends shouted in alarm and it slunk away, leaving him unharmed. He was plainly destined for great things.

Thankfully, for our purposes, he also had his wild side. As a young man in Rome, he was sued as the co-respondent in an adultery case, spoke in his own defence and got off. Returning home to Leptis Magna – also known as Lepcis – he married a woman named Paccia Marciana. To make sure that they had a good time on their wedding day, Faustina, the wayward wife of Marcus Aurelius, prepared the bridal chamber. Little more is known about Marciana as she died young and Severus remained a private citizen throughout their marriage. However, when he became emperor he erected statues of her. Soon after her death, he began asking around after young women who might make a suitable second wife. In the meantime he played the field "in the manner of soldiers" – though it is only said that he had two lovers before his second marriage.

Severus was a great believer in astrology. When an astrologer produced a chart that showed Severus had a tremendous future ahead of him, the star-man did not believe his own predictions and accused Severus of giving him the wrong birth information to base it on. But Severus insisted that the information he had given was correct. In that case, the astrologer said, everything he had foretold would come to pass.

Naturally, while he was looking for a second wife, Severus studied the horoscopes of any potential bride. He then heard that there was a woman in Syria whose horoscope foretold that she would marry a king, and sought her out. Her name was Julia Domna – which seems to indicate that she was dark-skinned or black. She was born in Emesa – modern Homs – on the River Orontes in Syria and her father, Julius Bassianus, was a priest of Baal, the fertility god that naughty woman Jezebel of Biblical fame tried to introduce to Israel.

Fortunately for the 41-year-old Severus, Julia was a *voluptatem Veneriam*. According to Gibbon, she "deserved all the stars could promise her. She possessed, even in an advanced age, the attractions of beauty, and united to a lively imagination, a firmness of mind and a strength of judgement seldom bestowed on her sex."

Through the mediation of friends he arranged to marry her and, soon after, she bore him a son whom they named Bassianus, after her father. Because this Syrian name translates into Latin roughly as "kiss arse", he was known by the nickname Caracalla, which means a long tunic or great coat – though it is not clear whether the garment was named after him or the other way around.

There is another confusion here, too. Ancient authors sometimes say that Bassianus was the son of Severus's first wife, Marciana, and that his second son, Geta, was the only child that Julia gave him. These sources also say that Caracalla "married" Julia, so whether he was Marciana's son or Julia's makes all the difference.

In Sicily, Severus was put on trial for consulting astrologers on whether he would become emperor. This was considered treason. He was acquitted, however, as Commodus was already becoming unpopular, and his accuser was executed.

The prefect of the Praetorian Guard, Aemilius Laetus, who had successfully conspired with Marcia to murder Commodus, recommended that Severus be given command of the army in Germany. From there he was all set to take over the empire when Julianus usurped the throne. Marching on Rome, he was greeted as the avenger of Pertinax.

Julianus did not give up easily though. Even when the army in Italy deserted him, he sent assassins to kill Severus, but these were intercepted and Julianus was murdered by one of his own men. Severus then sent his own assassins after Pescennius Niger, who had been proclaimed emperor by the legions in Syria, while Clodius Albinus had been picked in Britain. It was said that Severus's wife Julia helped foment both of these uprisings. *"Malo in consilio feminae vincunt viros,"* as the Latin saying has it.

Previously, Severus had praised Niger highly for disciplining the soldiers in Gaul when they had "turned their bedrooms into brothels". He was a tall, handsome man who "brushed his hair back gracefully toward the crown". However, his face was always ruddy because, according to his biographer, Aelius Spartianus, "he was very fond of wine, a sparing eater, and absolutely unacquainted with sex other than for begetting children". Indeed, he liked to participate in certain rites in Gaul where the person who was voted the chastest was lauded. Mind you, the deluded Commodus participated in similar rites.

Niger was a good soldier and would have served Severus well, if he had not been persuaded to make his own bid for imperial power by the ambitious Aurelianus, whose daughters were engaged to Niger's sons. Severus simply grabbed Niger's children and held them hostage until Niger himself was killed in battle.

The new emperor in Britain, Albinus, got his name from the fact that, rather than being a normal red, he was conspicuously white when he came from the womb – *albineus* means white in Latin. His claim to be emperor came from a letter from Commodus which gave him the right to call himself "Caesar", written, no doubt, when Commodus was having an off day and pretending to be an Amazon. *"Stultum facit fortuna quem vult perdere,"* as Publilicus Syrus had it.

Albinus was also given the right to wear imperial purple – though he refused these honours, infuriating Commodus, who began to favour Severus instead.

He was said to have been a great glutton and a great lover of fruit, eating at one sitting five hundred dried figs, 20 pounds of Labican grapes, ten Ostian melons, a hundred Campanian peaches, four hundred oysters and a hundred fig-peckers – no, not fruit penises but birds that peck figs. However, he was also said to be mean when it came to banquets, favouring quantity over quality.

He was thought to drink in moderation, though Severus claimed that he was drunk on wine even during battle.

"To his wife he was most hateful, to his slaves unjust, and he was brutal toward his soldiers," said Julius Capitolinus. "He often crucified centurions, even when they were on active service, although the charges against them did not require it. He never pardoned offences and those found guilty were frequently beaten with rods."

On the other hand, he was an elegant dresser, a leading lover and an accomplished womaniser. This was all the more remarkable as he had a high womanish voice that sounded almost like that of a eunuch. "But he remained innocent of unnatural sex and persecuted such practices," said Capitolinus.

Albinus was defeated in battle at Lugdunum (Lyon), though it was not recorded if he was *crapulentus* or not. He was dismembered. His wife and children were killed and their bodies were thrown in the Rhône, and the rest of his family was wiped out. The Senate had favoured Albinus and many senators also paid with their lives.

Just to annoy the Senate, Severus deified Commodus and had Narcissus, who had strangled him, thrown to the lions. Laetus was also killed, though Severus denied giving the order. Others were killed for making jokes, or for keeping silent, or for consulting astrologers about Severus's state of health.

When Severus was firmly in power, a woman turned up from Lepcis. She was barely able to speak Latin and Severus was very embarrassed about her presence. Nevertheless, her gave her numerous gifts and made her son a senator – then he told the two of them to return to their home town. They did and, soon after, the son died. We can only surmise that the woman was a former lover and that the son was the product of a youthful fling – such as the one that resulted in his trial for adultery. Severus then gave both his sons the name Antoninus – the adopted name of Marcus Aurelius – and, in doing so, effectively proclaimed that they would succeed him.

While Severus became famous for his cruelty, Julia kept her end up by becoming notorious for her adulteries. Gibbon said: "The great flattery of the learned has celebrated her virtues; but, if we may credit the scandal of ancient history, chastity was very far from being the most conspicuous virtue of the Empress Julia."

Her misdemeanours were brought to light by the prefect of the Praetorian Guard Gaius Fulvius Plautianius, a friend of Severus's from Africa. Plautianius brought specific charges against Julia and, in the course of the investigation, several Roman ladies were tortured on the orders of the emperor. The only charge that could be proved against her was that she had organised a scandalous gymnastics competition where, as in Ancient Sparta, the girls were to perform completely naked. Severus banned the repetition of any such event. *Podex*.

There was already bad blood between Plautianius and Julia. When they were out campaigning, Plautianius always seemed to have better quarters than Severus and once, when Plautianius fell ill and Severus went to visit him, Plautianius's men made the emperor enter alone, without his escort, seriously undermining his authority. Even Severus's own officials told him that they could not do certain things he wanted them to do unless they received orders from Plautianius.

Gossip circulated that Severus and Plautianius had been lovers. Severus even wrote in a letter: "I love that man so much I only pray that I die before him."

Plautianius's untrammelled power earned him the nickname "the fourth Caesar" – Severus and his two sons being the other three. He certainly acted like an emperor. According to Cassius Dio, Plautianius was a complete sensualist, gorging himself at banquets and freely indulging his lust with prostitutes of both sexes. So any accusation he levelled at Julia would have been a case of the pot calling the kettle black.

Meanwhile, Plautianius kept his wife more or less in purdah. Her male attendants were castrated and she was forbidden to see, or be seen, by anyone, including Severus and Julia. Julia particularly objected to this. She treated Plautianius with scorn. In response, he often abused her violently in front of Severus.

However, even before he pointed the finger at Julia, Plautianius had already overstepped the mark. A vain and ambitious man, he had had more buildings and statues erected in his own honour than were ascribed to Severus. Then, when Plautianius tried to have his own image placed among those of the imperial family, he quickly found himself in disgrace and all of his statues were demolished. Caracalla and Geta were particularly delighted to see the prefect, who had been a martinet, ousted from the palace. In celebration of Plautianius's downfall, they went on the rampage. The two lads "treated women shamefully, abused boys, embezzled money and hobnobbed with gladiators and charioteers", but a rivalry grew up between them and, during a fiercely contested chariot race, Caracalla fell and broke his leg.

Plautianius's disgrace did not last long, though. Severus had a soft spot for him. Even at the height of his unpopularity, those who called him a public enemy were banished. When he returned to favour, he murdered the other prefect and took sole control of the Praetorian Guard. Then, in AD 202, he married his daughter, Fulvia Plautilla, to Severus's son, Caracalla, who had recently been made co-emperor. However, Caracalla sided with Julia and refused to have sex with his new bride, no matter how much she, or her father, demanded it.

The following year, Plautianius became consul alongside Severus's other son, Geta, but Caracalla grew tired of his father-in-law's ambition. In 205, he suborned a centurion called Saturnius to warn Severus that Plautianius was planning to kill him. Severus believed the tale and sent for Plautianius. Realising that he was in mortal danger, Plautianius rushed to the palace so fast that the mule he was riding collapsed under him when he reached the palace courtyard. This was seen as an ill omen.

The emperor was disposed to be lenient. He merely chided Plautianius for his ingratitude and asked why he had wanted to kill him. Plautianius denied the accusations and would have got off if Caracalla had not leapt forward and struck him. Caracalla drew his sword and would have killed Plautianius there and then if Severus had not restrained him. But as Caracalla was co-emperor, Severus's hand had been forced. He called for a soldier to kill his favourite.

With Plautianius dead, Caracalla now aimed to kill his children – his own wife Plautilla and her brother Plautius. Severus, however, exiled them to the Lipari Islands instead – now called the Aeolian Islands – off the northeastern coast of Sicily, along with other supposed conspirators. Caracalla disposed of them later.

The charges against Julia were forgotten and she seems to have gotten away with her *improbitas* under the cloak of religion. She was, after all, the daughter of a priest of Jezebel's *improbus* fertility god Baal. In Greece, Julia was worshipped as Hera, the sister-wife of Zeus, or Demeter, another consort of Zeus who was responsible for fertility. A temple was erected to her in Aphrodisias in Caria, an ancient city in Anatolia, modern Turkey. The town of Plotinopolis in Thrace, northeast Greece, was renamed Domnopolis after her and, after Severus's corrupt successor Elagabalus deified her, she had a priestess of her very own in Naples.

The empress performed her religious "rites" with a small inner circle of women, who included her sister, the beautiful Julia Maesa, her nieces, Julia Soaemias and Julia Mamaea, and the respected woman philosopher Arria. A number of philosophers and intellectuals gathered around them.

"She was a patroness of every art, and a friend of every man of genius," said Gibbon.

Among them was Philostratus whom Julia commissioned to write the *Life of Apollonius*, based on the diaries of Apollonius Tyana's disciple Damis, which had fallen into Julia's hands. The *Life of Apollonius* bears a striking resemblance to the New Testament – complete with the annunciation, the virgin birth, a number of parables, lights being hidden under bushels, a St Peter-like figure in Damis himself and the preaching of forbearance for a woman caught in adultery.

After 18 years on the throne, Severus died in Eboracum, modern day York, in AD 211. He had, however, founded a new dynasty that ruled Rome for the next 24 years.

Mores Deteriores Increbescunt

Caracalla ruled jointly with his father from AD 198 to 211, then alone until 217 when he died. The son of a royal father, he fancied himself as the new Alexander the Great. And in the Senate he often praised the tyrants Sulla and Tiberius, giving them a hint of what they were in for.

Although Severus wanted Caracalla to rule jointly with his brother, he had Geta outlawed and then killed. He spread the rumour that Geta had tried to poison him and had been disrespectful to their mother, and he praised the men who had murdered him. Elements of the army were annoyed by the killing, saying that they had sworn allegiance to both the sons of Severus. Caracalla simply bought them off with huge bonuses. However, he soon found himself so unpopular that he found it necessary to wear a breastplate under his senatorial robes; when he addressed the Senate about his brother's supposed conspiracy, he took a military escort with him. Later, when he saw their mother and other women weeping over the death of Geta, he wanted to kill them and had to be held back. Then, Caracalla pretended to cry for Geta himself and had his murderers executed, along with those who sought honours for his dead brother.

Now we come to the allegation that Caracalla took Julia "as his wife". Even if she had been only his stepmother, this would have been illegal. Was Marciana his real mother? It is very difficult to make the dates work. Julia was a very beautiful and sexy woman, who was inordinately proud of her body. Feigning carelessness, she often let her robes fall open, exposing herself. Seeing her naked body, Caracalla was supposed to have said: "I would want to, if it was allowed."

And she was said to have replied: "If you wish it, it is allowed. Don't you realise that, as emperor, you make the laws and do not have to suffer under them?"

Apparently he took her at her word and married her – "adding incest to fratricide" to his indictment. Terrific though this story is, it ignores the fact that there is no dispute that Geta was her son. Would a woman, even a woman of Julia's dubious reputation, really marry a son or stepson who had killed her own flesh and blood – and who had wanted to kill her, too?

After the death of Geta, Caracalla went on a seemingly random killing spree. People were murdered at dinner and in the baths. It is estimated that he murdered some twenty thousand in all. Then he took his munificence out to the provinces. In Alexandria, he summoned the entire male populace to the gymnasium, then had them all slaughtered.

Caracalla was himself killed on the journey from Carrhae in Mesopotamia to Edessa – now Edhessa – in Greece when he got down from his horse to relieve his bladder. Other accounts suggest that he had a bad case of dysentery. For the sake of modesty, he kept his horse between himself and his bodyguards, who probably weren't too bothered anyway. This gave an assassin the opportunity to stab him to death.

Interestingly, Caracalla had been visiting Carrhae to prove his masculinity. The people there believed that whoever thought that the moon was feminine would be ruled by women and would always be subservient to them, while those who thought that the moon was masculine would dominate their wives and would not be won over by feminine wiles. The Romans worshipped Luna, the moon goddess. Caracalla, though, had been in Carrhae on his birthday to worship Lunus, the moon god. The Ancient Greeks also worshipped Luna, but called her a "god" – but then the Greeks were often confused over matters of gender.

The only good thing that Caracalla did during his reign was to complete the Caracalla Baths, which had been started by his father, Severus. They were the most luxurious baths in Rome and could accommodate one thousand six hundred bathers. More recently, they have been used as an open-air opera house, staging productions that require especially large casts such as Verdi's* *Aida* and Bizet's* *Carmen*. One can only hope that Caracalla liked singing in his baths.

Omnia Venalia Romae

Three days after the assassination of Caracalla, Marcus Opellius Macrinus was proclaimed emperor by the army. He was the first man to become emperor without achieving senatorial status first. Nevertheless, he loaded himself with titles and reigned as Caesar Marcus Opellius Severus Macrinus Augustus.

Although he was widely hated and was thought to be behind the murder of Caracalla, the Senate willingly accepted him as emperor, principally because Caracalla had been so unpopular.

"Anyone rather than the fratricide, anyone rather than the incestuous, anyone rather than the polluted, anyone rather than the murderer of the Senate and the people," went the cry. Snappy slogan.

However, there was one voice that spoke out against the low-born Macrinus. Aurelius Victor Pinio said that Macrinus had been a freedman under Commodus and a male prostitute who had been engaged in slave duties around the palace. In other words, he was one of Commodus's catamites.

"His honour was for sale and his life base," said Pinio.

Those words would have been enough to make an honourable Roman cringe, but given the emperors we've had so far, a bit of anal action on the *curriculum vitae* seems to have been the *sine qua non* for the position.

Under Severus, Macrinus had been dismissed and banished to Africa. After taking a series of lowly jobs, he worked his way up to being prefect of Caracalla's guard and, consequently, he would have been in the perfect position to have engineered his murder.

Although it was widely known that he was responsible for the death of Caracalla, Macrinus gave his own son Diadumenus the name Antoninus – Caracalla's adopted name – as if to deny the fact. Diadumenus Antoninus was also to rule at his side so that there would be an Antoninus on the team. Macrinus hoped that this would be enough to prevent any of the family of Antoninus Pius from rebelling against him. Meanwhile, Macrinus proclaimed that no one was "more fitted to avenge the murder of Bassianus" – Caracalla's real name – "than him, who would have been charged with punishing the conspiracy himself had he been able to detect it while he lived".

With Caracalla out of the way, though, no one was really bothered.

The Senate learnt very quickly that Macrinus was every bit as bad as Caracalla. He was arrogant and bloodthirsty and praised the strict rule of Severus. He crucified his own soldiers for minor offences and revelled in inflicting slaves' punishments on them. Faced with mutiny, he decimated his troops – that is, he killed one in ten of them. For mere grumbling, he only "centimated" them – that is, killed one in a hundred. This was merciful, he said, for troops who deserved to be decimated.

He was a stickler when it came to matters of sex, though. When he learnt that a number of his soldiers had had sex with a maidservant of their host, even though she had long had a reputation of being a good-time girl, he ordered two large oxen to be cut open and, without even asking the men whether the accusation was true, had them sewn up inside with their heads poking out so they could talk to each other as they died.

Julius Capitolinus commented: "Thus did he inflict a penalty on them, although punishments like this were not decreed even for adulteries by our ancestors or in these days."

While out fighting the Parthians in modern-day Iran, a tribune did not organise the watch properly. He was tied up and dragged under a wheeled carriage, at first alive and then dead. Floggings were frequent. Macrinus also reintroduced an ancient punishment of the Etruscan tyrant Mezentius, where a live person was tied to a corpse and left to die "consumed by slow putrefaction".

Runaway slaves were sentenced to sword fights in the arena at the games, where they were certain to die at the hands of the gladiators. Live men had walls built on top of them. Informers who did not prove their case were executed; those who did were given money and then sent away in disgrace. The worst punishment, though, was reserved for those caught in adultery. The couple would be bound together and then burnt to death. Macrinus was so sadistic that his own slaves called him *Macellinus* – "the butcher" – because the walls of his house were drenched with the blood of his household slaves and resembled a slaughterhouse.

On the other hand, he liked to hold banquets with literary men and refrained from drinking wine while discussing intellectual matters. However, he was greedy and if he had no literary guests in the evening, he would get roaring drunk.

Such human foibles did not save him. His cruelty was such that, after only 14 months in power, his men deserted him and his son Diadumenus Antoninus. Diadumenus was not much better than his father and it was said that he was only an Antoninus in his dreams. A satirical verse circulated about this:

> This too we saw in our dreams, unless I'm mistaken,
> Citizens: that boy the Antonine name had taken.
> Born of a father corrupt, but a chaste mother;

A hundred lovers she had, and chased a hundred others.
The bald head too was one, her spouse to be,
A Pius, a Marcus – Verus never he!

Macrinus, being a literary man, composed a riposte. Unfortunately it was lost in the coup that ousted him.

Diadumenus was a tall, good-looking boy. The biographer Aelius Lampridius said that he had "blond hair, black eyes, an aquiline nose, a chin shaped with all comeliness and a mouth ready for kisses". When a horoscope was drawn up for the infant and the astrologer proclaimed that he was the son of an emperor and an emperor himself, it was assumed that his mother, Nonis Celsa, had committed adultery, but he did grow up to become the son of an emperor and an emperor himself – but only for just over a year. Diadumenus was killed in the rebellion that his father Macrinus's sadism had provoked.

Early in his imperial career, Macrinus had made a fatal misjudgement. He had banished Julia Domna's sister, Julia Maesa, from Rome. She went back to Syria. Like Domna, she was well known for advancing her cause through her amorous intrigues, as were her two daughters Julia Soaemias and Julia Mamaea. Soaemias married Sextus Varius Marcellus. They had a son, called Varius Avitus Bassianus, who was known variously as Heliogabalus or Elagabalus.* When the army deserted Macrinus, it was Elagabalus that they turned to. Macrinus and Diadumenus fled with a small band of supporters. They were defeated in battle near Antioch, modern Antakya in Turkey, and subsequently were captured and executed. Meanwhile, Mamaea married Gessis Marcianus and gave birth to Gessius Bassianus Alexianus, who, as Severus Alexander, was to be Elagabalus's successor.

CHAPTER 15

According to the historian Charles Reginald Dawes, Elagabalus*
came to power because he was gay:

> The licentiousness and luxury of the army under Septimus Severus was
> notorious and at the time of Elagabalus, the soldiers were given up to
> every kind of vice, especially homosexuality. Indeed, it is stated that the
> beauty of Elagabalus and the unrestrained exercise of his all-pervading
> passion for pederasty so endeared him to the soldiers – who were
> themselves violently addicted to it – that they forthwith placed him
> upon the throne of the world.

That was not the whole story, though. Born Varius Avitus Bassianus in
Emesa, now Homs, Syria, Elagabalus was, like Julia Domna, one of the
family of the hereditary priest of the fertility god Baal, who was
worshipped locally as the sun-god Elah-Gabal. The boy became
identified with the god, so he was called Elagabalus in Latin and
Heliogabalus in Greek. In the name of the sun-god Elah-Gabal he
worshipped the phallus, both symbolically and in day-to-day life. His
sun worship also involved him acting as much like a lady as possible. He
was, it was said, "a prince who imbibed pleasure through all the cavities
of his body".

When the army deserted Macrinus, Elagabalus was just 14 years old
and spent his days "dancing indolently to the kiss of flutes". These were
played in the temple by scantily clad – if not naked – dancing girls. The

rites of his religion, Sol Invicta – also known as *Sol Cula* – were also said to include "a chorus of Syrian damsels performing lascivious dances to the sound of barbarian music". As priest, Elagabalus was not supposed to have been turned on by this. He was encouraged to dress and act in a feminine way while this tempting troupe danced around him.

A description of Elagabalus said that in his face was the "enigmatic beauty of gods and girls – the charm of the dissolute and the wayward, heightened by the divine". Surviving portraits show that he was very good looking. The third-century Syrian historian Herodian, who wrote in Greek, said: "In the flower of his youth, in beauty he surpassed all others of the same age. Since he combined youth, beauty and fine dress, he made men think of a beautiful picture of the young Bacchus."

He wore a crown on his head and a semi-transparent purple and gold tunic, whose "fine silk texture clung closely to his body and, swayed by his movements, revealed more than it obscured". He borrowed these translucent frocks from his mother, who had used them to delight her lovers – among whom, it was said, he was one.

The temple of Baal, where he presided, was large and opulent. It contained no statue or image of Elah-Gabal, only a large, black, stone phallus "which had fallen from above". This, plainly, was a dick-shaped meteorite. On it, it was said, if you looked closely, you could make out an image of Elah-Gabal, the Sun. *El Gabal* is the Arabic for a mountain or a high place, but it refers here to the phallus-shaped stone that came from a high place. So it might be fair to say then that Elagabalus was a *mentula*. He was also convinced that he was a god.

As a god, he was supposed to embody both the male and the female in one single divine being. There was no denying that he had the body of a boy, but, being effeminate in appearance, he thought of himself as a girl. This was no mere whim. It was part of his religion, but perhaps he got in touch with his feminine side slightly too much and could have done with a dash more male.

Before the death of Caracalla, a handful of his men passed through Emesa and, seeing Elagabalus, took him to be Eros, the god of love and the son of Aphrodite in Greek mythology. News of his beauty spread, bringing more soldiers to see him. Herodian described the scene: "When he did sacrifice and danced in the foreign way around the altar to the sound of flutes, pipes and other instruments, he took the eyes of all men – especially of soldiers, who knew that he was of royal birth. His youthful beauty fascinated those who saw him ... The soldiers used to come to the city often and, visiting the temple to attend service there, took pleasure in watching the young man."

A rumour soon spread that he was actually the son of Caracalla.

His grandmother, Julia Maesa, had stayed in Rome during the reign of Caracalla. During that period she had amassed great wealth. She was an ambitious woman and she might easily have persuaded her daughter to ingratiate herself with cousin Caracalla, who was already having it off with her aunt.

Under Macrinus, Julia Maesa had been banished and returned to Emesa. Seeing the effect that her young grandson had on disaffected Roman soldiers, she would easily have spotted her main chance. A young man variously known as Eutychianus and Gannys, a talented gymnast who had been brought up in her household, noticed that Elagabalus looked at lot like Caracalla who, now having proved to be not nearly as bad as Macrinus, was becoming popular again, particularly as he had allowed his men a certain amount of licence, especially in sexual matters. Julia Maesa did not hesitate to sacrifice the reputation of her daughter and claim that Elagabalus was, in fact, the son of Caracalla. Julia Soaemias's husband, Sextus Varius Marcellus, was a nonentity whose reputation could be discounted. Besides, Julia Soaemias was a woman of remarkable beauty and allure, and was already notorious for "granting her favours indiscriminately for the satisfaction of her own lust". Gannys himself, it seems, was one of her lovers and she was perfectly willing to go along with the story that she had had Elagabalus by Caracalla, as it might lead to power.

There may even have been some truth in this. Julia Soaemias was the type of assertive and lascivious woman that Caracalla would have fancied, and cousin sleeping with cousin was par for the course in imperial circles. Caracalla famously burnt to death a Vestal Virgin – not because she had broken her oath by surrendering her virginity, but because she had refused him. The poor girl protested the sentence on the grounds that she was perfectly willing to undergo the deflowering, but that he had failed to get *capulus rigidus* because Julia Soaemias had worn him out.

So Caracalla could well have been Elagabalus's father. However, an even bigger question mark has been raised over his paternity. The writer Aelius Lampridius suggested that Elagabalus – that is, Varius Avitus Bassianus – was given the name Varius by his schoolmates because his paternity was, well, various. A large number of gentlemen, it seems, contributed to the making of Julia Soaemias's child.

"She lived like a whore and practised baseness of all kinds," said Lampridius. "He was conceived by the seed of 'various' gentlemen, as happens with a whore."

Julia Maesa was enormously wealthy and showered gold on everyone who believed that Caracalla was Elagabalus's dad. This provoked the army to desert the emperor and rally to the young priest. Macrinus and Diadumenus were disposed of and, by the time he was 15, Elagabalus was Emperor of Rome, under the name Caesar Marcus Aurelius Antoninus Augustus.

Syrian male prostitutes already had a reputation in Rome and Elagabalus's family were famed as swingers. The Roman emissaries who visited him were captivated. It was said: "He charmed and fascinated all those in any way susceptible who came into contact with him … The soft, feminine delicacy and grace of his form and features, and his girlish beauty, is admitted by all, even his severest detractors."

After being proclaimed emperor, Elagabalus made his way at a leisurely pace towards Rome, hauling his great black stone penis with him. He wintered in Nicomedia in Asia Minor, where he "forced men to couple with him, and had himself possessed by them". It was said that he identified himself so much with his promiscuous mother that he wanted to know what it felt like to be penetrated by one man after another, and he fell into a bout of buggery and fellatio. He did this quite openly. Herodian said that Elagabalus "had no wish to sin in secret. He appeared in public with his eyes made up and rouged cheeks."

Although Elagabalus was not cruel or sadistic like Caligula or Nero, he murdered his mother's lover Gannys at Nicomedia, either fearing that he was becoming too powerful or simply out of jealousy. Killing her lover did not turn mommy dearest against him, though. It was said that, in bed, Gannys was no rival for Elagabalus himself. What mere man could hope to compete with a god? As well as being her son's lover, she also acted as his pander for the rest of his short life.

Rome knew what it was getting. In Nicomedia he had a full-length, life-sized portrait painted, showing him dressed in a flowing priest's robe and adorned with female jewellery. This was sent to Rome and hung in the Senate, where it was treated with due deference. When Elagabalus turned up in the Eternal City, though, accompanied by his family and symbols of his divinity, in the late spring of AD 219, he outshone even this image. He wore his see-through purple robe and was smothered with jewellery. A gem-ladened tiara flashed on his head. Great chains of pearls hung around his neck and costly bracelets graced his arms. And with his cheeks rouged and his eyebrows pencilled, he looked every inch a Syrian actress or courtesan. This was the new ruler of the world. No one, not even Caligula, had been quite this wacky.

Elagabalus had no interest in politics or power. He was, after all, a god. The business of government he left to his grandmother. He devoted himself to two things – his religion and homosexual love, which for him were basically the same thing. For him, to be emperor meant the unrestrained indulgence of his sexual fantasies.

As the worship of Elah-Gabal and the black stone was essentially phallic worship, he worshipped phalluses wherever he went. And he was enterprising. According to his biographer, Aelius Lampridius, he "devised different kinds of voluptuousness, excelling in this respect even the inventors of the spintrian postures familiar to the ancient emperors, for he certainly knew the refinements of Tiberius, Caligula and Nero".

"Spintrian" is defined by Thomas Blount's *Glossographia* of 1656 as "pertaining to those that seek out, or invent, new and monstrous actions of lust".

Cassius Dio said: "At night he would enter some low tavern, where, with false hair, he fulfilled the functions of a tavern girl. He resorted to the famous lupanars" – brothels – "where, after having evicted the courtesans, he gave himself up to prostitution, judging his own beauty by how much gold he took home. Finally, he established an apartment in the palace where he abandoned himself to incontinence, standing quite naked at the door of the chamber, like the prostitutes, drawing the curtain which was hung on rings of gold, and inviting passers-by with the effeminate voice of the courtesans. He had men there charged to let themselves be enticed. And, as for other things, he had for that purpose a host of emissaries whose occupation it was to seek out those who, by their lasciviousness and sexual power, could give him most pleasure. He drew money from them, and glorifying in his gains, was constantly in discussion with his companions in debauchery, pretending to have more lovers and to have earned more money than they had."

As well as donning the blonde wig of a whore, he liked to play act. His favourite role was that of Venus, or rather Aphrodite, in the "judgement of Paris" – where the Trojan hero Paris is charged by Zeus to determine which of the three goddesses, Hera, Athena or Aphrodite, is the most beautiful. He rejects the bribe of kingly power offered by Hera, and the military might offered by Athena. Instead he chooses Aphrodite, who promises to help him win the most beautiful woman alive. This turns out to be Helen, whom Paris abducts, starting the Trojan War.

In Elagabalus's tableau the action was pared down, with the emperor playing Aphrodite and Helen rolled into one. He would appear on stage, then, suddenly, all his clothes would fall to his feet. He would stand there naked in the classic pudic pose, with one hand placed across his "breasts" and the other covering his private parts. Then, according to Aelius Lampridius, he would kneel, naked, "with his buttocks projecting and thrust back on the front of his debaucher". Afterwards he would pose again as Aphrodite in the tableau, but this time he would expose his body, which was smooth and depilated with the hair removed from every part.

He also enjoyed watching theatrical performances, but ordered that the scenes of adultery that were normally simulated in Roman farces should be performed on stage for real.

With a constant desire for new lovers, he had public baths constructed in the imperial palace. This was open to the people and he bathed there himself, so that he could see the other men nude and choose those he liked the best. He was not selfish in his pleasures, though.

"He provided brothels at his house for his friends, clients and slaves," said Aelius Lampridius. And he reintroduced mixed bathing which had been banned under Hadrian. It seems that he liked seeing women naked, as long as they were young and beautiful. One of his extravagances was to be carried around the city in a gilded and bejewelled carriage drawn by teams of naked women, whose straining buttocks he would whip. He would have them halt, so that he could pick up a well-endowed boy or comment on a flower shop's riotous display. If he alighted, an attendant would have to sprinkle gold dust on the ground before him. He objected to treading on common-or-garden earth like ordinary mortals. And it was not just his feet that could not be sullied. He evacuated his bowels into a golden bowl and urinated into a vessel made of onyx.

He would take pity on prostitutes, buy them from their pimps and set them free. It was said that he had bought a famously beautiful prostitute for a hundred thousand sesterces – $8,000 – and "kept her untouched like a virgin". Money was no object. He often tore up expensive clothes and would not wear the same shoes – or even the same ring – twice, although he was happy to wander around the palace nude except for some exotic perfume.

Once it came up in discussion how many men with hernias there were in Rome. He ordered that all such men be marked out and put on display at the baths. He also searched the seedier districts of town and the riverfront along the Tiber, where sailors congregated for what he called "onobeli" – men built along the same lines as Commodus's *Onos*. It was said that Elagabalus "preferred men whose sole merit was their genital calibre and their amorous strength".

He was extremely fond of athletes and charioteers because of their powerful bodies. Two in particular – Protogenes and Cordius – "were mentioned among the companions of his voluptuousness". It was said generally, though, that "all those whose bodies pleased him, the most robust and best set up, he transferred from the circus and the arena to the palace".

Big men who were "vigorously constituted" were raised to high positions. When three ministers – the prefect of the city, the prefect of the watch and the prefect of provisions – were appointed solely for the huge size of their sexual organs, a saying from Petronius did the rounds: "It profits a man more to develop his penis than to develop his mind."

Elagabalus sent out emissaries to scour the empire for men with *mentulae magnae*. Finding an enormous specimen would earn the discoverer an enormous finder's fee. The find was then returned to Rome, where he would immediately be invited to visit the imperial baths so that the emperor could inspect the goods. If the man measured up, he would be invited to share the imperial bed. And when the emperor's lust was satisfied, the finder would earn a performance-related bonus.

On the other hand, things could go disastrously wrong, as in the case of Aurelius Zoticus, the son of a cook or master baker from Smyrna – modern Izmir in Turkey. As a youth, Zoticus had been an athlete and a wrestler, and had a very beautiful body. According to Cassius Dio, he also "surpassed all the world in the largeness of his private parts". Naturally, he came to the attention of Elagabalus's talent scouts, who whisked him off to Rome. Zoticus was received with all the regal pomp and dignity the city could offer, and he was given the title *cubucularius* – or gentleman of the bedchamber – before the emperor had even seen him, simply on the strength of his reputation.

Garlanded with flowers, he entered the imperial palace accompanied by a torchlit procession. Setting eyes on him for the first time, the emperor did a little dance for joy. Then Zoticus bowed low and said: "Hail, emperor, my master."

Elagabalus inclined his head gracefully like a girl and, with half-closed eyes, said: "Do not call me master. I am your mistress."

Zoticus was then whipped off to the baths, where Elagabalus found that he was everything he had been cracked up to be. The sight of Zoticus's naked appendage sent Elagabalus's ardour soaring to new peaks. Reclining on the cook's son's lap, he "supped upon his bosom like a love-sick girl".

However, Elagabalus was not exactly unattached. His favourite, Hierocles, grew jealous, so got his chums among the cupbearers to slip Zoticus a potion that "enervated him completely, and prevented his wonderful physique from being any use for the intended purpose of the emperor, who toiled and sweated in vain to achieve his desire". Discredited, Zoticus was stripped of all the gifts and honours Elagabalus had bestowed on him. He was chased out of the palace and kicked out of Rome, eventually having to flee Italy in disgrace to save his life. That, at least, was the story as Cassius Dio told it.

According to Aelius Lampridius, Zoticus was anything but incapable. He and Elagabalus got married and the emperor "submitted to the carnal act" while the bridesmaids – or rather bridesmen – cried out: "Push away, cook-boy," a reference to his father's profession.

However, it appears there was one show only. Once Zoticus performed the office which he had been brought to Rome for, Hierocles and the cupbearers' potions got to him. Lampridius said that Zoticus "was passionately loved and then hated by the emperor" – which was taken to mean that after whetting the emperor's appetite he found that he could not repeat the performance. And so the fair-haired Hierocles remained "the one romance of Elagabalus's life".

Hierocles was a slave from Caria in southwest Anatolia, who had risen to fame as a charioteer. According to Cassius Dio, one day at the circus, he was thrown from his chariot and landed against the *pulvinar* – that is, the ornate couch that the emperor reclined on. Hierocles lost his helmet, so Elagabalus could admire his beardless profile and his curly blond hair. Also because "the tunic had been upturned in the fall", the emperor could also see "certain other attributes with which the youth was bountifully supplied".

The missing helmet having been found, Elagabalus ordered that Hierocles be carried to the palace where, as Cassius Dio put it, he "still further enthralled the emperor by his nocturnal work". One nineteenth-century writer put it more romantically.

"On account of a similarity of taste," he said, "the intimacy soon ripened into love."

Cassius Dio reported that Elagabalus liked Hierocles so much that he "came into such a favour and was raised to such power that he had authority superior even to that of the emperor himself".

"Hierocles had abundant fair hair, a skin that was fair and smooth, fine features and glistening eyes, but to these somewhat effeminate traits were added the figure of a giant and the form of an athlete," ran one description. And of the meeting at the circus, the same author said: "Elagabalus had him carried off, all covered with sweat and dust; then, on emerging from the bath, he installed him in his own bedchamber, and on the morrow solemnly espoused him."

Not content with a clandestine affair, Elagabalus formally married Hierocles, who then became recognised as the "husband" of the emperor. This was no passing passion. Elagabalus refused all entreaties to give him up, saying that he would rather die first.

Cassius Dio said: "His affection for his lover was not a casual impulse, but a strong and deeply-rooted love." It also had a masochistic edge.

"Harsh treatment did not rouse his indignation, but rather increased his passion; he wished to give his lover the title of Caesar."

According to Aelius Lampridius, Elagabalus proclaimed his love for all to see by kissing Hierocles's private parts in public in a way "which it is indecent even to mention ... declaring that in his way, he celebrated the Floralia, or the festival of the goddess of spring, fecundity, rejuvenation and love". Hierocles, for his part, seemed not only proud of his newfound position, but also of the emperor's love for him, and stayed with him until the end.

Elagabalus was not faithful to his "husband". He was not the sort of man who would be content with one lover – indeed, he was as unfaithful as he could be, so much so that Hierocles would take it out on his hide.

"To more faithfully imitate the most libertine of women," it was said, "he committed adultery, for which he was beaten and punished by his husband."

Elagabalus organised his affairs deliberately so that he would be caught in the very act by Hierocles, who would then beat him and maltreat him for his infidelity. One of Elagabalus's favourite tricks was to be caught prostituting himself in one of Hierocles's favourite brothels; his actions were intended to produce a violent reaction and he would often appear in public with cuts, bruises and black eyes that would take days to disappear. However, that did not calm his desire for well-endowed men to be brought in from every province of the empire. Nor did it stop him from encouraging the rest of his entourage from entering into same-sex marriages.

Elagabalus loved to shave off the hair from his lovers' sexual parts with his own hand, and afterwards used the same razor to shave his own beard. He had himself carefully depilated, with all the hairs removed from every part of his body so that he "more closely resembled a woman and so that he could present himself all smooth and soft to his lovers".

He had been circumcised when he reached puberty. Some sources say that he had also been castrated, but that does not seem to have been the case. Many followers of Sol Invicta circumcised themselves, or castrated themselves and threw their severed sexual organs into the temple. At one point, it seems that Elagabalus did tie up his genitals ready for the chop, but that he then thought better of it.

The second-century Greek writer Lucian recorded one of these self-mutilation rites:

At the beginning of the spring, when the multitudes thronged to the sanctuary from Syria ... the flutes played, the drums beat and the eunuch priests slashed themselves with knives; the religious excitement spread like a wave among the crowd of onlookers, and many a one did that which he little thought to do when he came as a holiday spectator to the festival. For man after man, his veins throbbing with the music, his eyes fascinated by the sight of streaming blood, flung his garments from him, leapt forth with a shout, and, seizing one of the swords which stood ready for the purpose, castrated himself on the spot. Then he ran through the city, holding the bloody pieces in his hand until he threw them into one of the houses he passed in his mad dash. The household honoured this way had to give him an outfit of women's clothes and female adornments, which he wore for the rest of his life.

Ubi signo?

It was said that, like Nero's Sporus, Elagabalus wanted the doctors to cut an incision in his body, making an artificial vagina, so that he could be a hermaphrodite and truly experience what it was like to be both a man and a woman. However, it seems that this was not done.

Elagabalus also married a number of women. His first wife, Julia Cornelia Paula, was forced on him by his grandmother for political reasons. The wedding took place in July AD 219, soon after he had arrived in Rome. Royal weddings – then as now – were designed to make monarchs popular. Marrying a Roman woman made Elagabalus seem less like a strange foreigner. It also gave him a chance to distribute money to the populace, which was a Roman wedding custom. However, he was interested in neither the domestic side of life nor in procreating with women. None of his marriages bore fruit. He was too interested in being a *fructus* and practising his religion, that is, worshipping the phallus. In late 220 or at the beginning of 221, he divorced Julia Cornelia Paula. The reason given was that she had a secret blemish on her body. Apparently, it had taken her inattentive husband eighteen months to find it.

His second wife, Aquila Severa, was a Vestal Virgin.

"It is an appropriate act of religion for a priest to marry a priestess," he said.

The wedding would marry the cult of the sun to the cult of Vesta. Sol Invicta would then penetrate deeply into Roman spiritual life. Their union, he maintained, would produce a demi-god. There was little chance of that. Elagabalus did not even pick a pretty Vestal and, judging by her surviving portrait, Aquila Severa was no longer in the first flush of youth.

Their marriage did not unite their religions as Elagabalus had planned. It only succeeded in getting the Romans' backs up. By marrying a Vestal Virgin – even if he was not much of a threat to her virginity – he had violated all that the Romans had held holy for centuries. His wily grandmother, Julia Maesa, quickly managed to persuade the emperor to dissolve his marriage to Aquila Severa. Later that year, the now deeply unpopular Elagabalus married Annia Faustina, a granddaughter of Marcus Aurelius, in the hope that some of the lustre of his illustrious forebear would rub off. He was 18 and she was around 45, but she was a friend of his granny and recently widowed. Cassius Dio thought that Elagabalus was to blame, however. He said: "The inhuman monster would not allow Annia Faustina to spoil her beauty by weeping for her departed husband."

His marriage to Annia Faustina was also a symbolic marriage between Sol Invicta and the popular Carthaginian fertility cult of Dea Caelestis, which was closely tied to the sexy cults of Bon Dea and Dea Syria. The sacred image of the goddess Tanit was brought from North Africa for the ceremony. At the wedding, Roman senators and knights found themselves standing around in silken robes, watching the sacred dances of the young emperor surrounded by women of dubious character while men's severed wedding tackle was flung into the *Elagabalium*. This seemed to them both primitive and barbaric. If that was not bad enough, Elagabalus then began sacrificing children – "boys that were noble and good looking and had fathers and mothers still living". Aelius Lampridius said: "He inspected the children's innards and tortured the victims according to his own native ritual."

He often dressed as a woman and pretended to be one – to the point of hanging out among the women at the baths, swapping depilatory ointment. Even though he thought of himself as one of the girls, it is hard to see how he could have delivered a wholly convincing performance. You can only take a drag act so far. You can't be a female impersonator in a nudist colony. But they humoured him, allowing him to apply depilatory lotion on their pudenda, while using the same cream on his own beard.

Convening a large gathering of male and female prostitutes, and their pimps, he greeted the women in a woman's dress, then changed to welcome the men in the costume of a male prostitute. Addressing those assembled as "comrades", he lectured them on "postures and pleasures". Afterwards, he opened a discussion on all forms of lasciviousness and lust. It is not recorded whether he learned anything new. Finally, he gave each of them three gold coins in the way that other emperors might have rewarded their soldiers, then "asked them to pray to the gods that he might have others to commend to them". On another occasion, he went around Rome in disguise giving prostitutes gold pieces and receiving no service from them in return.

He swore constantly and made obscene gestures, and was equally immodest at both private receptions and public events. With a complete contempt for decency, he would receive guests while he was in bed with a lover and ask revered and dignified senators whether they enjoyed the particular form of sex that he was largely addicted to. When he travelled, he was accompanied by six hundred carriages filled with women, passive boy-prostitutes and active predators to minister to his pleasures. At banquets, he would fondle those next to him. He would often throw off all his clothes, except for rare items of costly jewellery that adorned various parts of his anatomy, and dance naked. The other guests were urged to follow his example and the feast would quickly degenerate into an orgy of nudity and homosexual lust.

He might have hosted a banquet serving, say, the brains of six hundred ostriches as just one of 22 courses. Between each course, he and his guests would bathe, then have intercourse with women – after which they would have to take an oath saying that they derived pleasure from it.

The Romans were not necessarily appalled by Elagabalus's sexual conduct – they were used to their emperors behaving that way – but they were offended by the foreign religion he was trying to foist on them. The Senate watched in horror as foreigners and men of lower rank achieved high office thanks to their sexual prowess. He further undermined their power by raising his mother and grandmother to senatorial rank and setting up a *senaculum*, or women's Senate, on the Quirinal Hill, with powers that rivalled their own.

Then Elagabalus contrived to make things even worse. He divorced Annia Faustina, whose kinship to Marcus Aurelius lent him some sort of legitimacy, and took two unnamed women as wives. The only reason for Elagabalus to take a wife, Aelius Lampridius said, was for companionship or as "a strumpet who could increase his knowledge of her art".

Given his proclivities, there is some dispute over how real these marriages were. Aelius Lampridius was sure that the marriages were consummated as he reckoned that Elagabalus swung both ways.

"He never had the same woman twice," Lampridius said, "except for his wife."

Given his belief in his own divinity, Elagabalus would only have sex with someone – at least as the active partner – once, no matter how pleasurable the encounter had been. According to Ovid's *Metamorphoses*, when a god gives himself to a human, it is a once and once-only experience.

Cassius Dio said that, after divorcing Annia Faustina, Elagabalus took back Aquila Severa, either as his wife or as his concubine. To defile a Vestal Virgin once, in the heat of passion, was bad enough, but to do it twice was a slap in the face for the Roman establishment. They began to switch their allegiance to the son of Julia Maesa's other daughter, the beautiful and alluring Julia Mamaea. As she had also had an affair with Caracalla, her son, Alexander, could also claim imperial blood.

Born Gessius Alexianus Bassianus, Mamaea changed his name to Marcus Aurelius Alexander, then persuaded Elagabalus to adopt him as his heir and added "Caesar" to her son's moniker. She also sheltered the boy from the emperor's excesses and took Julius Paulus, the father of Elagabalus's first wife, Julia Cornelia Paula, as his tutor. Julia Maesa then spread money around to ensure the popularity of the young Alexander, and soon everyone, including the army who had put him on the throne, turned against Elagabalus.

"They were disgusted when they saw his face made up more elaborately than any honest woman's," wrote Herodian, "and himself effeminately ornamented with golden necklaces and dainty clothes, dancing for all the world to see. So their minds began to incline toward Alexander: they placed more hope in him, because he had been decently and soberly brought up."

When Elagabalus realised that the boy was a rival, he tried to have him killed. This was too much for the Praetorian Guard, who had had to look on while the emperor indulged himself in every kind of vice. They turned on him. First his "associates in lewdness" were killed – "some they slaughtered by tearing out their vitals," said Aelius Lampridius, "and others they pierced up the anus, so that their death fitted their lives."

Hierocles was castrated and anally abused with a sword. Others of the emperor's circle were thrown to the mob who tore them to pieces.

Elagabalus fled. He and his mother were found cowering in the latrine outside the palace where they were killed. Their bodies were beheaded and thrown to the mob, who dragged them through the streets. After an unsuccessful attempt to push them down a sewer, whose opening proved too narrow, they were thrown in the Tiber. The 14-year-old Alexander then came to power as Marcus Aurelius Severus Alexander. His first act was to send Elagabalus's big black *facula* back to Emesa.

Dextra Mihi Deus

Alexander was too much under his mother's thumb to assert himself. When he was of age, she married him off to Sallustia Barbia Orbiana, the daughter of an impeccable aristocratic family. He was well satisfied with the choice and the couple lived happily together, but there was tension between mother and daughter-in-law. Mamaea became jealous when Alexander made Orbiana Augusta, raising her to the rank of Mamaea, who had been given the title when Alexander came to power. Then the mild-mannered Alexander proposed conferring the title of Caesar on Orbiana's father, Lucius Seius Sallustius. He was an old man and there was little chance of him succeeding Alexander, but Mamaea grew afraid that Alexander was favouring his wife's family over his own.

Mamaea drove Orbiana out of the palace and she went back home to her father in tears. Together they went to the Praetorian Guard, asking for their support against the emperor's mother and for help to avenge the insult to the emperor's wife. Alexander was put in a position where he had to choose between his mother and his wife. He chose his mother. He rode with supporters to the barracks. Waverers resumed their allegiance to the emperor; Orbiana and her father were arrested. Sallustius was executed straight away. The marriage was dissolved and Orbiana was banished to Africa, where she was later put to death. Alexander married again. His second wife, Memmia, was also picked by Mamaea, but was sensible enough to turn down the title of Augusta. They may have had a child that died young, but it seems as though it was a passionless marriage with Alexander constantly being nagged for spending too much time in the baths.

Soon there was trouble in the East. The king of one of Alexander's client states, Alsawad, was being besieged in a fortress by the Persian emperor Artaxerxes. The defenders resisted stoutly, but Artaxerxes knew that Alsawad had a daughter and proposed marriage to the princess. Alsawad rejected the proposal, but the princess herself quite fancied being Empress of Persia. By means of a note tied to an arrow, Artaxerxes got a message to her saying that if she let him know where the weakest part of the defences was, he would break in and make her his bride. She responded favourably and, after a volley of messages settling terms, she told him what he wanted to know.

Armed with the knowledge supplied by the princess, Artaxerxes stormed the fortress and took it. Good to his word, he married the princess, but soon he tired of her and set a simple trap for her. He asked her how her father had treated her. She said that her father had loved her more than anything in the world and that he had never given her the least cause for displeasure.

"Then you are unworthy to live," said Artaxerxes. "If you have betrayed your father who loved you and gave you not the least cause for displeasure, what fidelity can I expect from you? I will not expose myself to your treachery and you must be punished for the way you treated your father."

With that, he tied her by the hair to a wild horse, which galloped off at full speed, tearing the poor girl to pieces.

Taking Alsawad's fort provided Artaxerxes with a base from which he could invade Mesopotamia. Alexander counter-attacked, but was defeated in battle. Even so, the heavy losses suffered by the Persians forced them to withdraw.

Next Alexander went to Germany where the Alemanni tribe were attacking. He was not a popular figure with the army. By this time he was a dour character and had taken to praying to Christian statues, even though he did not understand the religion. Somewhat self-righteously, he tried to shame wrongdoers and stamp out homosexuality in the army. This alienated him even further from his troops. In AD 235, his sister's father-in-law, Maximinus, led a rebellion. Mamaea went to quell it and was cut down. When he heard this, Alexander knew it was all over. He was killed by swords that were still wet with his mother's blood.

After that things really came apart, with a succession of would-be emperors seizing power and losing it again. There were six emperors in AD 238 alone. Many did not hold on to power long enough for much to have been recorded about their private lives, and many spent their time fighting for their lives rather than enjoying the sexual side of them.

CHAPTER 16

T hings did not really settle down again until Valerian, who reigned from AD 253 to 260. This allowed his son Gallienus, who reigned from 260 to 268, to indulge himself as a youth. It was said that Gallienus "revived the luxury of the most effeminate emperors". His food was served on gold plates, encrusted with precious stones. His robes and shoes were covered with jewels and, like Lucius Verus the Younger, he powdered his hair with gold dust.

"He was so voluptuous and extravagant that he despised all ordinary pleasures, being delighted with nothing but what was difficult to be obtained, and he would eat no fruit but such as was out of its natural season," says one learned tome. "He did not limit his pleasures to these whims and fancies, but plunged into all those shameful debaucheries that are most apt to debilitate both body and mind."

"*Semper tibi pendeat hamus*," as Ovid enjoined.

His younger brother, named Valerian after his father, was also a bit *pulchri*: "In person he was perfectly well proportioned, had an agreeable countenance, and something so civil and affable in his behaviour that he won the hearts of all who approached him."

If you are good looking and charming you can get away with anything – and, it seems, Valerian did.

Realising how debauched his two sons were becoming, the Emperor Valerian decided to marry them off to two sisters from the town of Clazomenae in Ionia – Cornelia Supera and Cornelia Salonina.

Salonina, the wife of Gallienus, was beautiful, virtuous and well read. She gave her husband numerous children. He was named Caesar and she was honoured as an empress. However, even though marriage had weaned him away from the gay vices of his youth, he now became an inveterate womaniser, much to the displeasure of both his parents and his wife. Their constant nagging ultimately turned Gallienus against his father.

This divided the ruling family at the very moment when the empire was under attack again from the East. In 260, Valerian's army was ambushed by the great Persian despot Shapur I and was cut down. Valerian and his wife Mariniana were deliberately misused and humiliated. Shapur used the Roman emperor as a human footstool. When Shapur wanted to mount his horse, Valerian was forced to get down on all fours so that Shapur could step on his back.

With Valerian in that position, Shapur ruled that any citizen in his kingdom, down to the lowest beggar or leper, had the right to sodomise him. It has also been suggested that dogs were allowed to mount him from behind. Mariniana was treated in much the same way, often within sight of her husband. This went on for many years, until Valerian died of old age. His skin was then stripped from his body, decorated with coloured inks and hung in the Persian emperor's apartments. By this time, it is thought, Mariniana had also been relieved of her suffering.

While the capture of Valerian and Mariniana horrified the empire, Gallienus was indifferent to his parents' suffering. Instead of making plans to attack the Persians and rescue the unfortunate couple, he travelled from his army unit in Illyricum, in the northern Balkans, to Rome, where he "minded nothing but his infamous pleasures and debaucheries, passing the nights in brothels and the days in the baths". According to Gibbon: "When the great emergencies of state required his presence and attention, he was ... wasting his time in trifling or licentious pleasures."

Salonina was horrified. By now she was used to his passing affairs, but she suddenly found that she had a formidable rival in the shape of Pipara, the daughter of Attalus, King of the Marcomanni, a German tribe from the Main River valley. Pipara was a famous beauty and rumours circulated that Gallienus had conceived such a passion for her that he believed his life depended on possessing her beauty. Salonina was fiercely jealous.

Gallienus had a problem. Pipara was not a Roman subject, so she was not his to command, and Roman law did not permit him to marry a foreigner. Titus Antonius and Vespasian had both respected this law and sent away women they loved because they were foreigners. Gallienus, on the other hand, thought himself so much in love that he sought a way around the law.

He went to the Senate and listed the many enemies they now faced. He said that Rome's power was on the wane and that they could not hope to defeat such a roster of foes alone. So he proposed that they make an alliance with a foreign power, join forces and see off their enemies together. The obvious candidate, he said, was Attalus, King of the Marcomanni, and he was willing to cement the alliance by marrying his daughter. Gallienus knew that the Senate would not oppose him and they meekly passed the various amendments to the law needed to allow the marriage.

However, an alliance with Rome was not as desirable as it once had been. The Romans had been defeated on the battlefield and their emperor was now being used as a footstool in Persia. Attalus could afford to be circumspect.

He considered Gallienus's offer and decided that, for the hand of Pipara, he wanted not just an alliance with Rome but also part of Pannonia, the Roman province that comprised western Hungary, Slovenia, northern Croatia and parts of Austria and Serbia. Gallienus agreed and Pipara was sent to Rome. He was disappointed in neither her beauty nor her charm and was soon head-over-heels in love with her; he even carried a lock of her hair around with him. He also showed her the respect of a husband, even though, it seems, she only remained his concubine.

Meanwhile the jilted Salonina fumed, but she conducted herself with such dignity that no one could reproach her. When a jeweller sold her some fake gems, she had him arrested. The man was taken to the Colosseum and shoved out into the arena, where he imagined he would be torn apart by lions. He cried out in fear when the door to the dark cage where the lions were held opened and out came … chickens. Although the jeweller inevitably cacked himself, this was seen as an uproarious joke and spoke volumes about Salonina's *simpacio*. It is hard to imagine any other imperial personage letting an offender off so lightly. It made her very popular indeed.

CHAPTER 16

Despite his passionate affair with Pipara, or perhaps because of it, Gallienus was still seen as effeminate and deeply mired in "a voluptuous course of life". Instead of taking care of the affairs of the empire, it was said, he thought of nothing but how to please Pipara and win her affections, while "indulging himself in the most shameful debaucheries".

This invited rebellion, and there were numerous contenders for the throne. Even Gallienus's most trusted lieutenant, the governor of Gaul, Cassianus Postumus, turned against him. Gallienus had even trusted the education of his son Salonius to Postumus, but Postumus murdered Salonius and assumed the imperial purple in Cologne. The rebellion lasted for seven years.

In the East, though, Gallienus had an ally in Odenatus, King of Palmyra, in south-central Syria. He had tried to free Valerian and Mariniana by sending gifts to Shapur, but the Persian emperor considered this to be impertinent and threw them into the river. Egged on by his beautiful wife Zenobia, who claimed descent from Cleopatra, Odenatus won a great victory against Shapur. However, Odenatus and his heir Herodes were then murdered in an attempted coup. This may well have been a good thing, as Herodes would have made a bad ruler. There was already bad blood between Herodes, the son of Odenatus's first wife, and Zenobia. This had been exacerbated as the boy had been spoilt by his father, when he gave him the great riches he had taken from Shapur, including his numerous concubines. However, with Odenatus and Herodes now dead and with Shapur defeated, Zenobia became Queen of the East.

Odenatus's victory against the Persians shamed Gallienus into attacking Postumus, whom he defeated. Postumus was then replaced by Victorius, who was a great general but not much of a politician. He spent all his time seducing the wives of his officers and his mother, Victoria, ruled in his place.

It seemed that Gallienus was now sharing his empire with two women. This was a great shame for any Roman and prompted more rebellions. Piso assumed the purple in Thessaly, northern Greece; Valens in Greece itself; Aureolus in Illyria – Slovenia and Croatia; and Macrianus, backed by Ballista, in Egypt. Gallienus did not seem to be particularly bothered by this. He continued to live a life of debauchery in Rome. Zenobia was made of sterner stuff, though, and she started mopping up the rebels to the east.

Meanwhile, in Gaul, Victorius's cuckolded officers turned on him and stabbed him to death. Before he died he named his son as his successor, so the boy was killed, too. Seeking to hold onto power, Victoria named her armourer Marius the next emperor.

Marius immediately spoke out, condemning the "pleasures and effeminacy" of Gallienus, "who has tarnished the splendour of his birth by his infamous debaucheries". His sudden elevation made Marius arrogant, though. When a soldier dropped by the armoury to congratulate him, Marius treated the man with contempt. The soldier lost his temper and killed Marius on the spot, saying as he did so: "This is the very sword you made yourself."

Victoria then put Tetrius, a Roman senator, on the throne. She soon feared that he was plotting against her and planned to have him assassinated, but she died before she could put the plan into effect.

News reached Rome that the Scythians, a warlike tribe from northern Romania and southern Bulgaria, were making trouble in Illyria. This forced Gallienus to stir himself from his life of pleasure. Salonina, who feared that her husband's soft and effeminate behaviour might not go down too well with the troops, accompanied him on the campaign. However, when Gallienus went out to face the Scythians, he left his camp lightly guarded and the Scythians rode in and seized Salonina. She was a quick-witted woman, though, and persuaded them that Gallienus would not be at all worried if they took her. After all, he had done nothing to rescue his own mother who had been held by the Persians and subjected to years of humiliation and sexual abuse. It was Pipara they wanted. They released the smooth-talking Salonina and she went back to Rome.

More by luck than judgement, Gallienus won a great victory against the Scythians and followed Salonina home, but there was still discontent in the army, who blamed the rebellions around the empire on Gallienus's effeminacy. Seizing their moment, they murdered Gallienus, Salonina and their remaining son.

Aurelian Borealis

Gallienus was replaced by Claudius II, who found he now had to take on the Goths as well. However, he soon died of the plague. His brother,

Quintillus, took over, but he was murdered by his troops who put Aurelian in his place. Aurelian knew that his first task was to humble Zenobia. No Roman emperor could afford to see his authority challenged by a woman. He beat her on the battlefield and then besieged her in her capital. Eventually she surrendered and was brought to Rome in chains, along with Tetrius from Gaul, whom he had also defeated.

Aurelian managed to hold on to power for five years until he was murdered by his officers in AD 275. For that brief period of stability, he earned the title "restorer of the world"; the world, however, was far from restored. That came with Diocletian, and between 275 and 285 there was a series of competing emperors.

CHAPTER 17

Diocletian rose to power as one of the army chiefs of the Emperor Carinus, perhaps even as a member of his bodyguard. Carinus, who served from AD 283 to 285, it was said, "gave himself up to the vices and follies of an Elagabalus, accompanied by the cruelties of a Domitian". Nice guy.

Carinus Clunes

In the course of a few months Carinus married and divorced nine wives, one after the other, leaving most of them pregnant. This would have resulted in a nightmare for the succession. "Notwithstanding this legal inconsistency," said Gibbon, "he found time to indulge such a variety of appetites as brought dishonour on himself and on the noblest houses of Rome."

The palace – and even the imperial table – was filled with singers, dancers, prostitutes of both sexes "and all the various retinue of vice and folly". It was just like old times. Naturally, Carinus dismissed anyone from office worthy of holding the position and substituted them with one of his companions in vice. The prefect of the Praetorian Guard was murdered and replaced by one of Carinus's procurers. "Another who possessed the same or even a more infamous title to favour" was given the consulship, and Carinus appointed an "abandoned youth" with whom he always took his siesta as his secretary. All this led the fourth-century historian who used the pen name Flavius Vopiscus to sum Carinus up as "the most debauched of men, the most shameless of adulterers and corrupter of youth, who carried his infamy so far as to prostitute himself".

By tradition, Carinus was a bloodthirsty tyrant who murdered senators and raped their wives. He was particularly keen to execute all those who had teased him at school. He came to power jointly with his brother Numerianus, who died in mysterious circumstances, possibly struck by lightning. However, his father Carus was thought to have been killed by lightning too and it is not the sort of thing that runs in families. Diocletian succeeded Numerianus in the East and faced him at the Battle of Margus (now Morava) River near to modern-day Belgrade. Diocletian, it was said, lost the battle, but Carinus was killed by one of his men whose wife he had just bonked. Consequently Diocletian was proclaimed emperor on the battlefield.

Diocletian Diobolaris

Diocletian left his wife Prisca, a Christian, behind in Nicomedia when he went to Rome where he ruled alongside his mate Maximianus, the son of an Illyrian peasant. Naturally there were rumours that they were lovers, but Diocletian added the Trojan nobleman Constantius I Chlorus* and the former shepherd Galerius to form a tetrarchy. They all took the name Caesar, then Augustus. Their rule was also given a religious dimension when Diocletian took the name Jovius – Jove – and Maximianus took the name Herculius – Hercules – spawning the Jovii and Herculii dynasties.

Diocletian, it seems, was eager to divest himself of as much power as possible so that he could indulge himself in his great passion, gardening. This was a dumb move in those dangerous times and it was one that brought tragedy on both himself and his family. He also made all of his co-emperors' wives empresses, giving them the title "Augusta". So alongside the tetrarchy there was a titrarchy. Me dedo.

The Christian historian Lactantius Firmius, who was alive at the time, said in his On the Death of Persecutors that Diocletian's best mate, Maximianus, "plunged into the vices of the worst of tyrants".

"He did not scruple to carry off by force any young girls whom he took a fancy to, even in the sight of their parents, whom he compelled to be witnesses of their dishonour," said Firmius.

A courageous and violent man, he struck terror into the hearts of his enemies.

"His incontinence made it not less so to women of virtue in those places through which he passed," said Lactantius.

Together, Diocletian and Maximianus persecuted the Christians. After all, paganism as practised back then was a lot more fun.

Maximianus was a large and ugly man with a huge black beard. Nevertheless, he managed to marry the lovely Galeria Valeria Eutropia, who was thought to be related to his co-emperor Constantius. It was said: "She possessed great beauty, a cheerful temper, and an amorous temperament, and was very fond of pleasures and diversions."

Her first marriage was to a young Syrian. Nothing is known about him except that they had a daughter called Theodora together. He died soon after her birth.

"Eutropia's beauty suffered nothing from her deep mourning," said the historian Jacques Boergas de Serviez. "On the contrary, it seemed to be rather heightened."

She was an amiable and fun-loving widow, surrounded by admirers, "vying with each other who shall be the first to make amends for her loss". Meanwhile, "Eutropia paid such respect to the memory of her husband as fashion and the rules of decency required, but did not think herself obliged to carry on the farce further than she was obliged." She fooled around, discreetly.

Maximianus was not her sort at all, having a "most disagreeable appearance, and was more calculated to inspire fear than love; his mind was as uncultivated as his person, so that he was quite incapable of carrying on his amours gallantly".

Fortunately, a flash of the imperial purple did wonders and "made at least as deep an impression on the heart of Eutropia as the greatest accomplishments could have done".

Boergas de Serviez remarks: "A lover who wears a crown is always well received, and the eyes of his mistress, being fixed upon that splendid mark of his dignity, have no time to wander about to spy out the faults and deformities of his person."

So, even though she was surrounded by numerous suitors who were far more suitable than Maximianus, none of them stood a chance.

The dead hand of Diocletian was behind the match. If Maximianus married Eutropia, he would then be related to Constantius*, who was then obliged to put aside his concubine Helena* to marry Eutropia's daughter and Maximianus's stepdaughter, Theodora. She gave him six children. Meanwhile, Galerius divorced and married Diocletian's daughter, Valeria. Now the tetrarchy and the titrarchy was one big happy family.

Even Diocletian's wife Prisca was cool, although she maintained the purity of her Christian life while "Eutropia, on the contrary, indulged in such indecencies as were not at all to the advantage of her reputation".

With a husband like Maximianus, she had to be careful, at first. "But the characteristics of her own nation" – Syria – "added to her own natural temperament, soon prevailed, and she gave herself up to pleasures."

She was, after all, an empress and she could do what she liked.

Maximianus wanted a son, but they were still childless some years into their marriage. So Eutropia took up with a "polite and agreeable" young Syrian. He was also very handsome and "found the secret of insinuating himself into her good graces". He seems to have got into her pants as well – not that they wore any back then. And Eutropia was easy: she had neither "virtue nor resolution enough to withstand the solicitations of a lover who had everything she desired to recommend him".

She was soon pregnant. Maximianus, suspecting nothing, now fretted that the baby might be a girl, but no, she delivered a healthy boy whom the doting Maximianus called Maxentius.

"The credulous emperor received this present with the transports of joy, and caused this shameful production of his wife's libertinism to be educated with all possible care and expense," says Boergas de Serviez.

Other authors say that she actually gave birth to a girl, but knowing how much Maximianus wanted a son, substituted a boy. There are even those who say that Maxentius was really Maximianus's natural son all along, perhaps conceived with a mistress. Afterwards, Eutropia had a daughter called Fausta*. No one seems to know who the father was.

It has to be said that Maximianus was away a lot. As Diocletian's fearsome general, he was always riding off to suppress the Gauls, massacring Thebans or purging the ranks of his own legions of Christians in the most brutal ways imaginable. Prisca and her daughter Valeria, who had also converted to Christianity, tried to stay his hand, but Diocletian presided over the last and most brutal persecution of the Christians.

Much of this was overseen by Galerius. Despite being married to Valeria, it is said that his mother had instilled in him an implacable hatred of Christians. He also "had the vices of the worst of the emperors, and indulged them with the utmost brutality". During his first marriage, it was said that he "led a most dissolute life, nor were matters much better after his marriage with Valeria, for he had a favourite mistress whom he preferred infinitely to her".

Valeria was not the jealous type and bore his indifference without complaint. She accompanied him on his campaign against the Persians and, as they had no children, she adopted Candidianus, Galerius's natural son.

The only good one among the tetrarchy was said to be Constantius – "he honoured his nobility by the greatest virtues, especially sweetness of temper, affability, and the most engaging behaviour". He never filled his coffers with the riches of the provinces and he had such a good reputation in the army that "Carus judged him worthy of an empire". He was posh, though, and historians love a nob.

After Galerius won a great victory against the Persians, he persuaded Diocletian and Maximianus to abdicate. Diocletian retired to Salona in Dalmatia – now Split in Croatia – while Maximianus went into private life in Rome. Diocletian wanted Constantine, Constantius's son – not by his wife Theodora but by his mistress Helena – and Maxentius – who passed for the son of Maximianus – to be made Caesar, thus continuing the tetrarchy. Galerius rejected Diocletian's candidates. Hoping ultimately to make himself sole emperor, he completed the new tetrarchy with his nephew and adopted son, Galerius Valerius Maximinus, and his deputy Flaverius Valerius Severus. However, before Galerius could ease him out of the way and take over completely, Constantius died in York and Constantine stepped into his father's shoes.

CHAPTER 18

Constantine was the first Roman emperor to convert to Christianity. His mother, the concubine Helena, had been a bar girl in a wayside tavern when his father Constantius had picked her up. She was also a committed Christian and became St Helena when Constantine gave the empire over to the new faith.

Born Flavius Valerius Constantius on 27 February AD 271, 272 or 273 at Naissus in the province of Moesia Superior – present-day Nish in Serbia – Constantine was brought up in the eastern imperial court and, as a youth, fought in Egypt. When Maximianus stepped down on 1 May 305 Constantine's father, Constantius, succeed him as emperor in the west. When Constantius died, his troops in York proclaimed Constantine as emperor.

The ambitious Galerius, who aimed to make himself sole emperor, did not rate Constantine. Maximianus's putative son, Maxentius, seemed to be the greater threat. Galerius sent his right-hand man Severus against him. Maxentius was defeated and fled to Ravenna. Maximianus was now in a difficult position. He could not be seen to be supporting a traitor, so he ordered his son's execution, though privately he promised that he would spare his life. It did no good. Galerius declared war on Maximianus anyway.

Seeking an ally, Maximianus dangled his supposed daughter Fausta, who was scarcely more than a child, in front of Constantine. He promptly divorced his first wife Minervina, who had just given birth to his son Crispus,* and married the girl when she came of age. She gave him five children, three of whom would become Caesars.

Despite the family tie, Maximianus then turned against his son-in-law. Constantine got wind of it and forced Maximianus to commit suicide. Galerius died soon afterwards, thus terminating "by a shameful death a life which his cruelty and incontinence had made detestable". According to Lactantius Firmius: "He was smitten with a horrible disease in the most sensitive parts of his body, being devoured alive by worms, and such a stench proceeded from him as was offensive to those who were within the palace."

The virtuous Valeria held her nose and tended to her stricken husband. When he died – "without being regretted" – she and Candidianus were taken into the care of Valerius Licinianus Licinius, who was Galerius's deputy and now ruler in the West. Galerius's adopted son, Maximinus, was in charge in the East.

Constantine gingerly returned to the Continent and established his capital in Trier, in modern-day Germany. Like Galerius, Licinius did not perceive him to be much of a threat. His first priority was to take the eastern provinces. Valeria, who was still a very beautiful woman, was the key to this. Licinius thought that he could strengthen his position if he seduced her. She was, after all, Augusta, the widow of one tetrarch and the daughter of another, but the virtuous Valeria had been with Licinius for some time now and she had discovered that he was a bad character and a debauched pagan, very much in the mould of her dead husband. Being unmarried and fearing that Licinius might make some "disagreeable proposal" to her, she sought the protection of Maximinus, thus affording him the same opportunity to strengthen his imperial claim. Prisca was happy for her daughter to make the move. While Maximinus was no friend to Christianity, he was Valeria's adopted son. Prisca thought that Valeria might have more freedom to practise her faith in his court and joined her there. Diocletian was too busy tending to his garden at Salona to worry about it.

The two Christian women had made a bad error of judgement. Valeria had simply jumped out of the frying pan and into the fire. Maximinus was a brute, who spent most of his time drinking to excess, so "it cannot be wondered that he fell into all other sorts of irregularities and debaucheries; particularly, his incontinence was carried to such a pitch that there was no security against it". He would not take no for an answer.

"Her beauty kindled in the heart of Maximinus a flame that was not to be resisted," said a chronicler, "so that in fact he was rather her slave than her protector; and as he was not accustomed to curbing his passions, he gave himself up to the violence of his love, without considering whether it was lawful or not."

He was, of course, setting his cap at the widow of his uncle and his adopted mother, but he had unlimited power in his domain and was used to getting what he wanted. Not being a man versed in self-denial, he was not going to let her virtue stand in his way. Nor did he have the patience to wait until her period of mourning was over.

At first, Valeria was too innocent to realise what was going on. She took her nephew's attentions as filial concern. Meanwhile, he was growing more and more excited by her beauty and thought of nothing but gratifying his desires.

Skipping the whole dating, kissing and hand-holding stage, Maximinus sent an emissary who declared outright that he was going to divorce his wife and put Valeria on the throne beside him. The messenger did not fail to exaggerate the violence and sincerity of the emperor's love, and the great advantage that she would reap from such a match.

Valeria was thunderstruck. A pious Christian lady, she had just been proposed to by a libidinous emperor, whose hands she was in and who was eager to commit incest. She said no, thank you, but in the nicest possible way. She was, of course, obliged to the emperor for doing her so great an honour, but the ashes of her husband were still warm. Besides, the laws of decency insisted that she could only look on him with the eyes of his adopted mother. It would also have been unpardonable of her to deprive his current wife of her husband's affection; it would be the height of injustice for him to divorce a woman worthy of high esteem and who certainly did not deserve such treatment. Valeria added, for good measure, that she thought it unseemly for a woman of her rank to marry a second time and tarnish her womanhood with fresh, you know, activities – not that she had got much the first time around.

All this subtlety was lost on Maximinus. A no was a no. His love quickly turned into hate. If Valeria could not love him, she should fear him. He seized all her property and turfed her and her mother out of the palace. He then set about trying to sully their reputations "by accusing them of the very crime he would have persuaded her to commit, knowing that a woman of virtue is more sensible of the loss of her honour than of her life".

Maximinus promised a pardon to a notorious criminal if he would accuse Valeria and Prisca and appointed the notoriously cruel Eratinus, the governor of Nicaea, as the judge of a court set up to try the case. In court, the pardoned criminal accused both mother and daughter of "the most horrible prostitutions". And they weren't alone. Alongside them in the dock were two senators' wives, who were both related to the Empress Prisca, and another woman whose daughter was a Vestal Virgin and whom Valeria had a particular regard for. They too were charged with prostituting themselves to Maximinus while, in fact, all they had done was to resist his blandishments.

The judge found them guilty out of hand. Martyrs to their chastity, the senators' wives and the mother of the Vestal Virgin were summarily executed while the judge looked on.

Before Prisca and Valeria were sentenced, however, their accuser was arrested for some new crime and sentenced to death. In a further attempt to save his skin, he confessed that he had been put up to making false accusations by Maximinus himself. The judge had no alternative but to show them mercy. Instead of being executed, Prisca and Valeria were then banished to the Syrian desert, where they were dragged from town to town as an example of how the mighty are fallen. Diocletian sent an ambassador to Maximinus, demanding that he send his wife and daughter back. Maximinus merely laughed. Diocletian had stripped himself of power and handed it over to Galerius and Maximinus himself. Instead of returning the two women, Maximinus ordered that they be treated with even more cruelty. Hearing this, Diocletian fell ill.

Having lost the chance to marry Valeria, Licinius sought to make an alliance with Constantine by marrying his beloved sister Constantia. Both Constantine and Licinius wanted Diocletian to attend the wedding to lend his weight to the arrangement, but he wrote back saying that he was too poorly to do so. Constantine and Licinius took this badly and wrote him such a threatening letter that the old man killed himself.

Maximinus then picked a fight with Licinius, who defeated him at Adrianople – modern Edirne in European Turkey. Maximinus fled to Cappadocia where he killed himself. You might have expected things to get better for Prisca and Valeria after Maximinus's death, but they didn't. Candidianus presented himself at Licinius's court to pay his respects and to plead for his adopted mother and grandmother. Severus's son Severianus turned up, too. They were immediately seen as a threat and were executed on the spot. Licinius then sent a search party to track down Prisca and Valeria, who had escaped from their tormentors. They were pursued from province to province for 15 months before they were captured. As there was nothing they could be charged with, Licinius sent a corrupt judge who knew all too well that his duty was to condemn them to death. A huge crowd turned out to see the two empresses executed by a common hangman and their bodies thrown in the sea.

Eutropia escaped their fate. While Licinius had been taking over in the East, Constantine had invaded Italy and finished off Maxentius at the Battle of Milvian Bridge to the north of Rome. Although still a sun worshipper – though not quite in Elagabalus's league – Constantine fought the battle in the name of the Christian God. The night before the battle, it is said, Christ had appeared to him in a dream and told Constantine to place his sign on the shields of his soldiers. In another version of the story, Constantine had seen the cross in the sky accompanied by the legend "by this sign you will be victor". Constantine did as he was told and the new Roman battle standard became known as the *labarum*. This was topped with a gold and jewel-encrusted crown, a cross and the initial letters of the name of Jesus Christ.

The victory made Constantine the undisputed emperor in the West. Eutropia had escaped from Maximinus's court, dodged the murderous Licinius and come to live with her daughter Fausta and son-in-law Constantine. Now past the age where she could enjoy her former pleasures, she converted to Christianity.

When Constantine had married his half-sister Constantia to Licinius in Milan, he had made Licinius promise to give up the persecution of Christians. For a time, Licinius even pretended to believe in the Christian god himself, but then he returned to paganism. He banished

Christians from his court and "abandoned himself to all the abominations that are the natural fruits of idolatry".

"His insatiable passion for pleasure revived," wrote Jacques Boergas de Serviez. Tut tut. "He gave himself up to all manner of debauchery with so little reserve or restraint that ladies of the highest rank were compelled to submit to his infamous and brutal advances."

Constantia was upset by this: she remonstrated with him and begged him to mend his ways, but neither her eloquence nor her charm cut any ice; he had become such a slave to his passions that "he scrupled at nothing that could contribute to their gratification". Unable to find a marriage-guidance counsellor, Constantia reported all of this back to Constantine.

Not content with paying homage to Venus with all the ladies of the highest rank in the court, Licinius also wanted the beautiful young serving girl Glaphyra, who was Constantia's closest companion. She was a Christian and pious about it. Licinius made all sorts of overtures. He even promised to make Glaphyra empress in Constantia's place. Glaphyra refused, but it soon became clear that if she resisted much longer, Licinius would take what he wanted by force.

Constantia devised a plan and, like all good plans in the ancient world, it involved a bit of cross-dressing. She dressed Glaphyra up as a man and smuggled her out of the court on the pretext that she was a young nobleman who was on a secret mission. Glaphyra escaped from Nicomedia in drag and reached Amasia, the capital of Pontus in Anatolia. There the local king, taking her for an emissary from the emperor, offered her an apartment in the palace. Desperate to find someone she could confide in, she asked how Christianity was doing in those parts and was told that there was a particularly zealous bishop in the city called Basil. She made contact and told him all.

Glaphyra needed money to make good her escape, so Basil sent a letter to Constantia. The letter was intercepted by Licinius's men. Troops were sent to arrest Glaphyra, but, by the grace of God, she died – blissfully still a virgin – before they reached Amasia. Basil was brought back to Nicomedia where he was brutally martyred. Constantine saw this as a violation of the Treaty of Milan, where Licinius had promised to stop persecuting Christians, and declared war.

In AD 324, Constantine defeated Licinius in battles at Adrianople and

Chrysopolis – Edirne and Üsküdine in modern Turkey – to become emperor in both the East and West. Constantia made Constantine swear a solemn oath to spare her husband's life, but a few months later he ordered Licinius's execution. He also had the couple's nine-year-old son killed, leaving Constantine as the sole and undisputed master of the Roman world. Just to show that he was even-handed, Constantine also had his own son, Crispus,* and his wife Fausta* killed. They were strangled in the baths, after he suspected that there was an incestuous, and possibly treasonous, relationship going on between them. There were also allegations that Fausta had had it off with a slave and that Crispus had raped a girl. Constantine was adamantly opposed to that sort of thing, even though he had not minded summarily dumping his first wife to marry Fausta in the first place. Besides, murdering his errant wife was entirely unnecessary, as St Augustine* had given him a dispensation to take as many mistresses as he wanted.

With Licinius dead, Constantia joined Constantine's court, thus furthering the process of Christianisation. Constantine passed strict laws against abduction and rape – the very foundations of the Roman Empire. He also banned the taking of concubines, by married men at least.

On 8 November 324, less than two months after the death of Licinius, Constantine laid the foundations of his new capital city. He had decided to move the government of the empire from Rome eastwards to the ancient Greek city of Byzantium, which was renamed Constantinople – and, since 1930, Istanbul. The new walls were completed in 328 and the city was formally dedicated on 11 May 330. Constantinople resembled Rome. However, the pagan shrines had been replaced by Christian churches. He began the construction of the Hagia Sophia (Holy Wisdom) and Hagia Eirene (Holy Peace), and founded the Church of the Holy Apostles. Constantine himself did not convert until 337, however.

Soon after Easter that year, he began to feel ill and travelled to Drepanum – renamed Helenopolis (now Trapani, Sicily) in honour of his mother – to pray at the tomb of the martyr Lucian, who was his mother's favourite saint. He then went to Nicomedia, modern Izmit in Turkey, where he was baptised. A few weeks later, on the feast of Pentecost, 22 May 337, dressed in the white robes of a Christian neophyte, he died. As he had instructed, his body was returned to

Constantinople and placed in the Church of the Holy Apostles. His tomb was flanked by memorials to the Apostles themselves, six on each side.

Inconstans

Constantine was succeeded by his son Constans, who was just 17 years old when his father died. He had no time for Christianity and "revived the lowest vice of his pagan predecessors". He filled his palace with handsome boys, whom he either bought or who were attracted to the luxury of his court. There was trouble in store, though. Gibbon says: "His partiality toward some German captives, distinguished only by their charms of youth, was an object of scandal to the people."

Constans was murdered and his brother Constantius II* took over. He was no better. Gibbon said that Constantine's sons, "by their vices and weakness, soon lost the esteem and affections of their people". The empire was in terminal decline. In 395, less than 60 years after the death of Constantine, it was split in two. The Western empire then lasted for less than a century; the Eastern empire – the Byzantine Empire – lasted for over a millennium.

CHAPTER 19

The Roman Empire very nearly came together again under the Byzantine Emperor Justinian.* When he came to power in 527, the Western empire had already collapsed and the Eastern empire embraced the Balkans, Greece, Crete, Cyprus, modern Turkey, Syria, Israel, Palestine, Egypt and Cyrenia, a strip of Libya stretching a little past Benghazi. Justinian managed to regain Italy itself, North Africa, Sicily, Sardinia, Corsica, the Balearics and southern Spain. Only Gaul and Britain remained beyond his reach. In his attempt to achieve this great endeavour, he was helped by an extraordinary woman, his wife, the Empress Theodora.*

Born in Tauresium, Dardania – just south of modern Nis in Serbia – in 483, Justinian moved to Constantinople where his uncle Justin held high military command. Justin became emperor in 518 and, being childless, he adopted Justinian as his heir. Even though Justinian was influential in his uncle's administration, he was a bit of a tearaway. He joined the Blues, a rowdy street gang, who fought their bitter enemy, the Greens. No policeman dared to lay a hand on them.

They wore their hair short at the front and long at the back and had long moustaches and beards, like the Huns. They also wore Hun-style cloaks, shoes, riding breeches and tunics with leg-of-mutton sleeves. Armed with two-edged swords that they kept concealed under their cloaks, these hooligans would roam the streets at night robbing wealthy passers-by of their gold, brooches, silver buckles, belts and cloaks, and sometimes finishing them off with the thrust of a dagger. They also ran protection rackets and made money by blackmail, denouncing anyone who would not pay up.

The Blues were also interested in sex. According to the sixth-century Byzantine writer Procopius, who was there at the time: "It is said that a number of women were forced by their own slaves to yield to suggestions most repugnant to them ... Many unwilling boys, with full knowledge of their fathers, were forced into immoral relations with the partisans, and women who were happily married suffered the same humiliation."

Procopius also told of a woman who was sailing with her husband from one of the outlying suburbs to the mainland. The Blues intercepted them and forced the young woman into their boat, plainly intent on gangbanging her.

"Before going on board with the young men she whispered encouragement to her husband and told him to have no fear on her account; she would never submit to physical outrage," said Procopius. "Then, while her husband was still watching her through his tears, she jumped overboard, and from that moment was never seen again."

Justinian protected this gang of crooks and rapists. It was only in 524 or 525, when Justinian fell ill, that Justin found out what was going on. In the early throes of senility, Justin usually lived in seclusion in the Great Palace, and left day-to-day control to his nephew. On Justin's orders, the prefect of Constantinople, Theodotus Colocynthius – "the Pumpkin" – took control and hanged or burned alive many of the Blues.

It was through the Blues that Justinian met Theodora. She was some 15 years younger than him, though she never disclosed her age. Her father was a bear-keeper for the Greens. He organised bear fights and bear hunts, and put on performances where he would provoke a bear and escape its wrath by agility.

Theodora's mother was also a performer of some kind. This gave her a very low social status. Under Byzantine law, a man whose wife appeared on the stage without his consent was given an instant divorce. A senator was not allowed to marry an actress and any man who did marry an actress could not become a bishop – perhaps the origin of endless old jokes.

The couple had three daughters – Comito, Theodora and Anastasia.

Comito was just seven when their father died. Their mother quickly remarried in the hope that her new husband could take over the bear-keeping job and support the family, but another Green got the position and the family was left destitute. They had to beg for a living and the three girls appeared at the circus decked in flowers to solicit alms.

Ever anxious to score points over the Greens, the Blues took them under their protection and gave Theodora's stepfather a job. To bring in more money Comito went on the stage, quickly progressing to become a much sought-after courtesan. Theodora, being too young to go into business for herself, became her maid. Procopius said: "For the time being, Theodora was still too underdeveloped to be capable of sharing a man's bed or having intercourse like a woman; but she acted as a sort of male prostitute to satisfy customers of the lowest type." Clad as a slave-girl, she would perform oral sex or masturbate the slaves of the men who came to see her sister.

She also did a roaring trade at the theatre with slaves who, while their owners were watching the show, "seized their opportunity to divert themselves in this revolting fashion". It was obvious that she was adept at what she was doing, as Procopius records that "for some considerable time she remained in a brothel, given up to this unnatural bodily commerce".

As soon as she was old enough and fully developed, she joined her sister both on the stage and in her trade. Procopius says that as she was not a musician or even qualified to join a corps of dancers, "she merely sold her attractions to anyone who came along, putting her whole body at his disposal".

However, she was clever and witty and no one ever saw her taken aback. Soon she had a burgeoning career as an actress, partly because "she complied with the most outrageous demands without the slightest hesitation, and she was the sort of girl that if someone slapped her bottom or walloped her about the ears would make a joke of it and roar with laughter; and she would throw off her clothes and exhibit to all and sundry those parts, both in the front and behind, which the rules of decency require to be kept veiled and hidden from masculine eyes". Actresses like that remain popular.

Melior.

"She used to tease her lovers by keeping them waiting, and by constantly playing about with novel ways of intercourse she could always bring the lascivious to her feet."

She did not even wait to be asked. She would proposition anyone who came by with a dirty joke and a wiggle of the hips, especially if they were still "a beardless youth".

"Never was anyone so completely given up to unlimited self-indulgence," said Procopius. *"Disparis mores disparia studia sequuntur,"* as Cicero said.

"Often she would go to a dinner party with ten young men or more, all at the peak of their physical powers," the *peculium* Procopius continued. "When she had reduced them all to a state of total exhaustion, she would start on their servants, as many as 30 of them on some occasions, and copulated with every one of them." But not even that could satisfy her lust.

"And though she brought three bodily apertures into service, she often found fault with nature, grumbling that nature had not made the openings in her nipples wider than normal, so that she could devise another form of intercourse in that region. Naturally she was often pregnant, but by using all the tricks of the trade she was able to induce an abortion."

Even at drinking parties in the houses of distinguished citizens she would "pull up her dress in the most disgusting manner as she stood there, and brazenly display her lasciviousness". Procopius feigns shock, but her brazen behaviour was why she was invited. At that time in the Eastern empire it was not uncommon for young gentlemen to invite a number of strippers to their drinking parties. Such erotic entertainment was the order of the day.

"Often in the theatre too, in full view of all the people, she would throw off her clothes and stand naked in their midst, having only a ribbon around her private parts and groin – not because she was ashamed to expose these parts to the public, but because no one is allowed to appear completely naked and a ribbon covering the vulva is compulsory."

We now approach the climax of her act.

"With this minimum covering she would lie face upwards on the stage and spread herself out. Then servants, who had been especially hired for the task, would sprinkle grains of barley over her private parts and geese trained for the purpose would peck them off" – and peck her off – "with their beaks and swallow them."

"*Non enim posthac alia calebo Femina,*" as Horace said.

Without so much as a blush, Theodora would stand up and take a bow. Outraged, Procopius said she "actually seemed to be proud of this performance; for she was not only shameless herself, but did more than anyone else to encourage shamelessness".

The more cultured readers will immediately spot that her act was, in fact, a burlesque of the myth of Jupiter and Leda, where the king of the gods, disguised as a swan, seduces the lovely Leda – as a result of which the beautiful Helen of Troy is hatched from one of her eggs. "*Hoc discunt omnes ante alpha et beta,*" said Juvenal.

In more impromptu performances, she seems to have left off the G-string and was perfectly prepared – even eager – to put on a live show for the paying public.

"Many times she threw off her clothes and stood in the middle of the actors on the stage, leaning over backwards or pushing out her behind to invite both those who had already enjoyed her and those who had not yet had the pleasure to help her parade her own special form of gymnastics."

Nudity was widely appreciated in Byzantium, though. Paulus Silentarius, a court official of the Emperor Justinian, wrote:

> Full nakedness! Strip off your linen white,
> And clinging closely, limb to limb, unite.
> Off with these flimsy veils, for while they're on
> Between us stand the walls of Babylon.

Apparently Theodora also gave great *verpam comedo*. Procopius said: "With such lasciviousness did she misuse her body that she appeared to have her private parts not like other women in the place intended by nature, but in her face!"

Heia, morde citharam meam!

She got hitched up with a guy called Hecebolus from Tyre, modern Sur in southern Lebanon, and went with him when he was sent as governor of the Pentapolis, five cities in Libya, "in order to serve him in the most revolting capacity".

"Foeda est in coitu et brevis voluptas et taedet Veneris statim peractae," said Petronius.

Anyway, it was plain that she could not restrict herself to just one man and he kicked her out. She found herself without even the necessities of life "which from then on she provided for herself in her customary fashion by making her body the tool of her lawless trade". She went from city to city around the eastern Mediterranean, earning her fare back to Byzantium on her back. Procopius said that it was as if "some unseen power could not allow any spot on earth to be unaware of Theodora's depravity".

Procopius is not being entirely fair to her here, though. Theodora spent some time in Alexandria, where she seems to have met the Patriarch Timothy and the austere Greek theologian Severus of Antioch. She seems to have got religion. When she arrived back in Constantinople, she gave up the stage and made a living spinning wool in a small house near to the palace. Plainly she did not get that much religion as she soon became Justinian's mistress.

Apart from being heir to the throne, Justinian was not much of a catch. He was not very tall and had a heavy, somewhat florid face. Procopius said he looked like Domitian – that is, as far as he could tell from the statue made after Domitian's death, which was modelled from the corpse sewn together from all the bits of him that Domitia could find. It would be safe to say that Justinian was no looker.

He seems to have been a bit of a bad lad with the Blues in his youth, but after he met Theodora, when he was about 40, he cleaned up his act. Not even his worst enemy – and there were many – could accuse him of being unfaithful to her. From their first night together, he showered her with all the wealth of the Roman world and there is little doubt that he was the father of the daughter she bore soon after, who died young.

Theodora, by all accounts, was strikingly beautiful, though her face bore some evidence of the eventful life she had had up to that point. Her ready wit and her unfailing memory impressed all those she met. She had a talent for public appearances – even with her clothes on – and quoted the orator Isocrates to devastating effect.

At first Justinian intended to take her only as a mistress, though he persuaded his uncle to confer patrician rank on her so that she could own property and hang on to what he gave her.

"For as so often happens to men consumed with passion, it seemed in Justinian's eyes the most delightful thing in the world to lavish all his favours and all his wealth upon the object of his passion," wrote the old killjoy Procopius. "And the whole state became fuel for his passion."

Promoted to Caesar, Justinian could marry anyone in the empire he fancied and it was thought that he would pick some firm-breasted young virgin, not a wrinkled slapper who was fast approaching her sell-by date. While uncle Justin was not opposed to the match, his wife the Empress Euphemia, who normally played no part in public affairs, said that she would not have such a hussy in the palace – especially as Roman law specifically forbade the marriage of anyone of senatorial rank to a woman who had appeared on the stage, let alone performed the way Theodora had done. But, in 524, Euphemia died.

Soon after, Justin issued an edict saying that from then on actresses who had given up the stage could marry and that those who had high dignity conferred on them – such as patrician rank – could marry men of the highest standing – a Caesar, say. The law was specifically framed with Theodora in mind, though there was to be another beneficiary. It was also written in sonorous and circumlocutory Latin so that no one would realise what it said.

In 525, Justinian and Theodora married in the church of Hagia Sophia, built by Constantine two centuries earlier. It is thought that the Patriarch of Constantinople presided. Around the same time, Theodora's equally accomplished sister, Comito, took advantage of the actress edict to wed Justinian's old friend Sittas who was Master of Soldiers and the commander-in-chief of one of the regions of the empire. Soon after, Justinian was promoted again. On 1 April 527, with the old emperor now mortally ill, he was named Augustus, co-emperor. Three days later, in a huge ceremony that ended with a procession leading to the Hippodrome where the couple were greeted by cheering crowds, Justinian and Theodora were crowned emperor and empress by the Patriarch. The one-time slave gobbler was now Augusta.

It seems that only Procopius was appalled. He wrote:

Sad to say not even one member of the Senate, seeing the state saddling itself with this disgrace, saw fit to protest and to oppose such proceedings, though they would all have fallen down before her as if she were a goddess. There was not even one priest who showed her any disgust when they were obliged to address her as "Mistress". And the people who had previously watched her performances in the theatre thought it fit to be, both in name and in reality, her grovelling slaves. Nor did one soldier resent being called on to face danger on the battlefield for Theodora's benefit; nor did any living person oppose her.

She was, it seems, a very popular empress. Procopius puts this down to the fact that she still had a pretty face and a good figure, and that people accepted the roles that fate had assigned them. If fortune had chosen to lift up a fallen woman, good luck to her. In Procopius's mind, though, there was no question as to how Justinian got away with this – black magic.

"It is said that Justinian's own mother told some of her close friends that he was not the son of her husband Sabbatius or of any man at all," he said. "For when she was about to conceive she was visited by a demon, who was invisible but who gave her a distinct impression that he was really there with her like a man in bodily contact with a woman. Then he vanished like a dream."

He had no doubts about this because men of the highest possible character who had visited Justinian in his palace late at night had seen a "strange demonic form" in his place. One of them said that he had seen Justinian's head disappear more than once when he was walking around the throne room while the rest of the body continued on its way without it. Another man had seen the emperor suddenly transform into a shapeless lump of flesh that had no distinguishing features except the eyes and eyebrows, which were not in their normal place.

Procopius also remarked that Justinian must be a wild demon because he never satisfied his natural appetite for food, drink or sleep – and that he had a "demonic passion for the pleasures of Aphrodite". Well, with Theodora around, what do you expect?

"We understand too from some of Theodora's lovers," said Procopius, "that, when she was still on the stage, a demon of some sort swooped on them in the night and drove them from the room where they were spending the night with her."

And Theodora herself had told a fellow thespian, a dancing girl called Macedonia who belonged to the Blues in Antioch, that the night before she returned to Constantinople she had had a vivid dream in which she was told that she did not have to worry about money any more. When she reached Byzantium, she would go to bed with the King of Demons. The dream went on to say that she would live with him as his wedded wife and, as a result, would be mistress of all the money she desired.

All this is very strange as Justinian turned the old persecutions of the Christians on their head and began fining and torturing those who would not convert to Christianity. Astrologers were flogged and banished – I bet they didn't see that coming. He passed laws against buggering boys and pursued those who had enjoyed the practice in the past. The word of a single man or boy – even a slave – was enough to secure a conviction; those found guilty were castrated.

As empress, Theodora insisted on the repeal of all laws disadvantaging actresses and prostitutes, who often had no other way of earning an income. New laws freed them from the control of theatre owners and pimps, allowing 227 actresses to leave the stage for a new life. She even bought the freedom of some prostitutes with her own money so that the brothel owners would not be ruined.

Unfortunately, Theodora was soon fired with the zeal of the Christian convert. She began forcibly closing down the brothels where she had once made her living and shipped the girls out to convents. Five hundred prostitutes who had sold their services for a shilling a time in the Forum just to keep body and soul together were locked up in a convent known as the Repentance. Theodora was determined to make the prostitutes mend their ways there and sometimes the punishments she devised for them were so extreme that the women killed themselves rather than reform.

Despite her new-found faith, Theodora herself was not entirely reformed, according to Procopius at least.

"To her bodily needs she devoted quite unnecessary attention," he wrote, "though never enough to satisfy her." Well, a woman who can wear out 40 men in one session has special needs. "She was in a great hurry to get into her bath, and very unwilling to get out again." She was also very fond of her bed.

Just as she had once kept her clients waiting, she kept those who came to see her on state business waiting for hours on end in a stuffy anteroom.

"The nation became a community of slaves with Theodora as the slave-driver," said Procopius.

She liked having men, particularly those of noble birth, flogged before being banished or put to death. The flogging was often so brutal that it stripped the flesh from the bones. In her private apartments, she kept secret torture chambers. One innocent man was kept with his head in a manger, with a noose around his neck tied so tight that he could not move, in total darkness, for four months. He had to eat, sleep and perform all of his bodily functions in this position. He went mad and began to think that he was an ass. When he was finally released, he promptly died.

A woman called Amalasuntha fled from the Goths and sought asylum in Byzantium. When Theodora saw that her beauty rivalled her own and that she was of royal blood, she became jealous and had her strangled in her bath. It was also rumoured that she had fallen madly in love with a handsome young foreigner and that she had made him her steward. Then suddenly, on a whim, she had him flogged. No one knows what became of him afterwards.

A young Green called Vasianus made some uncomplimentary remarks about her. When she heard what he had said, she was so furious that he was forced to flee and he sought sanctuary in the Church of St Michael the Archangel. Theodora was determined to get her own back. She sent an officer to go and get him and to charge him, not with making rude remarks, but with buggering boys. The officer soon got Vasianus out of the church and "tortured him with an unendurable form of punishment". When his friends pleaded for him, she made his punishment worse – "she had his privy member cut off and destroyed him". His estate was then forfeited to the treasury, even though the man had never even been to trial.

Another Green called Diogenes was popular and even seemed to be a favourite of the emperor. Theodora turned against him and accused him of buggery, too. This time she did take him to court, suborning two of the household slaves to testify against him. However, the jury found that the evidence of the slaves, who were young boys, was not strong enough to convict. Theodora arrested one of his close friends. After the friend had refused many "flattering enticements" to testify against Diogenes, she resorted to prolonged torture. A strip of leather was wound around his head and twisted and tightened until he thought that his eyes were going to pop out of his head. Even so, he still refused to give evidence and the case was dismissed.

One day, Theodora's past caught up with her. A young man called John arrived in Constantinople, claiming that he was Theodora's son. While she had been a prostitute, she had been pregnant many times, but on one occasion the method she used to induce an abortion had failed and she had given birth to the infant. When the father of the child saw that she was upset because she "would no longer be able to use her body as before", he was afraid that she would kill the baby. So he took the child and went off to Arabia. The father had told the whole story to his son on his deathbed and John had returned to Byzantium to see his mum. Theodora invited him to visit her in her apartments, but she was so terrified that the story would come to the ears of Justinian that she had him murdered.

Like so many before her, power seems to have unhinged her. When Theodora heard that two young sisters of consul rank had been widowed, she arranged for them to marry the most revolting beggars that she could find. Appalled at the prospect, they took refuge in the Hagia Sophia.

"But such privations and sufferings did the empress inflict upon them that in their anxiety to escape the miseries of their confinement they became reconciled to the lesser evil of the proposed marriage," said Procopius.

So the two women were coerced into marrying far beneath their station. Later, Theodora thought better of it and gave their two husbands high offices in government. This was no consolation for the women, who had to suffer their loathsome conjugal attentions, and all those who came under the authority of these two louts suffered, too.

Theodora liked to interfere in marriages, arranging them as if by divine right. A man would suddenly find that he had a wife, even when he had no desire for one, and women were forced to live with men when they had not the slightest inclination to do so. She would even storm into a bridal chamber and remove the bride if she did not approve of the match.

A man called Saturnius had married his second cousin, a woman of good birth and excellent character. Her father had approved the marriage. However, the moment they had retired to the bridal chamber for the consummation, Theodora burst in, grabbed the groom and dragged him off to another bridal chamber where she married him, despite his protestations, to the daughter of her friend Chrysomallo. Like Theodora, Chrysomallo had been a dancer and a courtesan but, unlike the women who sold themselves for a shilling in the Forum, Theodora had invited Chrysomallo and some of her other high-class hooker friends to set up shop in the palace.

In spite of his broken heart, Saturnius did his duty with Chrysomallo's daughter and immediately discovered that she was not a virgin. He later complained that the girl was "damaged goods". His words reached the ears of Theodora, who sent for him and told him not to be so puffed up. Then she ordered her servants to bend him over like a schoolboy and gave him a sound thrashing.

Theodora was not so hard on women who committed adultery, though. All they had to do was come to her and bring a counter-suit against their husbands. The poor men would be dragged into court, forced to pay their wives twice the amount of dowry they had received, before being scourged and led away to prison. The women, now rich and free, behaved even more flagrantly with their paramours, some of whom even gained promotion for services rendered. As a consequence, cuckolded husbands kept quiet about it, preferring the humiliation of an openly unfaithful wife to penury, a scourging and prison.

While Theodora oversaw domestic policy in this idiosyncratic manner for 21 years, Justinian set about expanding the empire – under the generalship of Belisarius, the husband of Theodora's friend Antonina – so that it, briefly, encompassed Italy once again. And with Theodora's rampant promiscuity and pointless cruelty, it must have seemed quite like old times. A mosaic portrait of her can be seen in the Church of San Vitale in Ravenna. She died, possibly from cancer or gangrene, in 548. Justinian was mortified by her loss. His efforts to re-establish the Roman Empire ultimately failed, and with Christianity now well established throughout the region, emperors were never the same again.

*THE DAISY CHAIN

* Asterisks in the text indicate that the person has appeared in another book in the *Sex Lives* ... series. Starred figures, plus those who appear for the first time in this volume, appear in alphabetic order below, along with the titles of the books they've appeared in. Now you too can start to play Truman Capote's* game "International Daisy Chain" at home – or, even better, in bed. You could even play it for a forfeit – Strip Daisy Chain perhaps. Pick any two people from this list and see how many lovers you need to daisy chain between them. The player who can make the chain with the least lovers wins. According to Capote,* Mercedes De Acosta* – who gets a chapter to herself in *Sex Lives of the Famous Lesbians* – is the wild card. With Mercedes, he said: "You could get to anyone – from Pope John XXIII* to John F. Kennedy* – in one move." But remember, there are plenty more links in the chain out there in the rest of my *Sex Lives* ... series.

Acosta, Mercedes De – *Sex Lives of the Hollywood Goddesses, Sex Lives of the Famous Lesbians, Sex Lives of the Hollywood Idols*
Agrippina the Younger – *Sex Lives of the Famous Lesbians*
Augustine, St – *Sex Lives of the Popes*
Bizet, George – *Sex Lives of the Great Composers*
Bonaparte, Napoleon – *Sex Lives of the Great Dictators, Sex Lives of the Kings and Queens of England, Sex Lives of the Popes, Sex Lives of the Famous Gays, Sex Lives of the Famous Lesbians*
Caesar, Julius – *Sex Lives of the Famous Gays*
Capote, Truman – *Sex Lives of the Hollywood Goddesses, Sex Lives of the Hollywood Goddesses 2*
Clark, Lord Kenneth – *Sex Lives of the Great Artists*

CHRONOLOGICAL LIST OF ROMAN EMPERORS

31 BC–AD 14	Augustus
14–37	Tiberius
37–41	Gaius (Caligula)
41–54	Claudius
54–68	Nero
68–69	Galba
69	Otho
69	Vitellius
69–79	Vespasian
79–81	Titus
81–96	Domitian
96–98	Nerva
98–117	Trajan
117–138	Hadrian
138–161	Antoninus Pius
161–180	Marcus Aurelius
161–169	Lucius Verus
180–192	Commodus
192–193	Pertinax
193	Didius Julianus
193–211	Septimius Severus
193–194	Pescennius Niger
193–197	Clodius Albinus
211–217	Antoninus (Caracalla)
211	Geta
217–218	Macrinus

218	Diadumenus
218–22	Elagabalus
222–235	Severus Alexander
225–227	Lucius Seius Sallustius
235–238	Maximinus Thrax
238	Gordian I
	Gordian II
	Pupienus (Maximus)
	Balbinus
238–244	Gordian III
240	Sabinianus
244–249	Philip the Arab
248	Pacatianus
248	Iotapianus
	Silbannacus
	Sponsianus
247–249	Philip Iunior
249–251	Decius
250	T. Julius Priscus
250	Julius Valens Licinianus
251	Herennius Etruscus
251	Hostilian
251–253	Trebonianus Gallus
	Volusianus
253	Uranius Antoninus
253	Aemilius Aemilianus
253–260	Valerian
	Mareades
253–268	Gallienus
260	Ingenuus
260	Regalianus
260–261	Macrianus Senior
260–261	Macrianus Iunior
260–261	Quietus
261	Piso
261	Valens
261	Ballista

261	Mussius Aemilianus
262	Memor
262, 268	Aureolus
	Celsus
	Saturninus
268–270	Claudius II Gothicus
	Censorinus
270	Quintillus
270–271?	Felicissimus
270–275	Aurelian
271–272	Domitianus
271–272	Urbanus
271–272	Septimius
272	Vaballathus
273	Firmus
(260–274	Gallic Emperors)
260–269	Postumus
269	Laelianus
269	Marius
269–270	Victorinus
271–274	Tetricus I
273?–274	Tetricus II
274	Faustinus
275–276	Tacitus
276	Florianus
276–282	Probus
280	Bonosus
280–281	Proculus
281	Saturninus
282–283	Carus
283–284	Numerianus
283–285	Carinus
284–305	Diocletian
297 (296?)	L. Domitius Domitianus
297–298?	Aurelius Achilleus

303?	Eugenius
285–305	Maximianus Herculius
285 or 286	Amandus
285 or 286	Aelianus
c286–293	Iulianus

(286?–297?	British Emperors)
286/7–293	Carausius
293–296/7	Allectus

293–306	Constantius I Chlorus
293–311	Galerius
305–313	Maximinus Daia
305–307	Severus II
306–337	Constantine I
306–312	Maxentius
308–309	L. Domitius Alexander
308–324	Licinius
314 (316?)	Valens
324	Martinianus
337–350	Constans I
337–361	Constantius II
350–353	Magnentius
350	Nepotian
350	Vetranio
355	Silvanus
361–363	Julian
363–364	Jovian
364–375	Valentinian I
364–378	Valens
365–366	Procopius
366	Marcellus
367–383	Gratian
372?–374 or 375	Firmus
375–392	Valentinian II
378–395	Theodosius I the Great
383–388	Magnus Maximus

384–388	Flavius Victor
392–394	Eugenius
Partition	

The Western Empire

393–423	Honorius
406–407	Marcus
407	Gratian
407–411	Constantine III
409/10–411	Constans II
409–411	Maximus
409–410, 414–415	Priscus Attalus
411–413	Jovinus
412–413	Sebastianus
421	Constantius III
423–425	Johannes
425–455	Valentinian III
455	Petronius Maximus
455–456	Avitus
457–461	Majorian
461–465	Libius Severus
467–472	Anthemius
468	Arvandus
470	Romanus
472	Olybrius
473–474	Glycerius
474–475	Julius Nepos
475–476	Romulus Augustulus

The Eastern Empire

(395–457	Dynasty of Theodosius)
395–408	Arcadius
408–450	Theodosius II
450–457	Marcian

(457–518	Dynasty of Leo)
457–474	Leo I
474	Leo II
474–491	Zeno
475–476	Basiliscus
484–488	Leontius
491–518	Anastasius
(518–610	Dynasty of Justinian)
518–527	Justin
527–565	Justinian I
565–578	Justin II
578–582	Tiberius II (I) Constantine
582–602	Maurice
602–610	Phocas
(610–717	Dynasty of Heraclius)
610–641	Heraclius
641	Heraclonas
641	Constantine III
641–668	Constans II
646–647	Gregory
649–653	Olympius
669	Mezezius
668–685	Constantine IV
685–695	Justinian II (banished)
695–698	Leontius
698–705	Tiberius III (II)
705–711	Justinian II (restored)
711–713	Bardanes
713–716	Anastasius II
716–717	Theodosius III
(717–820	Isaurian Dynasty)
717–741	Leo III
741–775	Constantine V Copronymus
742–743	Artabasdus
775–780	Leo IV

780–797	Constantine VI
797–802	Irene
802–811	Nicephorus I
811	Strauracius
811–813	Michael I
813–820	Leo V
(820–867	Phrygian Dynasty)
820–821	Michael II
821–823	Thomas
829–842	Theophilus
842–867	Michael III
(867–1057	Macedonian Dynasty)
867–886	Basil I
869–879	Constantine
887–912	Leo VI
912–913	Alexander
913–959	Constantine VII Porphygenitus
920–944	Romanus I Lecapenus
921–931	Christopher
924–945	Stephen
959–963	Romanus II
963–969	Nicephorus II Phocas
969–976	John I Tzimiskes
976–1025	Basil II
1025–1028	Constantine VIII (IX) alone
1028–1034	Romanus III Argyrus
1034–1041	Michael IV the Paphlagonian
1041–1042	Michael V Calaphates
1042	Zoe and Theodora
1042–1055	Constantine IX Monomchus
1055–1056	Theodora alone
1056–1057	Michael VI Stratioticus
(1057–1081	Prelude to Comnenian Dynasty)
1057–1059	Isaac I Comnenos

1059–1067	Constantine X (IX) Ducas
1068–1071	Romanus IV Diogenes
1071–1078	Michael VII Ducas
1078–1081	Nicephorus III Botaniates
	Nicephorus Bryennius
	Nicephorus Basilacius
1080–1081	Nicephorus Melissenus
(1081–1191	Dynasty of the Comneni)
1081–1118	Alexius I Comnenus
1118–1143	John II Comenus
1143–1180	Manuel I
1180–1183	Alexius II
1183–1185	Andronicus I
1183–1191	Isaac, Emperor of Cyprus
(1185–1204	Dynasty of the Angeli)
1185–1195	Isaac II
1195–1203	Alexius III
1203–1204	Isaac II (restored) with Alexius IV
1204	Alexius V Ducas Murtzuphlus
(1204–1261	Lascarid Dynasty in Nicaea)
1204–1222	Theodore I Lascaris
1222–1254	John III Ducas Vatatzes
1254–1258	Theodore II Lascaris
1258–1261	John IV Lascaris
(1259–1453	Dynasty of the Palaeologi)
1259–1282	Michael VIII Paleologus
1282–1328	Andronicus II
1328–1341	Andronicus III
1341–1391	John V
1347–1354	John VI Cantancuzenus
1376–1379	Andronicus IV
1379–1391	John V (restored)
1390	John VII

1391–1425	Manuel II
1425–1448	John VIII
1449–1453	Constantine XI (XIII) Dragases

SELECTED BIBLIOGRAPHY

The African Emperor – Septimius Severus by Anthony R. Birley, B.T. Batsford, London, 1972

The Amazing Emperor Hegliogabalus by J. Stuart Hay, Macmillan, London, 1911

The Annals of Tacitus translated by Donald R. Dubley, Mentor Books, New York, 1966

An Apology for Raymond Sebond by Michel de Montaigne, Penguin, London, 1987

The Art of Love by Ovid, University of Michigan Press, Ann Arbor, 2000

The Beginnings of Rome – Italy and Rome from the Bronze Age to the Punic Wars (c1000–264 BC) by T.J. Cornell, Routledge, London, 1995

The Caesars' Wives – Above Suspicion? by Stewart Perowne, Hodder and Stoughton, London, 1974

Caligula: Divine Carnage – The Atrocities of the Roman Emperors by Stephen Barber and Jeremy Reed, Creation Books, New York, 2001

Commodus – An Emperor at the Crossroads by Oliver Hekster, J.C. Gieden, Amsterdam, 2002

Consent and Coercion to Sex and Marriage in Ancient and Medieval Society edited by Angeliki E. Laiou, Dumbarton Oaks, Washington, D.C., 1993

Constantine by Ramsay MacMullen, The Dial Press Inc, New York, 1969

The Cult of Sol Invictus by Gaston H. Halsberghe, E.J. Brill, Leiden, 1972

Daily Life in Ancient Rome – The People and the City at the Height of the Empire by Jérôme Carpcopino, Penguin, London, 1991

Daily Life of the Etruscans by Jacques Heurgon, Phoenix Press, London, 1989

Decline and Fall of the Roman Empire by Edward Gibbon, Penguin, London, 1994

Desire and Denial in Byzantium edited by Liz James, Ashgate/Variorum, Aldershot, 1997

Diocletian and the Roman Recovery by Stephen Williams, B.T. Batsford, London, 1985

Diocletian's Palace by Drazen Katunaric, Croatian P.E.N. Centre, Split, 1997

Diocletian (the Person and the Personality) and his Palace by Nenad Cambi, Croatian P.E.N. Centre, Split, 1997

Domitian – Tragic Tyrant by Pat Southern, Routledge, London, 1997

The Early History of Rome by Livy, Penguin, London, 2002

Early Rome and the Etruscans by R.M. Ogilvie, Fontana, London, 1976

The Emperor Constantine by Hans A. Pohlsander, Routledge, London, 1996

The Emperor Constantine by Michael Grant, Weidenfeld and Nicolson, London, 1993

The Emperor Domitian by Brian W. Jones, Routledge, London, 1992

The Emperor Titus by B.W. Jones, Croom Helm Ltd, Beckenham, Kent, 1984

Emperors and Biography – Studies in the Historia Augusta by Sir Ronald Syme, Clarendon Press, Oxford, 1971

The Empire of the Tetrarchs – Imperial Pronouncements and Government 284–324 AD by Simon Corcoran, Clarendon Press, Oxford, 1996

Etruscan Civilization – A Cultural History by Sybille Haynes, British Museum Press, London, 2000

The Etruscans by Graeme Barker and Tom Rasmussen, Blackwell, Oxford, 1998

The Etruscans by Mario Torelli, Thames and Hudson, London, 2000

Everyday Life in Ancient Rome by Lionel Casson, Johns Hopkins University Press, Baltimore, 1998

Following Hadrian – A Second-Century Journey Through the Roman Empire by Elizabeth Speller, Review, London, 2002

Galba, Otho and Vitellius by Charles L. Murison, Georg Olms, New York, 1993

The Garden of Priapus – Sexuality and Aggression in Roman Humour by Amy Richlin, Yale University Press, New Haven, Connecticut, 1983

Glossographia by Thomas Blount, The Scolar Press Ltd, Menston, England, 1969

Growing Up and Growing Old in Ancient Rome by Mary Harlow and Ray Laurence, Routledge, London, 2002

Gynecology by Soranos of Ephesus, Johns Hopkins University Press, Baltimore, 1956

Hadrian by Stewart Perowne, Croom Helm, London, 1960

Hadrian – The Restless Emperor by Anthony R. Birley, Routledge, London, 1997

Histories – Book One by Tacitus, Cambridge University Press, Cambridge, 2003

A History of Rome (Down to the Reign of Constantine) by M. Cary and H.H. Scullard, Macmillan, London, 1975

The Latin Sexual Vocabulary by J.N. Adams, Duckworth, London, 1982

The Life of Alexander Severus by R.V. Nind Hopkins, Cambridge University Press, Cambridge, 1907

Life of Constantine by Eusebius, Clarendon Press, Oxford, 1999

Life and Leisure in Ancient Rome by J.P.V.D. Balsdon, The Bodley Head, London, 1969

The Life and Reign of Lucius Septimius Severus by Maurice Platnauer, Oxford University Press, Oxford, 1918

Lives of Galba and Otho by Plutarch, Bristol Classical Press, London, 1994

The Lives of the Noble Grecians and Romans by Plutarch, Wordsworth, Ware, Hertfordshire, 1998

Lives of the Roman Empresses by Jacques Boergas de Serviez, Putnam, London, 1935

Lives of Twelve Caesars by Suetonius, Wordsworth, Ware, Hertfordshire, 1997

Love in the Ancient World by Christopher Miles with John Julius Norwich, Weidenfeld and Nicolson, London, 1997

Lucretius on Love and Sex by Robert D. Brown, E.J. Brill, New York, 1987

Marcus Aurelius – A Biography by Anthony Birley, B.T. Batsford, London, 1987

Metamorphoses by Ovid, Penguin, London, 2002

Natural Questions by Seneca, Ayer Company Inc, Salem, New Hampshire, 1984

Nerva and the Roman Succession Crisis of 96–99 AD by John D. Grainger, Routledge, London, 2003

On Benefits by Lucius Annaeus Seneca, George Bell and Sons, London, 1887

A Phase of Roman Life by Charles Reginald Dawes, typescript, British Library, London, 1914

The Policy of the Emperor Gallienus by Lukas de Blois, E.J. Brill, Leiden, 1976

The Roman Empire from Severus to Constantine by Pat Southern, Routledge, London, 2001

Roman History and Mythology edited by Henry A. Sanders, Macmillan, New York, 1910

The Roman History: The Reign of Augustus by Cassius Dio, Penguin, London, 1987

Roman Lives – A Selection of Eight Lives by Plutarch, Oxford University Press, Oxford, 1999

The Roman Mistress – Ancient and Modern Representations by Maria Wyke, Oxford University Press, Oxford, 2002

Roman Portraits – The Flavian-Trajanic Period by William C. McDermott and Anne E. Orentzel, University of Missouri Press, London, 1979

Roman Sexualities edited by Judith P. Hallett and Marilyn B. Skinner, Princeton University Press, Princeton, New Jersey, 1997

Roman Women – Their History and Habits by J.P.V.D. Balsdon, The Bodley Head, London, 1962

A Scandalous History of the Roman Emperors by Anthony Blond, Robinson, London, 2000

The Secret History by Procopius, The Folio Society, London, 1995

Sex and Difference in Ancient Greece and Rome edited by Mark Golden and Peter Toohey, Edinburgh University Press, Edinburgh, 2003

Sexual Life in Ancient Rome by Otto Kiefer, Kegan Paul International, London, 2000

S.P.Q.R. – The History and Social Life of Ancient Rome by E.C. Kennedy and G.W. White, Macmillan and Co, London, 1944

Suetonius: The Flavian Emperors – A Historical Commentary with Translation and Introduction by Brian Jones and Robert Milns, Bristol Classical Press, London, 2002

Theodosian Empresses – Women and Imperial Dominion in Late Antiquity by Kenneth G. Holum, University of California Press, Berkeley, 1982

The Syrian Princesses by Godfrey Turton, Cassel and Company, London, 1974

Trajan – Optimus Princeps by Julian Bennett, Routledge, London, 1997

Vespasian by Barbara Levick, Routledge, London, 1999

Women in Purple by Judith Herren, Weidenfeld and Nicolson, London, 2001

The Year of Four Emperors by P.A.L. Greenhalgh, Weidenfeld and Nicolson, London, 1975

INDEX